Tues 19th 2020

Dear Imogen,

This is my favourite ever
racing related book. I
really hope you will enjoy
it.

I feel so lucky we met-
hope our friendship will
last a lifetime

Love Meg
Xxx

THE
BLUEGRASS
CONSPIRACY

THE
BLUEGRASS
CONSPIRACY

AN INSIDE STORY OF POWER,
GREED, DRUGS, AND MURDER

SALLY
DENTON

DOUBLEDAY

NEW YORK LONDON TORONTO SYDNEY AUCKLAND

PUBLISHED BY DOUBLEDAY
a division of Bantam Doubleday Dell Publishing Group, Inc.
666 Fifth Avenue, New York, New York 10103

DOUBLEDAY and the portrayal of an anchor
with a dolphin are trademarks of Doubleday,
a division of Bantam Doubleday Dell
Publishing Group, Inc.

Library of Congress Cataloging-in-Publication Data

Denton, Sally.
    The bluegrass conspiracy : an inside story of
power, greed, drugs, and murder / by Sally Denton.
— 1st ed.
        p.   cm.
    1. Drug traffic—United States. 2. Drug traffic
—Kentucky. I. Title.
    HV5825.D46   1990
    363.4'5'09769—dc20   89-23618
                                                CIP

ISBN 0-385-26272-8
Printed in the United States of America

March 1990

First Edition
BVG

DESIGN BY SNAP•HAUS GRAPHICS/DIANE STEVENSON

CONTENTS

THE
BLUEGRASS
CONSPIRACY

3

For my parents, my husband, and my son

PROLOGUE

The red lights of the instrument panel glared in the pitch-black airplane cockpit. The pilot, forty-year-old Andrew Carter Thornton II, had rehearsed the steps a thousand times in his mind, plotted his strategy with the precision of a commando for the event he hoped would never happen. When he realized that two jets were on his tail, "Drew" knew that such specialized chase aircraft could only have been deployed by U.S. Customs. It was not in his nature to admit fear, but he wasn't optimistic about the forced switch to his contingency plan.

Moments earlier, the cold night air had blasted into the plane as Drew and his partner opened the door of the Cessna 404 and kicked the last parachute load into a remote section of Georgia forest. Then they prepared themselves for a jump into the black sky. Drew packed his Army duffel bag with a Browning 9-mm automatic pistol, a .22-caliber pistol, several clips of ammunition, a stiletto, forty-five hundred dollars in cash, six Krugerrands, food rations and vitamins, a compass, an altimeter, and identification papers in two different names. This time, his enemies on the ground were not the Viet Cong or Sandinistas, but U.S. drug enforcement agents.

Wearing a bulletproof vest and military-issue infrared night-vision goggles, he checked the straps to his parachute. The inspection was perfunctory, as Drew's paranoia of sabotage was so great that he did not allow anyone to touch his chute. The distant lights of Knoxville, Tennessee, twinkled on the horizon below, as he set the plane on automatic pilot, directed the aircraft to its crash destination in the remote mountains of North Carolina, and slid an extra ignition key into his pants pocket. His load, although heavy, was precisely the weight he thought his parachute could handle—not an ounce more or less.

Drew opened the door and jumped into the vast night, a free-falling flight as symbolic as America's spin from the 1950s into the 1980s.

■

Fred Myers always arose at 5:15 A.M. His routine, from which he rarely deviated, included reading the *Knoxville Journal* while awaiting a breakfast call from his two sisters, both in their nineties, who lived down the road. On this early autumn morning, the eighty-five-year-old retired engineer and guitar picker gazed out of his bathroom window while shaving. Across the apple orchard in the dawn light, he saw a dead body in his driveway. He telephoned his elderly sisters and described the strange sight. Fred Myers had always had an active imagination, and his sisters knew it. They told him to go back to bed. Instead, Myers called the police.

The crumpled heap in Myers' gravel driveway was Drew Thornton, a notorious narcotics agent turned drug smuggler.

"I saw the pack on him, and I knew right then he had too big a load for that little old parachute," Myers later told the news reporters who swarmed onto his property.

When the Knoxville police opened the three-and-a-half-foot-long duffel bag tied around Drew's waist, they discovered thirty-four football-sized bundles of cocaine. Another bag tied to his body held dehydrated food and other survival supplies. His main parachute was still in its pack, his right hand still gripped the rip cord of his partially deployed reserve chute. He was wearing combat-style fatigues and expensive Italian shoes—a seeming non sequitur to those getting their first glimpse into the bizarre world of the sexy, madcap Kentucky blueblood. His pockets contained a membership card to the Miami Jockey Club and a personal address book listing fewer than a dozen names and telephone numbers. Bruises and abrasions marked both legs and a trickle of blood had hardened on both cheeks. His spine and several ribs were fractured. A ruptured aorta had killed him.

Of the three epigrams he carried in his pocket, the most revealing read: "There is only one tactical principle not subject to change:

It is to inflict the maximum amount of wounds, death, and destruction on the enemy in the minimum amount of time."

Journalists and cops in Tennessee scratched their heads in bewilderment. They couldn't untangle the incongruities of the handsome man who had plunged to his death with $75 million worth of pure cocaine strapped to his waist and a failed parachute on his back.

But back home in Kentucky, Drew's wild and crashing demise seemed a logical conclusion to his life on the edge. Over the past twenty years, Drew had bounced from job to job, avocation to avocation. After a brief stint as an Army paratrooper, he dabbled in racehorse breeding, undercover police work, and the martial arts. He became a pilot, collected guns, and struggled through law school at night—obtaining a degree but few clients. He drove a white Jaguar sports car and played polo with other well-bred boyhood friends. He was an L. L. Bean-type dresser, sporting elegant flannels and expensive outdoor clothing. A health food fanatic and fitness freak, Drew smuggled tons of pot and cocaine into the country, while claiming never to "touch the stuff." As a kid, he wasn't athletic, wasn't a good student, and wasn't particularly popular. As a cop, he was a bully who enjoyed beating up the kids he busted, roughing up the drunks and hookers who put up little resistance, and practicing his karate on dogs. He believed in power through intimidation, thought he possessed supernatural abilities, and somehow persuaded an unlikely crew of misfits and sycophants from Lexington's seamier side of the tracks to become his fiercely loyal groupies.

He boasted of military decorations and courageous derring-do, hinting at ties to the CIA and dangerous escapades as a soldier and a mercenary. But his Army records described him as an unremarkable five-foot-eight-inch, 150-pound private who received basic training, spent two months in combat in the Dominican Republic (during which time he was shot in the left arm and received medals for having been wounded in action), who was exemplary in neither aptitude nor performance, and who was a disciplinary problem on at least one occasion.

The picture of Drew's dead body appeared on all three networks and went across the country's major news wires. Published photos from happier times showed a man in his prime—a tanned and fit man of action, handsome and flashy enough to be a star on "Miami Vice."

Drew Thornton wanted to be known as a guy with guts. He

wanted people to think he was tough and intelligent, cunning and sophisticated. His exploits would have been dismissed as those of a sec-
ond-class outlaw had he not been the son of what is known in the South
as a "good family" and possessed the political and social connections
inherent to such landed gentry.

■

To the average newspaper reader, Drew's bizarre death was just another
twisted statistic in the much-ballyhooed "War on Drugs." But Ralph
Edward Ross knew there was more. Ross knew that Drew Thornton was
a gunrunner whose tentacles extended into the highest levels of state
government, national law enforcement, and top-secret military installations; that his network included assassins, mercenaries, governors, and
federal drug agents; that his lieutenants and allies had penetrated the
inner sanctums of at least two Kentucky governors—John Y. Brown,
Jr., and Julian Carroll; and that his schemes were hatched and fulfilled
in places such as Las Vegas, Libya, Colombia, Costa Rica, Beirut, Honduras, El Salvador, Panama, and Angola.

Ralph Ross was possibly the least surprised of anybody at
Drew's absurd death. To say Ralph was happy about it might be going
too far, but he *did* feel that the son-of-a-bitch finally got what he deserved.

Ordinarily Ralph's mornings got off to a late start. Ever since he
had "retired"—been forced out was more like it—Ralph dawdled over
his newspaper and coffee. He still hadn't adjusted to his life as an
ostracized cop. Since his conviction three years earlier for illegal wiretapping, Ralph greeted most days like an empty canvas of white space.
A fifty-two-year-old man with nothing to do was a sorry sight in Ralph's
opinion. So he took his daily routine seriously, as if his life would
collapse without that semblance of structure, measly though it was.
Sooner or later, though, he would find himself alone with the tenacious
mind that refused to forget anything. From noon on, Ralph spent most
waking hours cursing Drew Thornton. "Just another darned blueblood
puttin' on airs," Ralph had thought upon first meeting Drew a decade
and a half earlier. Ralph's initial instincts would prove accurate: In the

end, Drew Thornton would be fatally hurled to earth, overburdened by his superiority complex and mythical self-perception.

When the phone rang at the crack of dawn on September 11, Ralph roused himself from a deep sleep.

"Drew's dead," the voice said. Though the caller didn't identify himself, Ralph recognized him as an informant from his past police work.

"He slammed into the ground in Knoxville when his parachute didn't open. At dawn I was driving north on Interstate 75 back to Lexington," Ralph's "source" continued. "Drew's friend, Rebecca Sharp, sped past me in a black stretch limousine with chemically darkened windows. She had somebody with her, but I didn't get a good look at him."

So began the denouement of the dramatic odyssey that began in 1970 when Ralph Ross and Drew Thornton embarked on their collision course.

Ralph recognized Drew's last jump as the climax before the resolution. Finally, the promise of a just conclusion to years of deadly conflict seemed imminent. Throughout the 1970s and early 1980s, the trails of Ralph and Drew had zigzagged across each other's territory. Both were Kentucky natives—one rich and one poor. But their backgrounds were not as dissimilar as their outcomes would later suggest, nor were their motivations and personality traits as polarized. Both were warriors, trained by the elite forces of the U.S. military. Both had entered manhood through combat in America's "lesser" wars—one in Korea and the other in the Caribbean. Both men returned home to Kentucky to serve as cops—one for the Lexington Police Department and the other for the Kentucky State Police. Both were trained in the most sophisticated undercover techniques of the time, attending some of the same law enforcement academies. Each had a reputation for patience and meticulousness, and each would rely upon the skills taught him by the U.S. Government to keep the other at bay.

Each viewed the other as his nemesis, and the obstacle to his mission.

■

Rebecca Sharp sheathed her petite hands in a pair of white cotton gloves she retrieved from her handbag.

"Drew taught me to wear these when I don't want to leave fingerprints," she said to the distinguished-looking older gentleman she recognized as Bertram Gordon and his remarkably handsome companion. Though she had never met Gordon, she had spoken with him over the telephone, and had been told by Drew that Gordon was a trusted associate. She also knew that Gordon had introduced Drew to the leaders of the Colombian cocaine monopoly known as the "Medellín Cartel," and that Drew had been living with Gordon at the Miami Jockey Club in recent weeks.

Rebecca fought the urge to blame Drew for bungling such a massive smuggling operation, leaving her with the labyrinthine puzzle of locating eight hundred pounds of cocaine strewn across thousands of acres of national forest. She had to find it, and then decide what to do with it. Meanwhile, she must try and persuade the Colombians who had "fronted" the coke to Drew that she was not the responsible party.

It did not come as a surprise, then, when, nine days after Drew's jump, Bertram Gordon appeared on the scene to "collect."

"I considered wearing a bulletproof vest," Rebecca said to Gordon.

The man driving the car introduced himself as James Vincent, an American representative of the Colombians, who were anxious to make arrangements to receive payment for the $80 million worth of cocaine Drew had guaranteed he would transport safely into the hands of the cartel's American distributors.

Rebecca handed Vincent a business card imprinted with the name "C. Fred Partin," referring to Partin as Drew's "good friend," and implying that Partin, and not she, was the individual to whom their questions should be directed.

"What happened?" Vincent asked her.

Rebecca had arranged for the getaway car for Drew in Knoxville, she told the men, and was awaiting his arrival at a prearranged local motel. Waiting at various "drop sites" in Georgia was the ground crew who intended to truck the cocaine that was thrown out attached to parachutes to Daytona, Florida. Included in that group was David "Cowboy" Williams—a Kentucky native turned Atlanta real estate magnate. Rebecca knew the plans had been bungled when a man claiming to be Drew's companion on the airplane appeared at the motel alone, and told Rebecca about the ugly turn of events that left Drew unaccounted for. She claimed not to know the identity of this individual.

With chilling detachment, Rebecca related the details of Drew's final hours, as had been told to her, she said, by Drew's mysteriously anonymous accomplice: The two dope transporters had left Colombia with twelve duffel bags full of cocaine on board. Upon crossing the U.S. border, they determined that they were being tracked by government aircraft. Vincent thought it odd that Rebecca specifically identified the chase planes as two Citation jets and a Black Hawk helicopter—aircraft recently acquired by U.S. Customs to interdict air smugglers—because it would have been impossible to see them from the cockpit.

Drew and his partner had divided nine of the bags into sets of three, she said, and attached a parachute to each set. They threw two more duffel bags out the airplane door attached to chutes; the bags were to be retrieved by crews waiting at designated sites. With their apprehension apparently imminent, Drew then tied the last duffel to his body and set the plane on automatic pilot. He gave his partner—a karate buff who had never parachuted—a quick rundown on the chute equipment, and pushed him out the door. Then Drew dropped out after him.

Rebecca told the men that when Drew's partner arrived at the Knoxville motel, the two of them waited several hours for Drew to turn up. She listened to the television, simultaneously hoping for and dreading news about Drew. When the 6 A.M. local news came on, she heard a report of a dead parachutist. Rebecca and Drew's accomplice then took off for Lexington, where, upon her arrival, she went directly to Drew's apartment. Accompanied by Drew's younger brother, she removed all incriminating evidence.

The man who had identified himself as Vincent impressed upon Rebecca that the Colombians were anxious to retrieve either their coke or their money.

Rebecca then assured Vincent and Bert Gordon that the situation, replete with extenuating circumstances, would be remedied under her watch. "Drew's people are honorable," she said, "and, if able, they will complete the deal. If they don't honor my promise, they know I will have them killed."

■

The bluegrass hills vibrated under the strong September sun as hundreds made their way past the Bourbon County grave site. The mourners made up a Who's Who of Kentucky aristocracy, a crowd of lawyers, socialites, and politicians. Thirteen floral arrangements decorated the rural cemetery, the largest of which was signed, "I will always love you, Rebecca."

Police were there. Horse breeders. Gamblers. Convicts. They were paying their last respects to Andrew Carter Thornton II—All-American boy. A cocaine commando spawned by the upper-crust serenity and refinement of the genteel South. A member of the Elvis Presley generation.

"He [Thornton] was very fond of the words of the oriental philosopher who said, 'Man can overcome any obstacle if he knows in his heart that he must and in his mind that he shall,' " the Reverend Cliff Pike of the tiny Episcopal church in Paris, Kentucky, said in his eulogy. Perhaps more than anyone, Thornton would have appreciated the absurdity of his death.

"He thought of himself as a purist, an innocent," said Betty Zaring, Thornton's former wife. Over lunch the previous summer, Betty had asked Thornton how he justified the violence, the paradoxes of his life. Thornton had replied that he meditated regularly, at which time he entered a world beyond good and evil. He told his ex-wife that he was of a hero-consciousness, that at another time in history he would have been a Genghis Khan, a ninja or a samurai, a valorous paragon of battle.

"He believed he was an *'Impeccable Warrior,'* " said Zaring, referring to Carlos Castaneda's term. "He was a philosophical, incredibly disciplined, extremely spiritual, and loyal warrior, with his own code of ethics, who thrived on excitement."

Others who knew him don't share this romanticized version. They say Drew Thornton thrived on vengeance and murder.

PART

BOOK ONE

ONE

THE
PREPPY
MAFIA

CHAPTER

ONE

Melanie Flynn was pleasantly surprised to hear her father's voice when she answered the phone at 4 P.M. on January 26, 1977.

A part-time referee, her father had called to ask Melanie for a directory of Kentucky's high school coaches which had been published by her employer, the Kentucky High School Athletic Association.

"I'll bring it home tonight," she assured him. Then, after a brief pause, added: "I love you, Daddy."

Melanie had completed her secretarial assignments early in order to arrive on time for her five-thirty appointment with her psychiatrist. She called her mother—her closest friend—to say she planned to join the family for a turkey dinner. Melanie cleared her desk, covered her typewriter, and said good-bye to her coworkers as she pulled on her red leather coat, preparing for the bitter six-degree weather. She nearly slipped on the ice as she made her way to her Ford Elite in the parking lot in the early darkness of Lexington's cold, gray winter.

But twenty-four-year-old Melanie never arrived home for dinner.

Former state senator Robert "Bobby" Flynn and his wife, Ella Ritchey Flynn, were not initially worried about their daughter. They had become accustomed to her independence and unscheduled comings and goings. For the past few years she had traveled extensively—to Florida, New York, Colorado, and the Caribbean—seeking employment as a singer or model. They knew she was a party girl who enjoyed a wild, extravagant life, and they gave her the leeway they believed an attractive, enthusiastic, high-strung young woman required. As do all parents, they watched in anguish as Melanie muddled through life's pitfalls. But they trusted her judgment and morality enough to believe she could pull herself through anything that happened.

Two days later, though, when her boss called the Flynns to find out where Melanie was, Bobby Flynn knew something was wrong. He started calling all of her friends he knew, including the man she had been dating—Lexington narcotics officer Bill Canan. The psychiatrist she had been scheduled to see had waited for nearly an hour for his patient. She seemed to have vanished.

On January 29 Bobby Flynn called the Lexington police and filed a missing persons report. Detective Canan agreed to "look into Melanie's disappearance," but hinted that she had voluntarily fled. The last time he had seen Melanie she had been drinking and taking pills, he said. Downplaying his relationship with Melanie, Canan acted as though they had been mere acquaintances, as though he was unconcerned about her safety or whereabouts. This surprised the Flynns, who thought she had become seriously involved with Canan. She even had told her family and friends that she and Canan intended to marry.

While Melanie had a history of running away, the Flynns believed she had outgrown that stage. No matter where Melanie had traveled in recent months, even if in the company of someone of whom her parents did not approve, or for reasons for which she would be ashamed, she called or wrote. Her mother pointed to disturbing signs—an income tax refund check remained in Melanie's bedroom; her favorite cosmetics, clothing, and beauty paraphernalia were also still there. Ella Flynn thought of the worst: Kidnapping, white slavery, even murder. She wondered if her trust in Bill Canan and the Lexington police was misplaced.

When Melanie's car surfaced a week later in a seedy apartment complex in north Lexington, the police became more interested. A suitcase full of clothes from Melanie's previous weekend trip to Louisville was found in the trunk, along with the leather coat she wore the day she disappeared. Her purse and keys were missing. The case was officially turned over to Lexington police detective John Bizzack. Her car was searched for blood, fingerprints, and other evidence.

Bobby Flynn told Bizzack everything about his daughter he thought might be relevant. She was particularly attracted to athletes—a leaning that ran in the family. Melanie's brother, Doug, was currently playing baseball for the New York Mets. She had a passion for horses as well, and for many years harbored an ambition to be a woman jockey. But those dreams were shattered in 1972 in a bizarre accident. While working as an "exercise girl" at the Kentucky Horse Center, Melanie was thrown from a high-spirited colt, landing on her head. She remained comatose for a few days, and was hospitalized for nearly five months. Those closest to her claimed she was never the same. Upon recovery, at the age of nineteen, she and the teenaged son of a wealthy horse breeder eloped. Early in the immature marriage, Melanie received another blow to the head, apparently inflicted by her husband. Following days of partial amnesia and loss of consciousness, she filed for divorce, and recuperated at her parents' comfortable home for several months.

Single again, she hooked up with a flamboyant Cuban-born horsebreeder and producer of B-grade movies named Mario Crespo. Crespo had appeared rather suddenly on the Lexington horse scene, purchasing a legendary mansion called "Corinthian" and entering the bloodstock business. Crespo hired Melanie along with several other women as grooms, whom he dressed in shocking pink hot pants, to display his thoroughbreds at the famous Keeneland Sales. Melanie seemed oblivious to the raised eyebrows of the old guard who thought Crespo's sales tactics vulgar and tacky. The thirty-seven-year-old, dark-haired entrepreneur felt a special affection for Melanie, who became his constant companion. Traveling with Crespo, she reveled in the opulence of the hotels they visited and boasted of her newfound jet-setting lifestyle. Bubbling with enthusiasm, she frequently called her parents. Despite their questions, she was intentionally vague about her role in Mario Crespo's life, implying that it was purely professional.

In 1975, Melanie had decided to embark on a singing career. With a repertoire of country rock songs and the stage name of Melanie O'Hara, she moved to Cincinnati, where her brother was playing pro ball with the Cincinnati Reds. She hooked up with an older, married man who paid her rent and travel expenses for a while. She apparently remained close to Crespo during this period. Again, the Flynns received regular phone calls and letters, even when Melanie was in Florida and New York auditioning for gigs.

A year later she returned to Lexington and took a job as a

secretary with the Kentucky Athletic Association, dissatisfied with her life as a professional singer and the success that eluded her.

Back in Lexington in 1976 Melanie's social life began revolving around two Lexington policemen—Bill Canan and Andrew Thornton. Canan and Thornton had gained a reputation for their fast-paced lives that included the best parties and nightclubs, flashy rolls of hundred-dollar bills, guns discreetly tucked into their ankle or shoulder holsters, and fast cars loaded with high-tech audio equipment—all, ostensibly, in the name of the war on drugs.

Like Drew, William Taulbee Canan wanted to be a legend in his own time. Born July 1, 1945, in Mount Sterling, Kentucky, he had returned to his home state in 1971 following a fourteen-month tour of duty with the U.S. Marines in Vietnam. Joining the Lexington police, he became the first undercover narcotics agent on the force, and the unofficial leader of the overzealous crew. Short and stocky, Canan used his muscular physique and icy blue eyes to intimidate his adversaries. He bragged about his Black Belt karate expertise, his macho command of all types of weapons, his purported ties to the CIA and DEA, and his supposed training by the military's elite special forces. On and off duty, he wore an eight-inch dagger on his belt and stalked his nervous suspects into local bars. As an undercover agent, he could wear jeans and long hair and drink alcohol during his shift.

Unlike Drew Thornton, Canan was not a native son of Lexington's prominent fathers. Though he possessed neither the breeding nor the manners that were second nature to Drew, the two men had found an instant affinity for one another.

Melanie's friends said she had fallen madly in love with Bill Canan. What Melanie found attractive about Canan puzzled many, for he was considered by most who knew him to be an egomaniacal misfit with a penchant for brutality. He relished the role of the super-narc, and was somehow able to inspire fanatical devotion from his fellow undercover team members. Canan also had become a devotee of mind control. Like Drew Thornton, though, Canan took himself much more seriously than anyone else did.

The irony of Melanie's uncommonly tight association with Drew and Canan was not lost on Detective Bizzack. Bizzack would not, however, humor the Flynns with speculation about the significance of such relationships. The investigation was in the most competent hands with the Lexington police and they would pursue every lead, Bizzack assured Flynn.

Less than two months later, Bizzack closed the case, announcing publicly that Melanie was alive and well, and living in Florida.

Ralph Ross didn't buy it.

Ralph felt certain Melanie had been murdered. The head of the Organized Crime and Intelligence units for the Kentucky State Police had sources and informants who told him that Drew Thornton and Bill Canan were responsible for Melanie's disappearance and death. But Ralph had no evidence, and his access to the Lexington Police Department's investigative files seemed to be blocked. Ralph's instincts told him the mystery was far from over.

In late May 1977, six weeks after Bizzack claimed to have solved the disappearance, Ella Flynn received a phone call from a woman who said her nephew had met a girl in Florida who identified herself as Melanie Flynn. Mrs. Flynn immediately called Bizzack. The Lexington police interviewed the witness, who said that he had been on vacation in Daytona Beach in March. He and his friends met four young women—one of whom said her name was Melanie Flynn. He remembered the name because he was familiar with Doug Flynn's baseball career. Although the witness was also from the Lexington area, he claimed not to have heard news reports of Melanie's disappearance until May.

Bizzack traveled to Florida to follow up on the man's statements. Returning immediately, he closed the case again, issuing a cursory statement that said ". . . the possibility of foul play as being a part of her disappearance has been eliminated and due to that elimination the investigation has ceased." Bizzack said Melanie Flynn had been identified through photographs, personal belongings, and activities, and that she had been living in Daytona Beach since March. Admitting that he never actually found her, Bizzack claimed to have interviewed six hundred people during his investigation, but refused to identify the witnesses or reveal any evidence to either the family or the media.

Frustrated, the Flynns mustered all of their political and social clout and implored other law enforcement agencies to enter the case. Doug Flynn discussed his missing sister with FBI agents in various National League cities during the season. Melanie's father beseeched former Kentucky governor "Happy" Chandler to exert his influence with the Kentucky State Police. But neither the FBI nor the state police had the statutory authority to open an official investigation unless white slavery, abduction, or some other federal crime was suspected.

Intrigued by Bizzack's hasty conclusion, Ralph decided to re-trace Bizzack's steps with the help of an FBI agent in Florida. That agent located and interviewed many of the same witnesses Bizzack had interviewed.

"It wasn't her," the agent told Ralph.

It was a delicate situation. The Lexington police had already announced that the case was solved, and the local papers had printed stories praising Bizzack's efforts. Ralph took his case file to a reporter at the *Lexington Leader.* "Read this," he told her. "Maybe you should go down to Florida and conduct your own investigation." The reporter declined to pursue the story.

The first week of August, the *Kentucky Post* published a contro-versial, four-part series of articles called "The Curious Case of the Missing Playgirl." In the photograph accompanying the article, Mela-nie's plunging neckline and give-anything-a-whirl gesture, intrigued even the most detached newspaper reader. In the article, Bill Canan denied a love or sexual relationship with Melanie, claiming instead that she had worked for him as an undercover narcotics informant. Canan said he had built a drug possession case against her, and then agreed not to prosecute her if she would help him infiltrate Lexington's drug culture. He was quick to point out that their professional relationship had ceased two years earlier, casting doubt that her disappearance could be related to her work as a "snitch." Canan, who was married, explained that Melanie told her friends and family she was engaged to Canan in order to provide herself with a cover.

Canan's disclosures shocked the Flynns, who no longer believed anything he said. Neither court records nor police department expense accounts verified Canan's claims that Melanie had been an informant.

Then, on August 13, a purse washed up on a boat dock on the Kentucky River during a flood. The purse was sent to the state police crime lab where its contents were analyzed. The partially decomposed purse contained two medicine bottles, a tube of lipstick, and a perfume atomizer. Ella Flynn identified one of the bottles as Melanie's antihistamine prescription—a fact that was subsequently confirmed by the state police crime lab.

Melanie's purse had been found outside Lexington's city limits. Finally, Ralph Ross had jurisdiction.

Shortly after Melanie's purse turned up, Doug Flynn granted an interview to the Lexington newspaper. Flynn said he " 'just couldn't understand why Canan would say that he and Melanie weren't close . . . it looks like somebody was trying to cover up something down at the police department . . . something's happened and I can't believe the FBI won't come in and help.' "

Ralph sent one of his men to interview Doug Flynn. But Doug was not forthcoming. He told the state police that his family was disgusted with the investigation, and had resigned themselves to the conclusion that Melanie's dead body would never be found. "We would like to know what happened," Doug Flynn told the trooper, "but it has gone on and on and on, and we finally just had to decide to leave it alone."

■

Drew Thornton had resigned from the Lexington police force just two weeks before Melanie vanished. Ralph reviewed Drew's personnel file, finding nothing exemplary in Drew's eight-and-a-half-year career as a city policeman. Drew had received no promotions, an average number of commendations, and one brutality lawsuit had been filed against him. The lack of disciplinary action against Drew seemed irrelevant, since Drew's social credentials outclassed the bloodlines of his superiors on the force. Funded by a federal grant, Drew had managed to enroll in a law enforcement course at Eastern Kentucky University, graduating in 1973 with a degree in law enforcement. The following September he had enrolled in law school, and transferred from narcotics to a mundane desk job in order to accommodate his academic schedule.

It appeared Drew never intended to make police work his life-long career. Drew did not, however, attempt to downplay his job as a cop. He drove a squad car to school and prominently displayed his weapons during class. He bragged to classmates about his involvement in what he called "high-level police work," and gained a reputation as a cavalier blueblood with mediocre scholastic aptitude.

Melanie Flynn's disappearance was not the beginning of Ralph's suspicions of the motives of Drew Thornton, but rather the impetus for an exploration of seven years of curious events. Reflecting on the number of times that the actions of Drew and his cronies—a handful of narcs—had come to his attention, Ralph began to see a pattern develop.

It was in 1971 that Ralph Ross initially learned that Drew Thornton and the Lexington police were selling drugs. The disappearance of a substantial amount of marijuana from the evidence room of the Lexington Police Department was the first incident to incite Ralph's suspicious nature. Following up on an informant's tip, Ralph's men had searched Drew Thornton's property for the stolen pot. The missing marijuana was found hidden in a fence row behind Drew's house. The packages were still marked with police evidence tags and case numbers. When no disciplinary or criminal action was initiated, even after the chief of police had been informed of the discovery, Ralph became convinced that Drew Thornton was being protected by high level officials in the Lexington Police Department.

A few months later, another of Ralph's undercover men filed a report with the state police about drug dealing by the Lexington police narcotics unit. In that report, a trooper claimed that one of the Lexington narcs admitted that he not only used drugs, but intended to leave law enforcement to enter the drug business using the contacts he had made as a cop. The Lexington cop then handed the trooper a chunk of hash.

Bill Canan was the unofficial tactician of the drug squad at the time, and notoriously encouraged the brutal and unrestrained conduct that became the unit's trademark. Though the narcotics unit was making hundreds of arrests, its minuscule conviction rate was raising eyebrows within the department, as well as within the city.

On the heels of the alleged hash incident, one of Drew's closest friends and lifelong associates—Henry Vance—was fired by the Fayette County sheriff. Vance was detailed on special assignment to work with the Lexington narcotics unit at the time. Vance had forged the sheriff's name on a purchase order for two dozen .44-magnum revolvers. The guns were to be shipped to New York, where they were allegedly to be received by Jay Silvestro—a former Lexington narc who had become a federal agent.

Henry Vance too escaped criminal prosecution—a fact Ralph attributed to his parents' social prominence. Vance's great-grandfather had been treasurer of Transylvania College; his grandfather had been a renowned surgeon and president of the state medical association; and his parents were pillars in the community. Henry Vance was the only child of Hank Vance—an insurance entrepreneur, and his wife Alice, who was active in Junior League. Around the same time, an informant told Ralph, Drew and Vance were selling large quantities of narcotics obtained from a local wholesale drug company. They would never be caught, Ralph's source claimed, because they operated under the auspices of law enforcement.

In those early years, Ralph had felt powerless to initiate a probe of the Lexington Police Department on drug-smuggling charges. He had been around Lexington enough to realize it was the kind of town where problems were often handled with one phone call to the right person. A country boy such as himself didn't stand a chance against the Lexington establishment. So he decided to pull his men out of Lexington, keep an eye on events from a distance, and bide his time until Drew and his cohorts made an inevitable error.

Immersing himself instead in statewide organized crime and racketeering cases, he was unsurprised at how frequently the tentacles of these investigations would lead back to Lexington. Whenever Ralph's men ventured into Lexington they were surveilled by the Lexington police, and a mutual distrust evolved between the two agencies.

Meanwhile, Ralph had ordered his Intelligence Unit to systematically collect and file bits and pieces of information on Drew Thornton's activities through the years. Ralph made a mental note of the close relationship that had developed, both professionally and socially, between Thornton and Harold Brown—the regional head of the federal Drug Enforcement Administration.

Ralph and Drew maintained their imposed distance, each becoming increasingly aware of the threat they posed to one another. When they met, they circled like male dogs, eyeing each other with curiosity while remaining on guard. Drew must have known that Ralph was chomping at the bit for him to slip up somehow. Drew probably didn't know, however, how transparent his actions were, and how badly Ralph wanted to catch him. Drew seemed to feel safe, as long as he operated within his own domain. In Lexington, insulated by his police credentials and high social standing, Drew thought he was invulnerable. Ralph recognized that insulation and realized the limitations of his jurisdiction. He watched patiently as Drew branched out across the state, relying more and more upon protection from his accomplice in the DEA, Harold Brown.

In the weeks prior to Melanie Flynn's disappearance in January 1977, Drew received his law degree, quit police work, and joined a legal practice of marginal legitimacy.

Ralph had been told by his informants in Lexington that Drew was plying his government-trained skills in the private sector—specifically in the profit-making world of drug peddling. If that were true, what would Drew's motive be in eliminating Melanie Flynn?

Ralph also speculated on the role con man Mario Crespo might have played in Melanie's disappearance, wondering if a relationship existed between Drew and Crespo. The two men would certainly have crossed paths in the horse industry, if not in other social circles as well.

Among Crespo's dicey business ventures was a thinly disguised escort service ring for which he solicited pretty Southern coeds to audition as "models and actresses." The applicants—seated alone in a small, dingy motel room—were asked to expose their breasts in the presence of a video camera anchored to a tripod. Melanie was among the "select few" who were chosen, and who were then transported to Florida and the Caribbean to tan their nude bodies. It was not long before Crespo's operations were awash in rumors of scandal. The FBI and state police were investigating reports that Crespo's girls were compromising state government officials on videotape for the purpose of extortion and blackmail. The nubile beauties lured the politicians to hotel rooms that had been wired for sound and equipped with hidden cameras. Weeks after the seduction was consummated, the damning evidence would turn up unexpectedly to haunt the unsuspecting state legislator or city councilman. Intimidated by the threat of public exposure, the married victims were forced to respond favorably to the subsequent political demands made upon them.

Such demands involved protection for organized crime elements who had immigrated to Kentucky from their homelands of Chicago, Detroit, Cleveland, and Miami. Had Melanie been a call girl for the mob? Ralph wondered.

By the time Melanie returned to Lexington in 1976 Crespo had been forced to sell his stud farm and mansion, and was on the verge of skipping town. One week before Melanie disappeared, Crespo had taken six Lexington girls to Florida. The girls were told they would be "trained" to film commercials, and would then be paid to model lingerie at the Library Lounge—Lexington's infamous disco and favorite hangout of drug dealers and police officers. Melanie had been scheduled to accompany them, but had failed to show up.

Drew and some of his police colleagues had moonlighted for Crespo, providing security for his horse farm in their off-duty hours. It wasn't clear how far such "security" extended, but it was an obvious conflict of interest for police officers to conduct private jobs for individuals they should have been investigating.

Such conflicts were not unique for the Lexington Police Department. Ralph thought the agency had historically been a tool of the elite, a puppet of the ruling class. It was the kind of department that routinely abandoned or initiated criminal investigations at the whim of the socially prominent. A well-placed phone call from a well-heeled citizen could stop a murder probe dead in its tracks. Ralph knew that a seemingly innocuous reference to a suspect such as "he's good people," could result in the casual disappearance of an entire case file.

■

Raymond James Ryan seemed to have the world by the tail on a downhill pull. He had outlived most of his enemies, he had money to burn, and he spent his days and nights doing whatever pleased him.

One pleasant day in October 1977, he walked out the back entrance of the Olympia Health Club into the bright Evansville, Indiana, sunshine. He looked at his watch and saw he had plenty of time to make his 1:30 P.M. appointment. He slid his tall, fit, seventy-three-year-old body behind the wheel of his Lincoln Continental Mark V and started the ignition. His eyes on the rearview mirror, he backed out of his parking space. Within seconds, an explosion ripped his body into indistinguishable shambles.

Ryan's movie-star good looks and high-stakes gambling had made him a legend in the underworld. He had learned the rackets as a kid, bouncing around northern Kentucky and other gaming hot spots. His organized crime ties were said to have originated with Frank Costello—the former head of the Mafia in New York. Ryan had invested his winnings in oil and real estate ventures, and was a partner of the actor William Holden in the plush Mount Kenya Safari Club in Africa. Famous for his betting, playing, and capacity to "lay off" record amounts, Ryan's wins and losses were romanticized. Oddsmaker Jimmy the Greek once wrote: ". . . in one afternoon Ryan had pissed away fifteen million dollars betting horses that ran second."

By 1977, the old hoodlum was enjoying a more sedate life than the hectic days of his youth. He spent most of his time in Palm Springs at the El Mirador Hotel he owned. Ryan also frequented his resort in Lake Malone, Kentucky, and was often seen publicly in the company of Lexington cops. A lot of people probably wanted Ryan dead. But his chief enemy was Marshall Caifano—a Chicago mobster and hit man. For a while, for several years actually, Ryan assumed he would be killed by Caifano. Seventeen years earlier, Caifano had tried to extort money from Ryan. "Caifano was shaking Ryan down and Ryan wouldn't shake," said an old-time gambler familiar with the situation, and in 1964, Ryan had testified against the mobster, which resulted in Caifano's conviction.

Ryan had just begun to think that he had escaped Caifano's wrath. He had apparently been mistaken. When the FBI dispatched laboratory experts from Washington, D.C., to the crime scene, the death was immediately labeled a "professional organized crime-type hit."

Ryan was killed, the FBI believed, in retaliation for his testimony against Caifano.

In October 1977, one of Drew's partners—a Lexington cop named Rex Hall—had approached Ryan peddling services that included round-the-clock bodyguards and an electronic security system. Hall owned and operated a private security firm called World Centurion, whose clients included Mario Crespo. His company, which employed off-duty Lexington police officers, provided security to several Lexington motels that were widely known for illegal prostitution and gambling—another blatant conflict of interest that was tolerated by Lexington Police Department higher-ups.

Ryan listened to Hall's proposal, and then agreed to travel to Lexington to pursue the financial negotiations. The two men met at the Hyatt Regency Hotel to discuss the security contract and to establish Hall's credentials with Ryan. The details of their discussion have never come to light.

A few weeks after Ryan's death, Hall telephoned the Evansville Police Department Intelligence Section and, falsely identifying himself, solicited information about the progress and status of the Ryan bombing investigation.

As head of the Organized Crime and Intelligence units of the Kentucky State Police, Ralph Ross had more than a passing interest in Ryan's murder, considering the mobster's long-standing ties to Kentucky. But it wasn't until April of 1978 that an FBI teletype message turned his interest into obsession: "[The] Evansville Police Department has developed suspects [in the Ryan murder] who are all former Lexington, Kentucky, police officers." Ralph took one look at the teletype and guessed what was coming next. He heaved a what-else-is-new sigh when he saw the two names—Rex Denver Hall and Andrew Carter Thornton.

A fingerprint taken from the steering wheel of Ryan's ill-fated blue Lincoln matched the left middle fingerprint of Drew Thornton.

Hall had resigned from the Lexington Police Department six weeks after the bombing. Ralph noted the convenience of both Rex Hall's and Drew Thornton's resignations at the height of the Ryan and Flynn investigations.

An Air Force veteran who had been trained by the FBI Academy, Hall had moved from Kentucky to Florida. Ralph tracked him to

Orlando, where Hall had recently been arrested for possession of a mini-arsenal of concealed weapons that included handguns, shotguns, an M-1 carbine, a Mauser 308-caliber rifle, handcuffs, wiretapping equipment, gas grenades, grenade launchers, and a significant quantity of ammunition. Tools of an assassin.

Though not directly related, the Flynn and Ryan cases shared a number of common traits. The most obvious link was Drew Thornton— a suspect in both incidents. Since the Ryan investigation was being handled by Alcohol, Tobacco and Firearms (ATF) and the FBI in Indiana, Ralph's participation in the probe was merely peripheral. But because the government's suspect was from Lexington, Kentucky, the federal agents working the case made frequent inquiries with Ralph about "Drew Thornton's gang." Ralph steered them in the right direction, providing access to the Drew Thornton dossier he had compiled, but he had no official involvement in the case.

Likewise, the Melanie Flynn case could be considered an ongoing state police investigation only in the broadest sense of the term. Not only was the trail of evidence cold by the time Ralph had legitimate jurisdictional access, but the Lexington Police Department systematically thwarted any attempts Ralph made to pursue leads in the Lexington area. Basically, there were three theories about Melanie's demise. Or four, if one included Sergeant Bizzack's claim that she was alive and well, which Ralph didn't bother entertaining. One—that Melanie had threatened to tell Bill Canan's wife about their love affair. Two—that she knew too much about the drug-smuggling activities of Drew Thornton and other members of the Lexington Police Department. Three— that she was on the verge of exposing the extortion and blackmail ring that had compromised dozens of public officials.

Ralph was inclined to believe that Melanie Flynn just knew too much about everything. One thing was clear: Drew Thornton's organization, in its most formative and burgeoning stage, could not risk a loose cannon such as Melanie. Though discretion had never been Melanie's strong suit, whatever semblance of propriety she possessed had been further dimmed by a drug and alcohol dependency.

Convinced of the relevance of Melanie's sex life to her current set of circumstances, Ralph decided to explore an avenue generally considered off-limits: He turned his attention to the queen of party-girl providers—the bluegrass baroness, Anita Madden.

■

Her stone house cannot be seen from Winchester Road, but once inside the gilded iron gates the awesome splendor of Hamburg Place is immediately felt. The grounds of the two-thousand-acre horse farm are immaculate, yet somehow eerie. Dark and tragic tales swirl around the fabled estate—tales of suicide and insanity, opulence and excess. Named for a famous thoroughbred, the estate was founded in 1897 by John E. Madden—nicknamed "The Wizard of the Turf." At one time, more Kentucky Derby winners had been foaled and bred at Hamburg Place than at any other farm—all of whom now rest in a horseshoe-shaped burial ground. Madden's son, J. E. Madden, Jr., didn't share his father's love for racing. When he acquired ownership and operation of the farm, he made it famous for the breeding of polo ponies. A gloomy, brooding man, J. E. Madden, Jr., committed suicide, leaving the farm to his sons Preston and Patrick.

By 1977, when it attracted the attention of Ralph Ross, Hamburg Place was notorious not for its horses or ponies, but for its outlandish mistress. Known for her cascade of platinum blond hair, her see-through gold lamé dresses and feather boas, her retinue of Las Vegas celebrities, hustlers, and showgirl types, and her million-dollar annual pre-Derby extravaganzas, Anita Madden possessed everything in the world to which Melanie Flynn aspired.

Anita wasn't born into the wealth of the Madden world. In fact, she came from as far on the other side of the tracks as possible. Raised in Ashland—Kentucky's steel, coal, oil, iron, and railroad center—Anita Myers was the epitome of what Lexingtonians considered an outsider. She came from a broken home with little money, but effervesced with cheerleader charm and friendliness. She attended Western Kentucky University for two years before transferring to the University of Kentucky in Lexington in 1952. Known as a free spirit on the University of Kentucky campus, Anita did not excel in academics. She began dating Patrick Madden, the eccentric heir to Hamburg Place, and, according to legend, she was on the verge of marrying Patrick when his handsome and dashing brother Preston literally snatched her away. "She jumped on the back of the motorcycle and came back home with me and has been with me ever since," Preston Madden once told the *Louisville Courier Journal.*

The couple moved into the stone house that was built in the 1930s by Preston's father as a guest dormitory for visiting polo teams. Patrick, a science fiction writer, continued living in the estate's main house, taking no part in the horse business. Patrick retreated into a life of solitary confinement, eventually taking an equally reclusive bride.

Preston, a military school graduate, was reputed to be a reckless and spoiled playboy who sought his thrills through the hazardous sports of rock climbing, skydiving, and car racing. The darkly attractive heir took to wearing a uniform consisting of a white knit turtleneck under a white shirt, with a black suit and black combat boots. His slicked-back hair, moody silences, and sardonic wit set him apart from Lexington's more gregarious country club set. Yet his bloodline cemented his membership in the very society that he scorned. Despite his rebellious stance, he was determined to follow the family tradition: To maintain the reputation of Hamburg Place as the most important horse-breeding farm in the Bluegrass.

Initially, Anita made an attempt to fit in with Preston's society. More understated in her earlier years, people gossiped about the barefooted, bleached blonde that Preston dragged home on a motorcycle. Ostracized by the traditionally staid horsey set, for many years she had remained a shy backdrop to the increasingly unsociable Preston. In 1964 she gave birth to their son Patrick. With her role as a mother, Anita finally seemed to have found her own voice. She immersed herself in the bloodstock business, voraciously reading everything that had been published on the subject. She came to realize that the breeding and training of racehorses was nothing more than a high-stakes gamble.

In the late 1960s, the Maddens started to run with the international jet set. They spent most of their time in New York and Los Angeles, where Anita felt more comfortable than in Lexington. She idolized the people she met—the television soap opera stars and sports figures, artists and entertainers—and invited them to Hamburg Place. She justified this lifestyle as promotion of her business: People who could afford to spend hundreds of thousands of dollars on frail and pampered Thoroughbreds did not run in mundane social circles, she contended.

Through her rich Lexington contacts Anita hooked into the Las Vegas crowd of gamblers, strippers, organized crime figures, and celebrities—a relationship that would irreversibly change the tenor of Lexington's party circuit from one of Southern civility to raucous vulgarity. In 1969, Caesars Palace opened the most gaudy, glitzy, outrageous establishment in Nevada's gaming history. Featuring fantasy suites and barely dressed waitresses, Caesars set a new standard of garishness even for Nevada gambling. Since the days of widespread illegal gambling in Kentucky, there had been a close connection between Kentucky and Las Vegas. Anita's friend Cliff Perlman owned Caesars, and had recruited numerous Kentucky natives for top casino positions. With the advent of Caesars, Anita began frequenting Vegas, where she met her new circle of friends.

She became particularly close to Leslie de Keyser, a designer of scandalous clothes who called herself Suzy Creamcheese. Defending the shocking outfits that had become Anita's trademark—leather jackets trimmed with rooster feathers; rhinestone-monogrammed sunglasses; sequined gowns plunging to burgeoning cleavage; capes covered with mirrors—Anita once remarked, "I do what pleases Anita."

She began hosting more and more parties, at which she made late entrances donning flamboyant Creamcheese creations. Her pre-Derby parties developed into annual bacchanals that gained international recognition. She considered horse racing a vehicle through which she could indulge the fantasies of her friends and clients and in the early 1970s she concocted erotic themes for her uninhibited bashes. The irony of these sexual obsessions, by a woman whose wealth was dependent upon the sexual performance of her studs and fecundity of her mares, was not lost on her guests. Preston, on the rare occasions when he attended Anita's parties, withdrew to the sidelines and watched his wife gyrate on the dance floor. Preston's haunting attendance, his contemptuous smile and black outfit, discomfited many guests.

Anita hired Omnibus Productions to create the environment for her elaborate festivals. The Philadelphia company that produced special events for Caesars Palace and other Vegas casinos attended to Anita's entertaining needs, to the tune of millions of dollars. Every year, the legendary estate was transformed to accommodate a new theme. At the "A Diamond as Big as the Ritz" party, based upon the elegant decadence of F. Scott Fitzgerald's novels, Anita wore a borrowed, 111-carat, coffee-colored diamond called the "Earth Star." In different years, themes included "The Great American Dream," at which Hamburg Place was decorated with oversized credit cards and thousand-dollar bills; "The Fountain of Youth," and "Dipsomania."

Photos of the celebrities drawn to the parties, including Muhammad Ali, Bert Parks, Sissy Spacek, Al Hirt, Ann-Margret, Mike Connors, Connie Stevens, Phyllis Diller, and more, received prominent placement in the *Lexington Herald.*

Members of Lexington's more sedate establishment were offended by the nude mermaids, the wrestlers wearing sado-masochistic uniforms, streakers, and erotic films. They chose to boycott Anita's, attending instead the more traditional annual events hosted by socialite Marylou (Mrs. Cornelius Vanderbilt) Whitney. The Whitneys—who are Anita's rival party-givers and competing horse breeders, held their parties on the same day, but the crowd was always decidedly more genteel: One comprised of diplomats, national political figures, and international industrialists. Her voice tinged with both naiveté and sarcasm, Mrs. Whitney once told a reporter the Madden's Derby Eve carnival was "nice for those who don't have a private party to go to."

Anita spent several evenings a week at the Library Lounge in Lexington, the disco owned by her good friend Jimmy Lambert. Wearing low-cut, clinging blouses with slit skirts and spike heels, the fiftyish woman danced uninhibitedly to rock-and-roll music. Rarely accompanied by Preston, Anita was usually flanked by University of Kentucky football players and wrestlers. The Library was Lexington's undeniable "in place," where narcs and druggies mingled and cops were provided with drinks on the house.

■

Ralph Ross had been receiving reports about Anita Madden's infamous parties for years. Not only were her parties attended regularly by governors, state legislators, mayors, and narcotics agents including Drew

Thornton and DEA regional head Harold Brown, but off-duty Lexington police officers moonlighted as security guards at the annual events. Ralph harbored the fantasy that one day he would have the clout to raid Hamburg Place.

The year Melanie disappeared, the one-thousand invitees to Anita's party were instructed to wear either black tie or "your favorite fantasy." "A Garden of Secret Delights" was held under a 150-foot yellow-striped circus tent decorated with exotic animals that had been stuffed by a famous Chicago taxidermist. Ms. Creamcheese wore whips and chains, and Anita wore a backless and sideless white crystal-beaded scrap of material.

Melanie's absence was conspicuous to Anita's inner circle. She had attended many of the previous parties, and had become a staple around Hamburg Place. Ralph knew that Melanie frequently used Anita's guest facilities as a refuge, and that the two women had become very close. Exactly how close was never actually determined. A Louisville reporter claimed to have been lunching with Anita in Lexington in the fall of 1976 when Melanie entered the restaurant. The two women were said to have engaged in a private conversation, leaving no doubt as to their intimacy. But following Melanie's disappearance, Anita, like Bill Canan, strove to deny all but the most casual of relationships. "I hardly knew her, of course," Anita told the *Kentucky Post,* "but she always seemed to be such a kind girl."

Police at one point in the investigation had asked to search Hamburg Place for evidence of Melanie, but politely retreated when Anita refused access. " 'I think the police must have actually believed I would hide her,' " she told the *Kentucky Post.* During the controversial August 1977 interview, reporter Tom Scheffey asked Anita Madden directly if she and Melanie Flynn had ever engaged in a lesbian affair. " 'Were you indeed lovers as she'd [Melanie] have her friends believe?' " Scheffey asked her.

" 'Lovers?!' A tangle of confusion and amusement swept around Mrs. Madden's clear handsome face.

"Her brow wrinkled in bafflement and she got up quickly to let out a dog—Dribbles—that was scratching at the door.

" 'No, I've never particularly gone for girls,' she said as she sat down again composed."

Detectives investigating Melanie's disappearance returned to Hamburg Place in the summer of 1977 when they implored Anita to help locate Sonny Collins—the former University of Kentucky football superstar and reputed lover of Anita whose name was in Melanie's address book. Anita refused to cooperate, and neglected to inform them that, in fact, Collins was en route to Hamburg Place at that very moment. Then a running back with the Atlanta Falcons, Collins was keeping a low profile since the recent surfacing of his name in connection with a kidnap, murder, drug, and point-shaving scandal at the University of Kentucky. Police eventually located and interviewed Collins about Melanie's disappearance, but the details of that interview were never revealed.

Though Ralph Ross suspected that Anita possessed valuable knowledge about Melanie—if not specifically about her disappearance, then at least about her lifestyle and enemies—he had neither the evidence nor the social standing necessary to infiltrate her web. What, if anything, Anita Madden told police about Melanie Flynn remains a secret, and was not provided to Ralph. He was forced to admit that the Flynn case was going nowhere. Except for graffiti messages that read *Bill Canan killed Melanie Flynn* spray-painted on walls near the University of Kentucky campus, the case had come to a standstill.

CHAPTER
THREE

Lexington, Kentucky, looks like paradise. Acres of grass as green and tender as a golf course putting green surround hilltop mansions. New Circle Road—a beltway enveloping the city's heartland like a moat—attempts to separate the wealthy landowners from the encroaching strip centers and fast-food joints that are symbolic of the rest of the state.

Little girls growing up in Paducah and Hazard focus their sights on Lexington as the Tara of their fantasies. Adolescent boys from the state's rural tobacco farms look to Lexington as an oasis in a state of poverty and ignorance—the lively playground of the idle rich. "Coloreds," as blacks are still called by most white Lexingtonians, look longingly from ramshackle rented houses on the west side of town to the manicured lawns and center-hall colonial manors situated along tree-lined boulevards.

Combining the traditional superior feelings of Southerners with the uniquely gorgeous landscape of the bluegrass, Lexingtonians consider themselves and their region the cream of the crop—not only of Kentucky, but of the nation.

Despite their feigned attempts to downplay their snobbery, Lexingtonians are as obsessed with family bloodlines as with the genealogy of their horses. They are boastful of their pedigrees and keenly aware of each others' places of birth. They judge each other on the basis of who their daddies and granddaddies were, and the counties from whence they came. What is confusing to outsiders is the graciousness and politeness with which these sometimes harsh judgments are dispensed. Describing a professional colleague, one lawyer said with a smile: "The acorn never falls far from the tree. His daddy was no-count so what more could he be?"

Horse traders and coal operators come and go. But the long-established families of central Kentucky—the scions of the original landowners—have never been unseated by the influx of wealthy Arabs and nouveau riche. Some relative newcomers, though, such as Jack Kent Cooke, Nelson Bunker Hunt, John Galbreath, and Cornelius Vanderbilt Whitney, have smoothly blended into the fold.

Money alone does not guarantee induction into Lexington's coveted inner circle. But it doesn't hurt. It is more common than not for the elite to entertain a mixed bag of power brokers, dotting their social events with public figures, prominent attorneys, successful businessmen, and local media celebrities. Despite the unassuming down-home charm, however, it does not go unnoticed at such affairs which guests seem awkward with the fingerbowls or oblivious to the appropriate placement of the tableware upon completion of dinner.

Claiming an affinity to England, Lexington society bestows the most dignified of names to their sons, names that sound as if they were rich sauces: Brownell, Breckenridge, Bentley, Cameron, Landon, Buckner, Preston, Catesby, Austin, Blake, Wickliffe. Their daughters—given sweet names such as Rebecca, Mary Jane, Sally Ann, and Betsy—are reared to be more free-spirited debutantes and hostesses than their staid Yankee counterparts. Even their homes are christened with names suggestive of royal dynasties: Beaconsfield, Buckram Oak, Castleton, Barrister Hall, Avondale, Paxton Place.

Blessed with a mild climate and perfect soil, Lexington is the reigning Thoroughbred horse capital of the world. Bred for the "sport of kings," the sleek and frail Thoroughbreds thrive on their bluegrass diet. Drinking the limestone-laced water and grazing on the special grass rich in phosphorous and minerals, the animals develop strong tendons, resilient muscles, and light but solid bones. Black and white plank fences glide gracefully, rising and falling over the lush greenery, separating paddocks and estates. Massive maple trees stand at the edge of clear pools of water, as groups of young horses prance in the pristine fields.

Long before the sexual prowess of four-legged animals became the cornerstone of the economy, Kentucky's early settlers used the unusual lime water to concoct a distinctive whiskey. During the Prohibition era, incestuous networks were created to transport the liquor to the infamous speakeasies of Chicago, Cleveland, Cincinnati, and New York. The connections were bequeathed to family heirs, becoming more and more sophisticated with the passage of time. The barges that bulged with whiskey barrels, moving slowly down the river under the cover of darkness, were replaced by houseboats that communicated with each other by two-way radio, and dropped off their drug loads at remote airstrips. Massive fields of marijuana were cultivated in the same fertile land that produced the world's richest tobacco.

The horse farms, too, have evolved with age. A spin-off of the Old South of the plantation days, Lexington land-owning society stubbornly resists change. Accustomed to a pampered lifestyle—made possible first by slaves and then by low-paid servants—many horse farm owners face increasing difficulty maintaining their image. They resent the influx of people, developers, and modern ideas. But the reality of modern America—with its high costs of wages, real estate, and provisions—was swallowing their way of life by the late 1970s. A fortune was needed to paint the miles of fences, to groom the fields, feed the horses, pay the trainers and domestic staff, and continue the lavish entertaining. To meet these extravagant financial demands, some farm owners have subdivided their property—once considered a fate worse than death. Others incorporated and sold shares.

Some turned to drug smuggling.

Against this backdrop, what happened to Andrew Carter Thornton II is not surprising. Raised on the picturesque Threave Main Stud horse farm, Drew had the good fortune to be included in Lexington's protected, leisured class. Somewhere along the way he acquired the belief that he was the King of the Walk, and that everyone outside his class was trash under his feet. He had access to the best Lexington had to offer: "The Club," the parties, the daughters of the wealthiest families. But that would not be enough for a guy with an innate sense of superiority. Drew Thornton had to prove that he was even better than the best.

■

Childhood friends recall nothing startling about Drew Thornton's youth that would be a prologue to his life on the razor's edge. Some remember him as a painfully self-conscious, clumsy, and shy lad who was embarrassed to be seen in his horn-rimmed glasses. Others say he exhibited a remarkable proclivity as a horse trainer from an early age.

But most who knew him in his seminal years have difficulty conjuring up anything more than an average, likable kid with the usual quotient of mischief. At what point in his life Drew became the thrill-seeker for which he would later become legendary is murky at best.

As a child, Drew was a loner. He stayed to himself, apparently immersed in his imagination. If he didn't know you well, he didn't know you at all. That distant personality became more pronounced as the years went by, mixing with a sense of bravado. Drew would always take the risk—ride the horse the fastest, take the first dive from the high board. At the age of ten he jumped out of a hayloft wearing nothing but a Superman cape. Knocked unconscious by the act, Drew was undeterred. Over the years, he would play war games with live ammunition; parachute illegally from television towers and cliffs; "pull low" while skydiving, waiting to open his chute within fifty feet of the ground; fly airplanes at altitudes beneath the radar level.

Whether by actual violence or carefully cultivated body language, Drew Thornton projected an air that he was not to be messed with. Obsessed with victory and domination, he became known in Lexington for the mind games he played. He seemed to gain personal power by intimidating others, and stories of Drew's implicit threats were rampant around Lexington. Surprisingly, the threats seem to have rarely materialized, begging one to wonder why he was capable of instilling so much fear.

On the one hand, he seemed to have derived pleasure from his blustering, but on the other, he was loved by many for his compassion, sensitivity, and loyalty. He enjoyed helping friends who had fallen on hard times, but his critics say he did so in order to command them, as well as to inflate his sense of self-worth. Once, he fractured his leg in a parachuting accident because he had taken measures to avoid children playing near his intended target.

Some girlfriends claim he beat them. Others say that physical violence against a woman or child was anathema to Drew, who they claim was the consummate Southern gentleman. What is consistent are references to his mercurial temper and a tendency toward violent outbursts—traits he apparently inherited from his father, Carter Thornton.

Born October 30, 1944, while his father was away in military service, Drew spent his infancy in Louisville at the home of his mother's parents. When his father returned from World War II, he claimed his tiny family and moved them to Paris in Bourbon County. Carter and his wife, Margaret Cummins, leased Threave Main Stud. Several years later, the Thorntons managed to buy the farm. The tranquil setting seemed an ironic site for the spawning of a vicious and mean-spirited boy.

Lexington's elite considered Carter and "Peggy" to be decent, hard-working people. Though they came from working stock and were not native Kentuckians—Carter was from New Jersey and Peggy from Connecticut—they were accepted as equals by the landed gentry, receiving all the significant social invitations, so respected were they for their perseverance and innate gentility. "They did everything within their means to raise their children right," said a longtime family friend, "and are some of the nicest people in the world." After meeting success in the bloodstock business, the Thorntons were invited to join the ranks of Lexington's blueblood society.

On the surface, Drew seems to have had the benefit of the finest upbringing. His parents were deeply involved with the small St. Peter's Episcopal Church, where Drew had been an acolyte, and they raised their three children in a traditional upper-middle-class manner. Drew worked with the horses on his father's farm, and became proficient in his training skills. He knew every nook and cranny of the farm's rolling hills, hunting rabbits and groundhogs for sport. He spent his summer days at the local Stoner Creek Country Club, where he played golf and tennis, or at the Madden's famous Hamburg Place, where he learned to play polo. He attended Southside Elementary School in Paris for five years before transferring to the prestigious Sayre School in Lexington —a country day school attended by the children of Lexington's horsey set.

But all must not have been as idyllic as it seemed, for Drew felt very ambivalent about his family. He confided in close friends that he feared his father, possessed mixed feelings about his mother, and worshiped his maternal grandmother, with whom he had lived as a baby. Some say Drew had always been slightly out of step with his parents, as well as with his brother and sister. He was uncomfortable with his nieces and nephews, sometimes watching them from the other side of a room with a look suggesting he couldn't fathom the point of having children.

Drew spent his freshman year at Bourbon County High School, where he received good grades with very little effort. When Drew wasn't challenged, his parents realized, he quickly became bored and stopped trying. One thing Carter Thornton couldn't abide was a quitter. Worried that the school was not intellectually challenging to Drew, Carter and Peggy decided to send him to the Sewanee Military Academy in Sewanee, Tennessee.

On the morning of September 7, 1959, Andrew Carter Thornton II—fourteen years old—entered the disciplined, regimented world of the cadets. Isolated in the Cumberland Mountains, Sewanee was an Episcopal academy affiliated with the University of the South. It was one of a handful of institutes and academies where Southern men of breeding were dispatched to receive their final polish.

The Sewanee curriculum was markedly more diverse and difficult than his hometown high school, and Drew was not an outstanding student in any subject. He nearly failed Latin and chemistry, and received a straight C average in religious studies, English, and history. An uncommitted, dilatory student, he didn't even excel in the subjects he most enjoyed—rifle and pistol shooting. Finishing sixty-second in a class of seventy-two, Drew's performance must have been a disappointment to his parents.

With more understatement than could possibly have been intended, one teacher described Drew as "inconsistent." Faculty members commented on Drew's laziness, while remarking on his intelligence and good intentions. Perhaps that first year in the sheltered seclusion of Sewanee was the turning point in Drew's life. It had become painfully clear to him and his parents that Drew was incapable of blending his intellect with his performance. Although he received formal disciplinary action only once—for threatening a younger student—Drew's legacy at Sewanee was that of a mediocre kid with a bad attitude. Drew thought his parents favored his younger brother, Tim. Tim was everything

Carter and Peggy wanted in a son: A smart, obedient, cheerful sort who had won the hearts of his parents.

Whatever was at play in the fertile, young imagination of Drew Thornton, it is clear that the devils in his mind were set loose during the years at Sewanee.

In 1962, when Drew was a senior, America was at the height of its cold war with Russia. The Russians had shot down an American U-2 spy plane and in 1960 John F. Kennedy had been elected President by a tiny majority, signifying the beginning of a new generation. The Berlin Wall had driven a wedge between Kennedy and Soviet Premier Nikita Khrushchev. Fidel Castro had become the leader of Cuba, and in 1961 Kennedy had been deeply embarrassed by the failed Bay of Pigs invasion. Tension was at an all-time high between the Americans and Russians, and Kennedy had called for a massive military buildup. In a televised speech, Kennedy had announced that the Russians were assisting the Cubans in constructing long-range-missile bases in Cuba and that he was ordering a blockade. Meanwhile, the world's two nuclear powers were racing each other to conquer space.

Sewanee, with its military history dating back to the Civil War, was a breeding ground for patriotic fervor. Its upper-crust cadets, who were the descendants of the most prosperous Southern families, strutted their conservative heritage proudly. In this highly political and emotional time, anti-communism became the rallying cry, and Drew Thornton's pulse quickened with a newfound purpose in life. To Drew, the *only* way was the American way.

Drew personally resented Castro's unruliness and was offended by his unkempt appearance and anti-American rhetoric. His belief in the superiority of those born to rule, coupled with the perceived threat to America, became his guiding torch. When the Army ROTC personnel instilled "kill, kill, kill" in order to win, a chord was struck in Drew's heart. At least one Sewanee instructor recognized, and worried about, Drew's gung-ho spirit. While most of the young cadets took their military training with a grain of salt—realizing that in a time of peace one prepares for war—others, like Drew, latched onto the killing instinct at their most impressionable age.

Upon high school graduation, Drew returned to Lexington to attend the University of Kentucky. But he felt like a fish out of water on the quiet, relaxed university campus. He saw himself and his generation on the threshold of a new and exciting frontier. Yet nothing seemed to have changed back home in Lexington. His peers weren't responding to the same passions that fomented a restlessness and sense of mission in Drew.

After failing most of his classes in the first semester, Drew sought reinforcement for his warrior instincts. One cold February day in 1963, he drove himself to Louisville and enlisted in the Regular Army. Asked about any special interests or qualifications, Drew didn't hesitate before responding: He wanted to join the airborne division. To become an Army paratrooper stirred Drew's romantic longings. As a sky diver, Drew would finally be able to integrate his brawn with his brains. From that point forward, Drew's friends thought he was unable to distinguish between peace and war environments, fantasy and real-life situations.

Assigned to the 82nd Airborne Division at Fort Bragg, North Carolina, Drew was a member of the invading forces who quashed an insurgency against the ruling dictatorship of the Dominican Republic. He was awarded a Purple Heart and an Oak Leaf Cluster when he was shot in the arm there. This led to an honorable discharge in 1965, and his much-romanticized military career came to a premature end.

When Betty Zaring met Drew he was nursing his wounds, training horses, and thinking of becoming a policeman. A beautiful coed from Shelby County, Betty was the kind of small-town Southern beauty whom boys like Drew were expected to marry. She found his boyish charm, blue eyes and stocky physique, to be irresistible. Head over heels in love with him, she watched from the sidelines as Drew searched for ways to recapture the thrill he was missing in civilian life. She dated him as he recuperated—both physically and emotionally— and she encouraged him to spend his free time parachuting and learning to fly. Eventually he obtained his pilot's license, and embarked on plans to buy his own plane.

In the middle of one of the country's most troubled decades, Drew felt caught in the cross fire. The patriotism that had been epidemic in his youth had given way to widespread domestic turmoil. The hatred and distrust that a short time earlier had been aimed at the Communists had now turned inward. Civil rights disturbances had rocked Birmingham, Savannah, Selma, Chicago, Philadelphia, and

Watts. Then, the resumption of bombing raids in North Vietnam had brought massive demonstrations nationwide. By early 1968, the buildup of U.S. forces in Vietnam was at an all-time high, and college students were demonstrating en masse against the war and the draft.

That year, Drew was taking political science courses at the university. He had no tolerance for the vociferous anti-war protestors, and despised his long-haired, blue-jean-clad peers. After the excitement of battle, he felt let down, left out, at a loss. He was a member of the limbo generation—the group who came of age after the Korean War, but before Vietnam. He thought of himself as a war hero, but no one else seemed to have heard of the skirmish in the Caribbean that he took so seriously. He had no clear idea of what he wanted to do, and so, after a year, he was back working for his father, training Thoroughbreds.

Drew and Betty were married in July 1968, and a month later Drew joined the Lexington police. Betty thought he went into the police force so that he could do battle. She knew that he was happiest when he was testing himself—when he was on the cutting edge. Others thought Drew was attracted to the local police force because he could be a big spoke on a little wheel.

Their marriage was strained almost from the start. Betty was much more complacent and self-satisfied than Drew. Described as a "knock-down, gorgeous beauty" by an acquaintance, life came easier to Betty than to Drew. A schoolteacher and pacifist, Betty had a rich inner life that kept her on an even keel. She believed that she had psychic powers, and Drew was fascinated with her uncanny intuition. It was a bittersweet marriage that was doomed to failure. Here was a woman who was at peace with herself, married to a man who was raging around in confusion.

Betty blamed their problems on Drew's inability to find a niche in modern American society. She accepted his obsession with violence, blaming it on the military. She thought the U.S. Government had taken a tender soul—not a natural killer—and turned him into an efficiently trained warrior. He told Betty, and others close to him, that he had been secretly recruited by the CIA during these most turbulent of times and that being a cop was just a cover. He recounted tales of his participation in military operations in which American assassins were dispatched to kill American prisoners of war in Vietnam who knew too much about U.S. covert operations. On the one hand, Drew had trouble reconciling the obvious paradoxes of such operations, while on the other hand he lusted for the intrigue. Though Betty and his family believed Drew when he claimed to be a government assassin, they were forced to rely upon his word, for the government would never admit to such acts. *I did it for my country* would become a catch-all phrase Drew would use throughout life to explain his questionable, and often illegal, actions.

As a rookie with the Lexington Police Department, Drew worked long hours and became increasingly secretive about his professional life. He was frequently sent out of town to training seminars, where he learned lock-picking and surveillance techniques. Assigned to the Intelligence Unit, Drew worked mostly on the University of Kentucky campus. Guy Mendes, a reporter for an underground newspaper on campus, remembered Drew Thornton as a policeman who was vehemently opposed to college anti-war demonstrators. Rather than work undercover, Drew proudly refused to camouflage his normal militaristic, macho, short-haired appearance. He made no attempt to hide his right-wing reactionism, and made the campus leftists aware that he was out to get them because of their liberal ideology and activism. Drew quickly gained the reputation as a cop who was to be feared and avoided. He swaggered with his sense of purpose, his mandate to intimidate hippies and counterculture types.

By 1970, political activity on campus was at its peak. Four students had been killed at Kent State in Ohio, and hundreds of universities were on strike to protest military action in Cambodia. Kentucky was no exception. Final exams were canceled due to rallies, marches, and moratoriums, and the National Guard was called in to keep peace. The Students for a Democratic Society (SDS) threw eggs at Kentucky's Patterson School of Diplomacy because of that school's alleged involvement with a violent coup in Indonesia.

That year, Drew was assigned to the city's first narcotics squad, sending a clear message to university pot smokers. "It became common knowledge at that time," Mendes said, "that Drew Thornton would bust people for dope and then sell what he confiscated." Drew claimed he had the power and license to do anything he wanted, pointing to his scrape with death in the Dominican Republic as evidence that his life was charmed. Rumors abounded about his physical excesses and brutality against those he arrested. Yet he was never disciplined by his superiors in the department.

Betty watched as her husband became more and more a James Bond character. Discarding his eyeglasses for contact lenses, he adopted a new self-confidence. His obsession with physical appearance became absurd, and he started collecting bizarre spy gadgets and instruments. He took to calling himself "ACT II," which were his initials, and spoke in cryptic parables. Betty found it increasingly difficult to relate to her husband. With time, she found she had more in common with his enemies than with him. In many ways, Drew was a loving, gentle, and supportive husband who was very protective of the people close to him. She knew that he loved her, but he resented having a wife, for the domestic simplicity betrayed his image as the larger than life man against the world. The spy who had to forsake his personal life in order to serve his country. How much was real and how much delusion would never be known.

They were divorced that year—1970. Though Betty and Drew parted friends, she couldn't help feeling sorry for him. She had come to believe that Drew would be destined to a life of longing and loneliness.

Drew had been trained in the basics of martial arts in the Army, and in 1970 decided to pursue karate with vigor. As a committed disciple, he became a fanatic about his physical strength and ability. He studied human anatomy—the circulatory and nervous systems—so that he could accurately target his victims' weaknesses. He became obsessed with the Eastern philosophy behind karate, immersing himself in *t'ai chi* and meditation techniques. He developed and refined a moral and religious code based upon ancient Chinese and Japanese systems. Intrigued with the oriental secret societies, he perceived himself as a kindred spirit of the ninjas—the spy-assassins who did the bidding of the aristocrats.

He studied the modern ninja techniques of concealment, experimented with smoke bombs and exotic poisons, dwelt on the sect's superstitious beliefs, and, eventually, believed he was part of the myth. The most brutal of all the martial arts, the ninja training helped Drew justify his own viciousness.

He flaunted his soldier-of-fortune idealogy, his professional and political connections, his skydiving exploits, and his love of guns. He took to hanging out at Lexington bars known for their offbeat clientele —gay men and bodybuilders; local TV and radio personalities; druggies and up-and-coming yuppie restaurateurs; the kind of criminal defense attorneys who scrounge up cases by loitering in courthouse corridors. Though he tried to be discreet, he couldn't resist flexing his muscles and bulging wallet.

Unencumbered by a mundane marriage, in the early 1970s Drew embarked upon a crime spree that would last fifteen years and become infamous for its heinousness. His trademark would be the perverse pleasure he derived from the "overkill" sense of violence that accompanied his acts.

His inseparable friendships with fellow members of the narcotics squad would further shape his character and serve as a lifelong brotherhood. Like-minded in their belief that they were above the law, the bonds between them would become stronger than blood, and their deeds more gruesome with the passage of time.

What better way to utilize his paramilitary skills in everyday American life than to pursue a profession of drug smuggling, gunrunning, assassinations, and law enforcement? Such pursuits, it seemed to Drew, went hand in hand.

What he *didn't* take into consideration was the threat posed by Ralph Ross.

CHAPTER
FOUR

By the time Ralph Ross was eight years old, he had visited Lexington enough times to know that that was where the rich snobs lived. His life, on the other hand, had not been so privileged.

Born in 1933, Ralph was the third of six offspring who were all born at home on the farm. His father raised tobacco, corn, and maize, and bartered his services as a mechanic to neighboring farms. They raised a few horses—work horses, not the pampered Thoroughbreds that grazed the bluegrass fields twenty miles to the north. His parents grew up on adjacent farms, near the same dried-up creek where Ralph entered the world. Several generations before them had lived within a mile of those farms, and it was the only life Ralph's ancestors knew. His mom took care of Ralph and his five siblings, and everything they raised, while his father managed the business end of the farm. She did the canning, made cream and butter, killed all of her own cows and hogs and chickens, and made buttermilk biscuits every day from store-bought flour and sugar, and sewed clothes for her brood. The kids were responsible for milking the cows and feeding the livestock. Ralph was expected to take care of the runts—the baby lambs, piglets, and calves whose mothers ignored them—by inducing them to drink from a baby bottle. Ralph became attached to the orphan calves, the stray lambs, and little pigs the old sows had rejected, and for many years couldn't bring himself to eat beef. For some reason, he didn't muster up an abundance of compassion for hogs and chickens, but could be brought to tears by the slaughter of a cow. The big event of every year was when the farmers butchered their pigs. Ralph would watch, and be expected to help, as his father and the neighbor men gutted the big animals and then hung them so the blood drained from their veins.

Ralph had two older sisters to contend with—Vernice and Sara —who, Ralph thought, acted like they hung the moon. Then there were Thelma and Shirley, who were younger than he, and his baby brother Lynn. Lynn would disappear after high school, leaving no trail. Throughout his life, from time to time Ralph would hear that Lynn had been arrested out West. But Lynn would never return to Dry Branch, Kentucky.

His father had moved the entire family into the five-bedroom main house on the property after Ralph's grandmother died. His parents took one bedroom, his grandfather another, and the rest of the kids shuffled for themselves. Four fireplaces were the only source of heat against the bitter-cold Kentucky winter, and the hearths became the focal point for evening conversation. Sometimes, in the days before electricity, Ralph's dad would hook up a radio to a battery that had been charging all day long, and the family would listen to championship boxing matches. Entertainment was not as hard to come by in the late 1940s, though, when Ralph's family became the first in Mercer County to own a television.

A taciturn disciplinarian, Ralph's father instilled fear in his children without raising his voice or striking them—a trait that Ralph would inherit. With his head cocked a certain way, his lips slightly parted, and his eyebrows raised, one look from Ralph's father would let the kids know if they were in trouble. He left the spankings to Ralph's mother, who kept a supply of maple switches for meting out her punishment and inspiring impeccable manners. "You could figure on two or three whippings a week until you were about ten years old," Ralph would remember in later years. His mother handled the day-to-day problems with the kids, dispensing permission and penalty alike. (Breakfast, lunch, and supper were all scheduled events, with each Ross kid expected to wash up before taking his place at the rectangular oak table.) One of the tasks Ralph's dad took most seriously was planning the family vacation. His quiet, reserved manner must have belied an active imagination, for it seemed to Ralph his dad was constantly dreaming about the ocean. Every chance he got, Ralph's dad loaded his family into the car and headed for the coast. "The crew of us young uns would be fightin' and carryin' on in the backseat the whole way," Ralph remembered.

Though both his parents made every effort to keep him in line, Ralph had the good fortune to have two sets of grandparents living on the adjacent property. "I went to their house for spoilin'," Ralph recalled.

He attended a one-room schoolhouse in nearby Harrodsburg, the county seat, where he was taught, among other things, to say: "Yes, sir," and "Yes, ma'am"—a habit Ralph would never shake. There were six grades there, and when the time came for the students to get their lessons for the day, each one got up, walked to the front of the room, and took a seat on the stage. One teacher taught all six grades, while the students were expected to sit in silence until everyone had finished.

Ralph's father decided to send all of his kids to Harrodsburg High School, which reputedly maintained high educational standards. Neither parent had had the advantages of a high school education, yet placed a high value on learning.

Ralph, nicknamed "Buster," was a strong, lanky boy—all arms and legs in his adolescence. His soul mate was his sister Thelma. The two of them used to invent games in search of some comic relief. They'd get up in the morning, eat breakfast, and each grab a hoe. With their dog—a conglomeration of breeds—they would head out to hunt snakes in the parched creek that ran through the farm. "We'd pick up them rocks with them hoes, the dog would jump in the middle of 'em, and the snakes would come crawling out and we'd go after 'em with the hoes. It was nothing to get two or three water moccasins out from under one rock."

Ralph was the kind of Southern man who had been indoctrinated with a sense of independence and self-reliance. He grew up fast, having been expected to take care of himself from a very early age. Kentucky men of his generation and rural heritage were not afforded the luxury of pondering their future. Upon graduation from high school in 1950 he was drafted into the Army. After nearly three years with the artillery outfit at Fort Knox, Kentucky, Ralph decided he was interested in communications. He wanted to become a code-breaker. Since the Army offered little advancement in that area, he switched to a four-year tour in the Air Force where he was trained in International Morse Code and communications basics. Before long he was an expert in encoding and decoding. Charged with communicating with the Philippines, Okinawa, Korea, Japan, and the Seventh Fleet of the Navy, Ralph's unit roamed all over the world. He found himself most frequently in desolate areas where he worked out of the back of a pickup truck. Ultimately, he wound up at the Air Defense Control Center at Johnson Air Force Base in Japan where he sat in an enormous room filled with plastic boards monitoring unidentified aircraft. Although his outfit was stationed in Korea, Ralph was in constant motion, traveling to the various satellite and early-warning stations.

Ralph had become a well-built man, whose six-foot-three height and large hands exuded self-confidence. A dead-ringer for the actor Robert Mitchum, he had been approached more than once for his autograph. War had made him more appreciative of Kentucky's blue skies, languid hills, and lush greenery. A finicky eater, he longed for the sausage biscuits, salt-cured ham, corn bread and collard greens, and Kentucky bourbon. When he returned to Dry Branch in 1955, he had no desire to see any more of the world.

He spent the first three months after his return wandering around central Kentucky, dating girls from Boyle, Mercer, and Anderson counties. In November 1955, Ralph and two buddies drove to Hartsville, South Carolina, where they had arranged three blind dates. A year later he was married to his date—a petite South Carolina native named Vivian.

Having been trained by the military in the most sophisticated communications techniques of the time, Ralph Ross was unsure how he would apply his technical skills to civilian life. One thing he was sure of: He didn't want to be a cop.

One day he accompanied a friend who had decided to apply for employment with the Kentucky State Police. Ralph leafed through a magazine while waiting in an anteroom for his friend to complete his interview. A first sergeant came out and said to him: "Hello there. Put your application in." Ralph replied: "Hell no! I don't want to be no police officer!" But when the sergeant continued badgering him, Ralph finally succumbed and agreed to an interview. Two weeks later, he found himself at the police academy in Frankfort—the state capital.

Ralph's first assignment in 1956 was to the "Tip Top Post"—located at the intersection of U.S. 31W and Highway 60. Situated at the edge of the Fort Knox Army base, it seemed to Ralph as if he were policing an entire city. There was no typical day in the life of a trooper, Ralph quickly found out, as state police duties included a little bit of everything. Nicknamed the "Dixie Die-Way" because of the rampant bloodshed on the dangerous stretch of road, Ralph became accustomed to working all hours of the day and night. When he wasn't investigating car accidents, Ralph was responding to homicides and assaults. He was faced with an exorbitant number of shootings, "where the GIs got off the base and brawled with each other."

Ralph spent the next ten years as a trooper, patrolling Kentucky's state roads in various rural counties. Transferred from one post to another, sometimes with very little notice, Ralph would pack his little family and dutifully follow orders. First in Stanford, then in Lebanon, he personally built new homes for his wife and two toddler girls. He played basketball twice a week with a regular group of guys at the local high school gymnasium, which kept him in immaculate physical condition into middle age.

By the mid-1960s, Ralph was tired of moving, and bored with traffic and homicides. Law enforcement was changing. Political assassinations, race riots, and student protests suddenly dominated the scene, challenging the nation's police forces, which were ill-equipped to handle internal violence. The CIA's Office of Security in 1966 began training certain police officers throughout the United States, and had made overtures to him. The training courses, held at the CIA's compound near Washington, D.C., included declassification of materials, foreign weapons, counteraudio measures, explosive devices and detection techniques, basic theories of intelligence and clandestine collection of information, covert photography, and photoanalysis, and Ralph found that he was a quick study.

In 1968 Congress created a special appendage of the Justice Department to financially assist state and local police departments in battling the new, complex national crime wave that had accompanied the riots and demonstrations. President Richard Nixon announced drugs to be the evil force destroying American society, and made funds available for his much-publicized *War on Drugs*.

Every police agency in the country scrambled to obtain the Law Enforcement Assistance Administration money allocated by the federal government, which was dished out only to agencies that established intelligence units. In 1969, Ralph became one of a handful of officers assigned to the first such unit created by the Kentucky State Police. The more violent and rebellious American society became, the more federal funds became available for training. Ralph's superiors saw in him the right mix of intellect and levelheadedness. Inspiring their confidence, he was handpicked time and again as the state police designate-trainee to attend the country's most renowned law enforcement academies. Before long, he had learned everything there was to know about lock-picking and wiretapping.

In addition to the FBI and CIA programs, Ralph attended training courses offered by manufacturers of state-of-the-art electronic audio and video equipment. Even Smith & Wesson, which had primarily been an arms manufacturer, entered the business of night-vision cameras and scopes, recorders, and transmitters, offering training to its customers. Ralph was the Kentucky State Police representative at all the schools, including the National Intelligence Academy (NIA) in Fort Lauderdale, Florida. Long rumored to be CIA-sponsored, NIA offered twenty-first-century training and technology to elite units of U.S. and Latin American police forces. Founded by a Kentucky native named Jack Holcomb, NIA existed hand-in-hand with Audio Intelligence Devices (AID), the manufacturer of the spy equipment used by NIA students. It was at NIA that Ralph perfected his electronic eavesdropping expertise.

Ralph then became the tactician of the squad, training his unit in surveillance, countersurveillance, and most other investigative techniques, except for telephone wires. He guarded that specialty, keeping details of these unique abilities to himself.

Soon he was not only the technical adviser, but also the strategist for the unit. The key to a successful probe, Ralph had come to believe, was in the accumulation of relevant intelligence information.

As drugs began seeping into Kentucky, the Intelligence Division expanded to include investigations of narcotics trafficking and corruption of public officials. In 1971, Ralph was named the head of the larger, more inclusive division that was now called the Organized Crime Unit. Until then, the Kentucky State Police had been more like the FBI —it didn't tackle big-time corruption cases. Corruption had always existed in Kentucky—from slavery to bootlegging to illegal gambling— and organized crime had operated openly for decades. But neither the feds nor the locals had ever taken them on. Now, the Organized Crime Unit of the state police would operate less like the FBI and more like the CIA—methodically and systematically collecting and analyzing data.

For the first time in Kentucky history, a faction housed within the state police had become less a manipulative tool of the political machinery and more an autonomous mechanism that only a few men, including Ralph Ross, understood.

It was in this climate that Ralph Ross learned that Drew Thornton and other members of the Lexington Police Department were dealing dope. As had become Ralph's custom, he assigned his men to gather intelligence on their counterparts.

Ralph considered police officers a strange breed. Some were zealots. Some were driven by a passion for truth and justice. Some were naive about the shortcomings of democracy, of politics, of human nature. Some were on a personal mission to clean up the world. Some enjoyed the power of a uniform, the discipline of a male-dominated organization. Some were motivated by ego and the desire to be revered as authority figures. Some were honest men dedicating their lives to public service.

He hadn't yet decided which category Drew fit into.

Ralph Ross was himself an enigma. He was a seemingly uncomplicated man who believed he knew the difference between right and wrong and considered himself a peace officer in the truest sense of the word. He would be described as overzealous many times during his career, but no one would ever call Ralph Ross anything but honest. He was a good old boy who believed in doing his job well and going home to his family at night. But the bulldog commitment that accompanied those simple beliefs would prove to be a deadly challenge to Ralph's adversaries.

Ralph had come to enjoy a statewide reputation for his integrity and down-home charm. His lack of a formal higher education, which resulted in horrendous spelling on official reports and an often comical mispronunciation of words, coupled with a Southern drawl and rural colloquial expressions led some to dismiss him as a lightweight. But anyone who had an opportunity to work for or with him, as well as anyone who had the misfortune to be investigated by him, quickly had his doubts dispelled about Ralph's intelligence and professionalism. Nobody ever considered Ralph to be dull in mind or spirit.

For a man who didn't want to be a police officer, Ralph had become the consummate cop. He had faith in his organization, he believed in the law enforcement and judicial systems—warts and all. He thought, perhaps naively, that he could make a dent in the war on drugs, and he considered it his duty to work long hours for little pay. He didn't realize it at the time, but he was sacrificing his marriage for his profession. As the years went by, he returned home later and later at night, until, finally, Vivian and the girls hardly saw him at all.

■

By the time Melanie Flynn disappeared in 1977, infiltrating Lexington's elite had become one of Ralph's favorite pastimes. The progeny of wealthy Northeastern families, heirs to industrial fortunes, oversaw their empires from their mansions in the Bluegrass that had lawns the size of parks. Ralph thought that the Scotch-Irish blood of Lexington's natives had commingled with that of America's Anglo-Saxon gentility, producing a new breed of flighty, eccentric patricians.

In spite of the pretense and unabashed emulation of the world's more refined societies, Ralph knew there existed in Lexington an insidious underbelly that was not without a certain diamond-in-the-rough charm. Though it cultivated correct form and good manners, gentlemanly grace and feminine sweetness and light, Ralph saw that as a facade to a decidedly offbeat society. As far as Ralph was concerned, Lexington's rich had made their money off the blood and sweat of others. Before horse racing there had been moonshine. And before that, slave trading. To Ralph, it was all the same and not something of which the heirs should be proud. He knew that the same routes along the Kentucky River that were used to smuggle slaves and bourbon were now being used to transport guns, pot, bombs, and cocaine. He figured that Lexington's big drug smugglers had learned the tricks of the trade from their bootlegger granddads.

By 1977, Ralph had reformulated his view of the drug problem in Kentucky and started to take it much more seriously. Something had changed, and with that change had come an increase in violence. The days of campus marijuana smoking—which he never considered as big a deal as his colleagues did—had given way to a literal epidemic of cocaine.

When the floodgates from Colombia opened, unleashing a torrent of the provocative white powder, Lexington's elite was waiting with open arms. Not only did the humongous profit margin seduce even the most cautious investors, but the party-going horse crowd latched onto the luxury drug with fervor. Overnight cocaine had become a status drug, and Lexingtonians, not to be outclassed, were forerunners in incorporating the drug into high society.

The traffickers, Ralph noticed, were no longer University of Kentucky hippies whacking up bricks of marijuana, but lawyers and bankers, preppies and businessmen, horsemen and socialites, who were financing million-dollar loads of cocaine.

Ralph had successfully avoided the drug interdiction level of law enforcement for nearly ten years. He didn't believe in the traditional "buy-bust" methods that were in vogue. To him, it was similar to buying a half pint of whisky from a moonshiner in Pikeville. Narcotics enforcement was attracting a bunch of "cowboys" who liked to wear gold chains and flash buy money. Ralph had realized early on that he just wasn't the "narc" type.

But by the end of the 1970s, Ralph was astounded by the plethora of guns and explosives that accompanied the new cocaine trade. Not just a few guns here and there that the cocaine crowd carried for security. But lots and lots of guns. Enough guns to destabilize a continent.

Shortly before Melanie Flynn disappeared, Ralph had infiltrated a gunrunning organization in Lexington. The fact that the group was also involved in drug smuggling was of only passing interest to Ralph.

One of Ralph's informants—a former military pilot from outside the state—told Ralph he had been hired to escort a load of guns from Kentucky to South America. Ralph directed him to accept the job and to report back on the details of the trip.

Ralph breathed a sigh of relief when his informant returned alive. As he listened to his story, Ralph realized for the first time the significance of the escapades of the Lexington group. His undercover source had driven from Lexington to Huntington, West Virginia, where he boarded a cargo plane that was filled with weapons—AR-15s, Ingrams, Uzis, AK-47s, and military-type explosives. Ralph's source was not told the destination of the plane, but was charged with making sure the load arrived safely.

Twenty-four hours after takeoff, the plane landed at a remote landing strip located in a tropical jungle. Several three-quarter-ton military vehicles were awaiting the aircraft, and, upon their arrival, uniformed guards off-loaded the weapons. Ralph's informant began his twenty-four-hour return flight to Kentucky within an hour.

Although the informant could not identify the country to which the arms were taken, he recognized that the soldiers were speaking Spanish.

Ralph's long-standing suspicions were confirmed, for the person who had hired his source for the job had a high-level position on the Lexington police force.

Ralph immediately realized that an operation of that magnitude had more far-reaching implications than fell under his purview. First, he set up meetings with the FBI and turned over his information to them. He hoped that agency would have the wherewithal to take on the Lexington Police Department. A few days later, he met with Customs agents, who, Ralph knew, would be interested in neutrality violations.

After a couple of weeks had passed—long enough, Ralph thought, for the FBI and Customs to have made some progress in the probe—Ralph called a contact at the CIA. He told the CIA about the incident, primarily to let the intelligence agency know that he had infiltrated the network because he had a sneaking suspicion that maybe he had inadvertently landed in the middle of a CIA deal. "Look," Ralph told his contact, "if this is your operation, maybe you should be getting in touch with FBI and Customs, because I already turned it over to them."

As is customary with the CIA, they neither confirmed nor denied any knowledge or involvement. But Ralph wasn't looking for confirmation or denial. He was merely trying to keep them apprised.

Suddenly, Ralph's informant disappeared. Inquiries Ralph made into his whereabouts were met with silence. Though he knew it was possible that he had been killed, Ralph assumed that one of the federal agencies had co-opted him to work for them.

That incident started Ralph thinking about guns. Where were

they coming from? His suspicions led him to cast a wary eye toward a wholesale Lexington gun dealer who seemed to have an inordinate supply of weapons warehoused. Licensed to supply the official handguns to all the major police departments in Kentucky, Florida, West Virginia, and Tennessee, the outfit had a perfect cover for arms-trafficking.

Phillip Gall & Sons had established a pattern with the Kentucky State Police that was suspect to Ralph. Every year, Gall ordered a thousand magnum pistols from the Smith & Wesson factory. Since guns could legally be purchased in such massive quantity from a gun manufacturer only if they were to be sold to police departments, Gall made arrangements for the weapons to be sold to the Kentucky State Police. The following year, Gall would order a thousand brand-new guns from Smith & Wesson, claiming they would be provided to the Kentucky State Police. When the guns arrived, Gall would distribute them to the state troopers free of charge, in exchange for the previous year's weapons.

Such a scenario, Ralph reasoned, provided the Gall company with a surplus of unreported weapons available for private sale.

Following his hunch, Ralph checked with friends at ATF, from whom he learned that the company had a long-standing history of shoddy paperwork and delinquency in filing reports required by the federal government. But, like so many other occurrences in Lexington, the gun dealer had never been the subject of a criminal investigation. To the contrary, the company's owners enjoyed the social benefits generally bestowed upon reputable, successful businessmen.

Ralph found it particularly noteworthy that Drew Thornton was one of Gall's steadiest customers. That fact in and of itself was not especially remarkable, since police officers are frequently avid gun enthusiasts. But Ralph had come to believe that Melanie Flynn's disappearance was integrally tied to the gun and cocaine trade currently flourishing in Lexington, and that she had fallen into fatal quicksand at the hands of the Lexington police.

At the heart of it all, Ralph suspected, was Drew Thornton.

Ralph set out to locate and interview Drew—a task that turned out to be more difficult than he anticipated. Drew's colleagues on the police force—Canan and others—refused to cooperate with Ralph.

Even the chief of police was recalcitrant when called upon to assist in determining Drew's whereabouts.

Despite the roadblocks and cover-ups thrown into Ralph's path, he soon learned that Drew was spending all of his time up in Philadelphia with his childhood friend and erstwhile military school cadet— Bradley Fred Bryant.

P A R T

BOOK
TWO

ONE

THE
COMPANY

CHAPTER
FIVE

As Drew approached the curved driveway of Bradley Bryant's seven-acre estate, he could see that outdoor tables had been set among the huge oak trees where a group of well-dressed guests were already mingling. An off-duty policeman was waiting to offer valet parking to Drew and others. Black waiters wearing white dinner jackets were taking drink orders near a buffet table. The guests—an odd mixture of police types and high-society elements—must have been reminiscent to Drew of Lexington's royalty. Standing near the champagne fountain, women drifting toward him as if pulled by an invisible magnet, Bradley was, as usual, the most handsome, intriguing man in the crowd.

When Drew Thornton joined his best friend Bradley Bryant in Pennsylvania in 1977, Bradley had been living there for nearly a decade. Known by his neighbors as the perfect Southern gentleman, who hosted lavish parties, a shrewd and successful businessman, a devoted father to three small children and loyal husband to a blond beauty, few saw beneath his veneer.

But to those aware of Bradley's darker side, his outer facade was peeling, exposing a mysterious man whose marriage was on the rocks, whose enterprises were on the wrong side of the law, and whose exploits had strayed beyond the boundaries accepted by everyday American life.

One of Lexington's native sons, Bradley grew up in enviable upper-middle-class circumstances, in a tree-shaded neighborhood near the estate of statesman Henry Clay. The second of four children, Bradley was the son of a businessman and the grandson of a former Lexington mayor. As a toddler, he was breathtakingly adorable—his chocolate brown eyes and sweet smile, his shy, yet engaging demeanor prompted one family friend to describe Bradley as the most beautiful little boy she had ever known. He spent his adolescent summers at a family retreat on the shores of a remote Kentucky lake, attended cotillion with the other upper-class children, and grew into a tall, tanned, athletic, attractive young man whose sexy earnestness made him popular with the girls in his high school. A born leader, Bradley had the type of personality that attracted and intimidated at the same time. Gregarious but cool. Affable but unapproachable.

Though Bradley's childhood was enviable, it was not without its blights. His grandfather's suicide brought shame and confusion to the family, and his father—a used car salesman—went into a professional and personal slump as a result. Domestic events tumbled out of control for Bradley's family during the 1950s, and inevitably led to the divorce of his parents in 1958. Living with his mother, Bradley became the family leader—a role for which he was not quite prepared at fourteen years of age. His lack of a strong, masculine model took a toll on Bradley's personality and, his mother feared, on his academic capacities. In 1960, during Bradley's sophomore year, his mother decided he should transfer to Sewanee Military Academy. Several of Lexington's privileged youth were attending the institute, including the son of "those lovely people, Carter and Peggy Thornton," so it would be easy, she reasoned for Bradley to fit in. She hoped a military environment would prove an adequate substitute for a weak father figure.

At Sewanee, Bradley and Drew forged an alliance that confounded some observers. They assumed roles that would last for nearly twenty years—Bradley the leader and Drew the follower.

Bradley was everything Drew wanted to be, but could never quite achieve—smart, goal-directed, incredibly good-looking, and popular. He received good grades and won the Team Spirit Award three years in a row. What Bradley and Drew had in common was an eagerness to become men, to prove to themselves and to their parents that they were able to take control of their lives. Each felt like a misfit within his own family unit—firstborn sons who were conflicted by the male role models they saw in their fathers. These ambiguous feelings drove them both to never-ending searches for shortcuts to surpassing their fathers' successes and failures. For nearly twenty years, the two young men would attempt to beat the system that their fathers symbolized.

After graduation in 1962, Bradley stayed at Sewanee for an extra year of trigonometry and physics, hoping to qualify for the Naval Academy at Annapolis, but he was rejected. Following a short and unremarkable stint with the U.S. Marines, Bradley returned to Lexington to study architecture at the University of Kentucky. But he found he had neither the discipline nor the endurance much less the finances to pursue his dream of becoming an architect. During this period, he socialized almost exclusively with Drew and Betty, and when he met Callie Grace—a stunning blond coed—he fell head over heels in love. Bradley married Callie in 1967, and the next year Drew followed suit, as if, he were waiting to take his cue from Bradley. Drew chose Bradley as his best man, even though Bradley had not bestowed the same honor upon Drew.

The two couples became the closest of friends, even after Bradley and Callie moved to Philadelphia where Bradley had obtained a high-paying corporate executive's position, thanks to his friendship with John Young Brown, Jr.—the fast-food wizard who had made millions with his Kentucky Fried Chicken empire. Bradley had gotten to know Brown when his younger sister Lynne married one of Brown's best friends—Dan Chandler. Chandler, the wayward son of former Kentucky governor A. B. "Happy" Chandler, worked for "John Y.," as everyone called the chicken magnate, in the franchise business. The marriage of Lynne Bryant to Dan Chandler signaled Bradley's inclusion into a slightly older, and more solidly entrenched, generation of bluebloods. Chandler and Brown were like big brothers to Bradley, and their fast crowd of jet-setters and gamblers appealed to Bradley's adventurous streak. Through them, Bradley met his future partner—a Philadelphia multimillionaire named Edward "Biff" Halloran, who was a regular at the Kentucky Derby. Chandler was more than happy to take credit for launching Bradley's career. When Chandler and Brown introduced Bradley to Halloran, Bradley was working as a flack in Frankfort for state government—a patronage position Chandler had helped Bradley land. Disenchanted with his menial bureaucratic salary and bored with his duties, Bradley was looking for a windfall. He felt insecure and uncertain about his lifetime goals and lack of professional experience. Since neither Annapolis nor architecture had panned out for him, Bradley was more than willing to entertain offers of any kind.

Biff Halloran had extensive oil and real estate holdings, including a racetrack in Atlantic City, New Jersey, and was looking for someone to run his industrial cleaning service. Individuals familiar with Halloran's operations said later that Halloran needed to hide his ownership in the company, called the Armstrong Corporation, because of conflicts of interest in the awarding of government contracts to construction firms owned by Halloran's family. So in order to avoid bad publicity and the scorn of both his competitors and government prosecutors, Halloran selected Bradley Bryant as the perfect front man to disguise Halloran's involvement with the company.

Bradley jumped at Halloran's offer, and made immediate arrangements in 1970 to move his wife, Callie, and son Bradley, to Pennsylvania, where they bought a run-down, Georgian mansion on Philadelphia's Main Line, and began renovating it one room at a time.

The Armstrong Corporation was an immediate success, given Bradley's enthusiasm and Halloran's financial backing, and Bradley's life was perfect for a while. The first major strains on his marriage apparently began with the birth of Brandon, in 1971, who was born with a cleft palate. While president of Armstrong Corporation, he bought a 5 percent interest in a waste oil reclamation company, and in 1973 his wife bore him a little girl. By the mid-seventies, Bradley was exhibiting the confidence of a successful businessman and the restlessness of an unhappily married man. Friends point to this era as the turning point in Bradley's life—a time when ideas percolated in his mind for ways to make big money—and in 1975 he actually managed to start his own company. Drawing upon what he had learned with Halloran, he founded Bryson Environmental Services, Inc.

Bradley was not satisfied to live on the periphery of wealth and power. His grandfather's prominence had been his ticket to the cotillions, the country clubs, the debutante balls. But the suicide, coupled with his father's failings as a businessman and family man, had marred Bradley's credentials. His kinship to Chandler had opened worlds previously closed to Bradley Bryant, yet he always felt as if he were an observer rather than a participant. John Y. Brown and Dan Chandler seemed to Bradley to be of a higher caliber: John Y., a self-made millionaire at the age of thirty-three, possessed the glamorous lifestyle unique to rich, young entrepreneurs; Chandler had the rare protection of his daddy's immense national political power.

When John Y. Brown bought Lums Restaurants in 1974—the corporation that owned Caesars Palace in Las Vegas—Brown insisted that Chandler be given a top-level job at the casino, which meant that Bradley had carte blanche access to the garish casino. Bradley frequently visited his sister and Chandler at Caesars, where his every desire was "comped." The casino, under Chandler's reign, picked up the tab for Bradley's meals, drinks, suites, and women. In Vegas, Bradley rubbed elbows with high rollers and mobsters, and crossed paths with other Lexingtonians such as Anita and Preston Madden. To Bradley, the Vegas casino scene was but one more example of a life he could experience, but not quite command.

It was the Vegas connection that would send the partnership of Bradley Bryant and Drew Thornton into the big leagues.

What had started as a two-man operation in which Bradley and Drew sold small quantities of drugs stolen from police evidence and from suspects that Drew had arrested, was being transformed into a large-scale operation by 1977.

They both came to the realization at approximately the same point in time that perhaps they were ready to try a test run of smuggling their own load of marijuana. Drew decided to leave the police force in order to devote full attention to their enterprise and begin a search for appropriate aircraft. It had been a convenient time for Drew to resign from the Lexington Police Department, though he seemed undaunted by the investigations of both the Flynn disappearance and the Ryan murder.

Drew told close associates that Melanie Flynn had followed in the footsteps of Jimmy Hoffa, referring to the missing, and presumed dead, labor leader. He boasted of inside knowledge of the Ryan investigation, for his network of police associates kept him apprised of all developments. He knew that his lone fingerprint on Ryan's steering wheel would never comprise enough evidence to justify criminal charges against him. Drew felt untouchable. As it turned out, he was right.

When Drew attended the party at Bradley's Devon, Pennsylvania, home in 1977—shortly after his resignation—the two men had a secret agenda. Bradley introduced Drew to the guests at his party: real estate magnates, casino executives, DEA and FBI agents, cops from Mississippi and Florida, jockeys and Thoroughbred horse trainers, lawyers and corporate climbers. The eclectic crowd was the nexus of their own secret company, the network upon which they would rely to expand their business goals.

Drew had learned a great deal during his years as a policeman; and he certainly knew how to avoid detection and apprehension by other cops. Now, he knew the legal ropes as well. In short, Drew felt his military and law enforcement training, his law degree, his tightly knit Lexington organization, his DEA and Lexington Police connections, his professed relationship with CIA assets and operatives, his piloting, parachuting, and martial arts expertise, his knowledge of various types of aircraft, his legendary courage, and his excellent physical condition, qualified him as major player on the international gun and drug circuit.

Bradley, too, had expanded his horizons during the past decade. Bryson Environmental—the industrial cleaning firm that he formed with his brother, Earl—had quickly mushroomed, with offices in Pennsylvania, Georgia, Alabama, and Colorado. Meanwhile his marriage to Callie was coming to an end.

But most of all he had met people at Caesars Palace in Las Vegas who had offered to invest in their operation. The Vegas crowd were scammers—high-rolling gamblers looking for places to hide their money. Bradley told Drew about men he met who would drop half a million dollars on the table in one night. Bradley convinced Drew that the two of them could create a smuggling organization that could make them both millionaires.

During the mid-1970s, Bradley and Drew had become deeply involved with what is known as "the SOF crowd"—a group of freelance military advisers and mercenaries whose unofficial leader is Robert Brown, the publisher of *Soldier of Fortune* magazine. How that association developed is not clear. Since both Bradley and Drew had been gung ho military types who fancied themselves as paramilitary experts, the SOF crowd was a natural melting pot. At the annual Las Vegas convention of soldiers of fortune, Bradley and Drew came into contact with a number of Vietnam veterans who were looking for action.

It was time, Bradley convinced Drew in 1977, to use those

contacts for profit. Under the auspices of a private security firm, hiring
independent contractors through the classified advertisements in *Soldier
of Fortune,* they would find a retinue of pilots who weren't afraid of the
risks and danger—pilots who enjoyed the challenge of flying below
radar in the middle of the night and into remote jungle landing strips of
foreign countries to pick up a load.

Bradley and Drew had formed Executive Protection Ltd. in
1975—a corporation owned and operated by Bradley Bryant and Drew
Thornton to which they would refer in private conversations as "the
Company." But it wasn't until 1977 that the two men felt capable of
putting "the Company" into full-scale action. They recruited operatives,
drawing from a pool of former police officers and drug agents from
various state, local, and federal agencies.

"The Company" could serve two purposes for them: to provide
cover for drug-smuggling ventures and to serve as a legitimate private
security service. Bradley had met dozens of people, through Chandler in
Vegas and through Halloran in Philadelphia, who had the need and
wherewithal to pay hundreds of thousands of dollars for sophisticated
bodyguard protection. Through their allies in the law enforcement and
SOF world, they had plenty of contract employees to perform both
security and drug-trafficking services.

Meanwhile the security company provided a perfect cover for
acquiring weapons, assimilating a private army of enforcers and obtaining airplanes ostensibly needed to shuttle clients into foreign countries, from which Bradley and Drew could then import marijuana back
to the United States.

Their first major purchase for "the Company" would be an airplane which they would modify by removing the seats, adding extra fuel
tanks for long-range flights, and modernizing the radar equipment.

They had spent several years amassing the tools of their trade:
AR-15s, Uzis, AK-47s, Ingrams, Walther PPKs, cartons of ammo, electronic surveillance equipment, nightscopes, explosives, night-vision
goggles. Now it was time to put them to use.

Bradley claimed that his cousin, Larry Bryant, would help them
add to their cache of arms, using his top-secret Defense Department
security clearance to embezzle scopes and radar equipment from the

highly restricted Navy weapons-testing center at China Lake in California's Mojave Desert.

Forging a subsidiary partnership with his police colleague, Bill Canan, Drew bought a remote farm on a bluff overlooking the Kentucky River, where they would train their employees in guerrilla war tactics and hide their growing stash of weapons.

Bradley and Drew also had a ready-made client base to buy their product. They had access to Kentucky's big-money horse crowd, the Philadelphia Main Line group, and the Vegas gamblers. Their blueblood connections proved even stronger than they had anticipated, as they found Lexington society to be a huge market for illicit drugs. In fact, it was a larger market than they could supply.

Both men considered Kentucky their strong and secret asset. Kentucky was a haven of remote landing strips, nonexistent law enforcement, crooked politicians, lax airports, and rivers leading to the Gulf of Mexico.

Between the two of them, they believed they had covered nearly every base for a fail-safe organization. At their company meetings, it was understood that Drew was in charge of procurement and transportation. He was responsible for the supply side of the operation through the drug traffickers he had met while working as a narc. But Drew didn't like being reliant upon middle men for his supply of pot. He knew that if he and Bradley had their own "source" in Colombia or Mexico, they would be able to buy a kilo of marijuana for as little as a couple of hundred dollars, marking it up threefold once it arrived in the United States.

It irked both men to pay a cut to some scumbag trafficker. Through his contacts Drew set out on a task of finding a South American contact who would "front" him a load of pot, without which Drew and Bradley would be forever dependent upon brokers.

Bradley, it was agreed, would find investors, set up a distribution network in Lexington, Philadelphia, and Vegas, and arrange to launder the profits through casinos. While Drew searched for a supplier, Bradley would round up some seed money to help get their larger dreams off the ground.

■

Bradley, and therefore Drew's, life took a significant turn in the fall of
1978, when a midnight fire swept through the Bryants' Pennsylvania
mansion. Bradley had taken his family to Disney World in Florida, and
neither the butler nor the maid were present when the blaze demolished
the house.

　　　Many valuable items, including Bradley's stockpile of weapons,
had conveniently been removed prior to the fire, prompting insurance
investigators to suspect arson. State Farm Insurance Company detectives had contacted Ralph Ross, seeking information on Bradley and his
associates, and seemed particularly interested in Drew, who they believed had torched the house. Local investigators, however, blamed the
fire on faulty wiring, leaving State Farm with little recourse but to
quietly settle with the Bryants. Paying $400,000 for the loss, the settle-
ment became the single largest homeowner insurance payment ever
made in the state of Pennsylvania. Callie, who was said to be devastated
by the incident, filed for divorce almost immediately. She moved her
three children to another Philadelphia suburb and remarried.

　　　Now, it would seem, "the Company" had the needed capital to
finance its operation.

　　　Forging Callie's name on the insurance check that had been
issued to both of them, Bradley used the $400,000 to purchase an
International Harvester truck dealership in Savannah, Georgia. The
truck company would provide "the Company" with the heavy equipment necessary to offload their bulky aircraft shipments of pot.

　　　Bradley moved to Savannah when he split with Callie, and a
large part of "the Company's" business was transacted out of the historic 1790 Inn. At the corner of President and Lincoln, its parking area
full of Jaguars, BMWs, and Mercedes-Benzes, the 1790 was an in place
for the young entrepreneurs of the South.

　　　Bradley took to holding court in the dining room of the 1790.
Round and square tables placed a discreet distance from each other
filled the room built of stone. Bradley's table—a round one at the back
of the room with a panoramic view of the restaurant—was always set
with linens, crystal, and a lantern.

　　　Chris Jurgenson, the German-born owner of the 1790, took very
good care of his best customer, Bradley Bryant. Jurgenson made sure
that the well-dressed gentleman, whose trademark seemed to be his

expensive cowboy boots, received first-class treatment. Jurgenson saw to it that Bradley's special table remained vacant except for Bradley, recognizing Bradley's great desire to keep his eye on the door. Jurgenson claimed he knew nothing about Bradley's business and thought Bradley was the most generous man he had known. He was a lavish tipper, inspiring attentive service by the waiters and waitresses. He once surprised Jurgenson with a private flight to Tampa to view the World Cup via satellite because he knew of Jurgenson's strong wish to see the games.

When Bradley first moved to Savannah, he rented a house from Jurgenson and surrounded the entire property with a fence. At the same time, Jurgenson began construction on a room at the inn to be used exclusively by Bradley. A striking blonde named Wendy had the dubious distinction of being known as Bradley's girlfriend, but it was not a monogamous relationship, as he also dated other women in Lexington, Las Vegas, and Philadelphia. "When Bradley first moved to Savannah, he seemed to be in pain from his divorce," Jurgenson recalled. "He missed his wife and kids a lot. He was extremely jealous and protective of Wendy, who was completely devoted to him. He kept her locked up, away from other men. No one envied Wendy's position."

Over a period of several months, Jurgenson saw Bradley on a daily basis, and was struck by some of Bradley's peculiar characteristics. He had an absolute phobia about being touched physically, by either a man or a woman, making it difficult for friends to imagine that his sexual relationships were normal.

He also had a violent temper that usually flared up when his subordinates disobeyed him. Jurgenson witnessed an incident when Bradley lost a bet—a substantial amount over something incredibly insignificant. "He took a pile of money, hundred-dollar bills, and began throwing them into the fireplace in the 1790 dining room," Jurgenson remembered. Jan Fisher, one of Bradley's errand boys, jumped up and began retrieving the money. Disregarding Bradley's commands to let the money burn, Fisher said: "It's stupid to burn cash, Brad!" With that, Bradley grabbed Fisher and ordered him to throw the money back into the fire or "I'll throw you in."

Fisher obeyed, but Bradley never forgave Fisher for his perfidiousness.

Fisher, a former Lexington civilian police employee, believed that Bradley would have killed him there on the spot had he continued to defy Bradley's order. Though Fisher despised the groveling characteristics Bradley required from the employees in his organization, he didn't have the courage to walk away from such lucrative employment.

Though Drew regularly accompanied Bradley to the 1790, there was never any question in Jurgenson's mind that Bradley was the main man. Jurgenson had no reason to believe that Drew was any higher on the ladder of Bradley's group than the other Lexingtonians who visited Bradley at the 1790, nightclub owner Jimmy Lambert, and the Kentucky governor's aide, Henry Vance.

When he witnessed Bradley and Drew toasting each other with champagne, Jurgenson had no comprehension of the depth and complexity of their partnership. With Bradley ensconced in Savannah, and Drew flying in and out for his missions abroad, reporting the results of his activities to Bradley, their patchwork pasts of Melanie Flynn, Ray Ryan, Sewanee, Callie, and Betty seemed far behind them. Like the adolescents they had once been—enamored with the drills, the marches, the war games, the rituals, the guns, the discipline of military school—they translated their proclivities into grown-up life. Best of all, they made up the rules as they went along.

Bradley and Drew proved to be a formidable team for law enforcement, so connected were they to various police agencies. They used their police employees to run counterintelligence in order to detect infiltration by cops or competing drug groups and to install private wiretaps.

Educating and familiarizing themselves with such laws as the Bank Secrecy Act, they learned that as long as their deposits in "friendly" Kentucky banks totaled less than $10,000 per transaction, no one would tip off U.S. Treasury officials about their money-laundering activities. Lexington bank tellers began gossiping about Drew Thornton carrying briefcases containing $9,999.00 in cash to their windows.

Their contacts in the DEA and Lexington Police tipped them off to any ongoing investigations of them or their associates, and of any inquiries from other agencies.

It is not known how many loads of marijuana Drew and Bradley smuggled into the United States in the one-year period from 1977 to the fall of 1978, but they had apparently been successful enough to focus on more long-term goals. They planned to acquire marijuana plantations and cocaine-processing laboratories of their own.

Through Bradley's contacts in the mob—some of whom he had met while visiting his brother-in-law Chandler in Vegas and others through his Philadelphia associates—the two felt confident that they had a receptive market.

In the fall of 1978, Bradley Bryant, dressed like a transplanted East Coast cowboy with alligator boots and eelskin belt, and his preppy-looking partner, Andrew Carter Thornton II, set out to translate their New Age fantasies into reality.

■

The warm desert air slapped Bradley Bryant's face as he emerged from McCarran International Airport terminal. The dry heat was a change from the Savannah humidity. Finally, it seemed, "the Company" was about to acquire what they most needed: a good connection in Colombia.

A limousine greeted him and his bodyguard, and whisked them down the Strip toward Caesars Palace, where Dan Chandler had promised him he would meet two men who would change his life—Lee and Jimmy Chagra.

Lee Chagra was an El Paso attorney famous throughout the Southwest for his successful defense of drug dealers. Wearing a black cowboy hat and gold necklace that spelled "Freedom," the Texan known as the Black Striker was one of the Strip's most flamboyant high rollers. The flashy gambler was also thought by drug agents to have masterminded hundreds of cocaine, heroin, and marijuana deals— many of which originated in Lebanon, the homeland of Chagra's ancestors.

"F. Lee" Chagra, so nicknamed for his brilliant courtroom antics, had defended a multitude of international smuggling rings, continually locking horns with Justice Department prosecutors and DEA agents. The federal government had spent hundreds of thousands of dollars compiling a dossier on Lee Chagra, but the closest they ever came to prosecution was a 1973 indictment against him for his participation in a marijuana operation based in Tennessee. The case against him was dropped and Chagra went on to represent members of the "Columbus Air Force"—a brigade of self-styled cowboys who supplied the Southwest with regular loads of marijuana and cocaine.

His black Stetson, his small-town country affability, his reputation as a freedom-fighter for the downtrodden, his leadership in the tightly knit Lebanese clan of south Texas, combined with his astute legal mind, won the hearts of many a jury, and made him a formidable adversary for government prosecutors.

Lee was said to be powerful enough to pick up the telephone and order a man killed. But Lee had so much heat on him that he was forced to consider passing the torch to one of his younger brothers.

Jamiel "Jimmy" Chagra had been envious and jealous of Lee since their childhood. Other family members say that Jimmy took secret pleasure in Lee's sudden turn of fortune. Under federal investigation in Texas for his role in smuggling activities, Lee's once-flourishing law practice was on the skids as a result. Potential clients knew the feds wanted Lee badly—so badly that it became anathema for anyone to seek his legal expertise. To be associated with Lee Chagra—every smuggler came to believe—was the kiss of death.

Reluctantly entrusting Jimmy with more control over the daily activities of his operations, Lee had serious doubts about Jimmy's competence. Jimmy had always had a big mouth, and, Lee knew, such lack of discretion in the drug business carried a particularly high price.

But Jimmy proved to be a quick study, and he seemed to relish the role of emulating his brother. Lee introduced Jimmy to the people in Vegas who had always taken care of him—the casino hosts and executives at his favorite money-laundering spots. Caesars had long been Lee's most steady hangout, where he received VIP treatment from casino bigwigs.

Through Lee, Jimmy met Dan Chandler, who arranged for an $8 million credit line in Jimmy's name. Chandler also provided Jimmy with several Caesars credit cards in the names of aliases—a mechanism that facilitated the laundering of illegal drug proceeds at the gaming tables. Caesars furnished him with a limousine and Lear Jet, and an army of security. Sporting a black mustache, diamond rings, heavy gold chains, a cigar, and cowboy boots, Jimmy played blackjack or baccarat at tables the casino roped off for him and his entourage. Before long, Jimmy was attracting even more attention to himself than Lee had.

"We knew he was laundering millions of drug dollars through the casino," said a DEA agent who was on Jimmy Chagra's trail, "but we couldn't get near him."

During an undercover investigation of Chagra code-named Operation Jaeger, one DEA agent reported, "It was impossible to wiretap or trail Chagra, since Caesars provided him with residency, the use of various aliases to record his casino transactions, armed guards, and a secluded penthouse suite." The DEA believed that Jimmy had become the kingpin in a criminal organization that imported heroin from Lebanon and cocaine from South America, and that Caesars facilitated Chagra's illegal activities by offering him safe harbor. They documented numerous incidents in which Chagra was flown by charter jet from Mexico to Las Vegas, where he was met on the tarmac by a Caesars Palace limousine and taken directly to the casino—thereby avoiding U.S. Customs. The Chagra family's ties to organized crime figures throughout the U.S.—particularly to Raymond Patriarca in New England and Tony Spilotro in Chicago—were well known to the feds. Yet they couldn't make a case against either Jimmy or Lee Chagra or Caesars executives. In an internal investigative report the DEA ultimately admitted that "the magnitude, scope, and complexity of the [Chagra/Caesars] operations exceeds DEA field capabilities."

Bradley Bryant must have been elated that Chandler had agreed to introduce him to the legendary pair of Texans. At his first meeting Bradley watched an ecstatic Jimmy Chagra scoop up half a million dollars from the green-felt craps table. Corporate security then escorted the two men to Chagra's car, a polished black Cadillac. Sliding into the driver's seat, Jimmy headed the car past the fountains and neon glitter toward the $900,000 home he had built in Paradise Valley. He told Bradley he was lucky that night. Not only at craps, but he had also won several hundred thousand dollars on sports bets. Jimmy bragged about his winnings from "Amarillo Slim" Preston's recent high-stakes poker game. Bradley was apparently impressed by Chagra's vulgar display of wealth.

The meeting of Bradley Bryant and Jimmy Chagra was a fortuitous combination of like-minded souls. Though the organization of Bradley and Drew had met with success, they couldn't have dreamed up a better association. In 1978 the Chagras were considered by DEA to be the kingpins in the country's largest heroin, cocaine, marijuana, and firearms distribution system. Not only did the Chagras have their own cocaine and marijuana suppliers in Colombia, a source for Lebanese heroin, and connections to Middle Eastern terrorists, but their organized-crime connections in the United States were said to be at the highest levels of the traditional La Cosa Nostra.

The bona fides of Bradley and Drew must have carried some weight, for "the Company" and the Chagras entered into a mutually beneficial arrangement whereby the Chagras provided the dope and "the Company" provided the transportation and distribution.

At the same time, Jimmy Chagra was but one of the Caesars habitues to whom Chandler introduced Bradley. The feds suspected that Bradley had also become a trusted courier of illegal bets and payoffs for the mob, in addition to, or perhaps as part of, his drug activity.

During the remainder of 1978, Bradley made frequent trips to Vegas to meet with the Chagras while the Chagras were under investigation, prompting law enforcement authorities to suspect that Bradley had become a key lieutenant in Jimmy Chagra's drug organization—at the time considered one of the largest in the country.

Drew Thornton thought Jimmy Chagra was a loudmouthed liability—an egomaniac obsessed with outshining his older brother. But Bradley was adamant: Chagra's drug connections, both in Colombia and the United States, were a valuable asset. Bradley even went as far as to tell Drew that if he didn't like being associated with Chagra he was free to leave the organization.

Drew begrudgingly agreed to stay with "the Company," but he began bad-mouthing Bradley behind his back. Despite his misgivings and bruised ego, Drew went ahead with the necessary planning for the importation of ten tons of marijuana into Lexington.

Dismissing Drew's concerns about Chagra, Bradley told Drew to focus on the transportation end of the business, specifically to make sure the DC-4 aircraft was able to handle the heavy load Drew would be flying from South America to Kentucky during the 1978 Christmas holidays.

Bradley was also making frequent trips to South America with Jimmy Chagra, where he met Chagra's drug suppliers. Rumors were flying in El Paso and San Antonio about Jimmy Chagra's imminent indictment, so Chagra introduced Bradley to his U.S. distributors, and it became evident to everyone in the operation that Bradley was the heir apparent.

Jimmy attributed his problems to an assistant U.S. attorney in Texas named James Kerr, blaming Kerr for the ubiquitous "leaks" to the news media that were increasingly crimping his style and *modus operandi*. Kerr was making no secret of his grand jury vendetta against the Chagra criminal organization. Normally Jimmy would have relied upon his brother Lee to defuse such an explosive situation. But this time it seemed Lee had a world of troubles all his own. Lee was also a target, and all of his legal machinations were falling on deaf ears.

On the morning of November 21, 1978, as Kerr waited at a San Antonio intersection on his way to the federal courthouse, two gunmen opened fire on Kerr's Lincoln Continental from the back of a van. Nineteen rounds of ammunition riddled Kerr's car before the van sped away. Miraculously Kerr escaped injury. Certain the Chagras had been responsible for the assault, Kerr vowed to pursue their prosecution with vengeance.

■

Bradley's and Drew's alliance with the Chagras was the rocket booster that launched "the Company." In the overall scheme of things, Bradley's responsibilities were more expansive and demanding, while Drew's hands-on relationship to the drugs was more risky.

Combining their assets with those of the Chagras, "the Company" almost immediately had enough money to command a cadre of electronics and weapons experts; aircraft brokers; wheeled-vehicle suppliers; retired military pilots; ground crews; polygraph examiners to test the loyalty of their drones; attorneys; recruiters; flight engineers and mechanics; couriers; bag men to pay off cops and politicians; and financiers. All transactions were made with cold cash, and their trips to local banks became so frequent they had to search for more discreet ways to hide their money.

Through Chagra's mob connections, "the Company" hooked up with distributors in New York, Chicago, Florida, Texas, Cleveland, and Cincinnati.

Simultaneously their private security operation was flourishing and their clients included competing drug organizations, Mafia figures, and government operatives who could not fulfill their goals within the parameters of their agency's guidelines.

Friends and family say that in the fall and winter of 1978, Bradley and Drew moved more and more into the shadowy, violent world of mercenaries and international drug smugglers. The society they now traveled in was one in which individuals perfected their survival skills through self-defense. They stockpiled paramilitary weapons, freeze-dried foods, gold coins. Drew wore camouflage fatigues and swastikas and bulletproof vests, and talked about revenge and the end of the world. Bradley wore skintight Levis and cowboy boots, and surrounded himself with homosexual weight lifters and body builders. Any challenges to his manliness, however, brought a venomous display of macho superiority.

The two men began bickering incessantly. Bradley saw himself as the brains and Drew as the brawn—a perception that Drew was apparently willing to tolerate in the early years. Though they were ostensibly equal partners, their employees considered Bradley Bryant both the president and chief executive officer.

They considered themselves invulnerable. The only thorn in their side was the Kentucky State Police or, particularly, Ralph Ross. Drew felt assured that Ralph was not a serious threat, thanks to sources like Henry Vance in Governor Julian Carroll's administration who could keep them apprised of any State Police activity.

They knew that Ralph was oblivious to the magnitude of the partnership they had cemented with the Chagras, and that Ralph underestimated the abilities of Drew and Bradley to pull off as large a scam as they had in mind.

A pair of country boys reared in the Camelot world of the South, Bradley and Drew immersed themselves ever deeper in the opaque world of espionage and narcotics, where drug dealers and spies find common ground—a world where one government agency inevitably breaks the laws that another government agency tries to enforce. A world where American military equipment is bartered in Third World nations and international narcotics organizations and governments are one and the same. A revolving door world where CIA-trained employees enter civilian life, skilled in techniques that are illegal in the United States but are in demand abroad. A world where multibillion-dollar drug profits make it easy to buy corruption—at any level. A world of temptation, glamor, and intrigue that is often impossible for underpaid cops and spies to resist.

■

On December 23, 1978, Lee Chagra's wife surprised him with a block of tickets to the Sun Bowl football game. He had bet fifteen thousand dollars on his alma mater, the University of Texas, against Maryland. Ecstatic about the gift, he told his wife he would meet her at the stadium after first spending a couple of hours at his electronically guarded law office.

Two hours later, the charismatic attorney was dying slowly on the carpet beneath a stained-glass window in his fortress-like office. Both lungs had been sliced by an assassin's .22-caliber bullet. After writhing in a sticky pool of blood for almost an hour, Lee Chagra finally died.

Three months earlier, Lee Chagra had taken the offensive in his war against the government. He had retained two Boston lawyers to bring a lawsuit against the DEA, charging the agency had launched a conspiracy to entrap and harass him. That suit died with Lee.

Even before a medical examiner was called in to inspect the body, El Paso police and DEA agents sealed off the murder scene and began rifling through thousands of manila folders containing information on Chagra's drug-smuggling clients. They confiscated cassette recordings of his privileged conversations with clients, receipt books, files, and cash totaling anywhere between $100,000 and $2.5 million, according to varying reports. Envelopes full of cash had been found strewn throughout the law office—apparent bets from local bankers and businessmen.

Jimmy Chagra was a terrified man when he called Bradley Bryant to relate details of his brother's brutal slaying. He needed Bradley to provide him with protection as soon as possible. Lee's assassin remained at large; the rest of the family could be targeted next. Bradley personally arranged for Jimmy Chagra's protection, assigning two of his employees to serve as Chagra's secret service.

The death was bad timing, all the way around. Two days before Christmas, Bradley Bryant and Drew Thornton were in the final stages of importing 20,000 pounds of pot into Lexington. The new heat on Chagra—Lee's murder and the assault on Kerr—made Drew even more nervous. He had more faith in his and Bradley's original organization— it was smaller, its members more loyal, and fewer things could go wrong. But Bradley had violated their pact by bringing Chagra into the fold. He had then poured salt on the wound by siding with Chagra over Drew. It seemed to Drew that Bradley had sold out the Company to a bigger corporation, and by doing so had forsaken his partner.

Bradley had carefully patterned the organization after the CIA, compartmentalizing its various facets. Although his personal bodyguards, mainly weight lifters and karate instructors recruited from various spas, accompanied him everywhere, they were never included in business meetings. Pilots he hired to fly drug loads were not the same pilots he used for ferrying aircraft across the country. Bryson employees were separated from Executive Protection employees, and different offices and staff were maintained. He hired individuals who were paid six thousand dollars per month to forward mail from a post office box in one city to boxes in other cities. Bradley insulated himself from his inferiors, often playing them against each other to instill loyalty and fear. He had painstakingly created a system of deniability—a quagmire that only *he* understood.

To Drew, smuggling was the most exciting, challenging, adrenaline-activating venture that existed in peacetime society. The risk, the thrill, the payoff—everything else in life paled in comparison. Organizing and planning the dope runs were the least captivating, most mundane pastimes to Drew. Drew took care of the airplanes he'd fly, the parachute he'd use, and his personal weapons and survival supplies. He preferred to leave the rest of the details to the ubiquitous sycophants who surrounded Bradley.

Bradley's employees in Executive Protection Ltd. were charged with the more sensitive arrangements of the drug deals. For menial

tasks that required little or no knowledge on the part of the participants, Bradley relied upon employees from his ersatz legitimate truck
enterprise—Bryson International.

Jack Hillard and Don Leach were two of Bradley's more trusted
subordinates. Hillard, a former captain with the Lexington Police Department had served seventeen years on the force before Drew recruited
him as head of Executive Protection Ltd. Leach, a former Pennsylvania
policeman, was the muscle of the operation.

Johnny Trussell, a former Mississippi state trooper, had been a
pilot operating out of the Savannah airport for several years when he
was first approached by Hillard in December 1978 and was asked to fly
for Bradley. Trussell had been suggested to Hillard by mutual friends.
Trussell knew Bradley only as a handsome Philadelphia businessman
who was flashing money around Savannah's high-class night spots. He
told Hillard he would take the offer under consideration.

Two days later Bradley appeared at the airport. He told Trussell
he was offering him an opportunity for early retirement. Trussell indicated he was interested and Bradley arranged a second meeting to be
held within a week.

Trussell went to the Bryson International offices on the appointed date, and was surprised to be greeted by Don Leach instead of
Bradley. Leach informed Trussell that he would be given a "couple of
tests," and led Trussell to a back room where he was hooked up to a
polygraph machine and asked questions designed to reveal his propen-
sity to become an informant, and any prior activities as a narc. Following the lie detector test, Trussell was given a psychological stress evalu-
ation to test his reactions under pressure, using scenarios such as being
chased by U.S. Customs, interrogated by cops, ripped off by smugglers,
barraged by gunfire, and other skirmishes typical of the front lines of
the drug war.

Sweating it out for a week, Trussell didn't know how he had
fared with Bradley's mind games. Then, in late December, he was summoned again to Bradley's inner sanctum. Peeling two thousand dollars
in crisp hundred-dollar bills from his pocket, Bradley dispatched Trussell to Muskogee, Oklahoma, for his first assignment: To inspect a DC-4
aircraft Bradley was considering purchasing. Trussell was told he would

be flown to Oklahoma on a Lear Jet belonging to one of Bradley's other employees.

When Trussell reported back that the aircraft was capable of hauling several thousand pounds of marijuana, Bradley ordered him to sit tight. A few days later, Don Leach arrived in Oklahoma with $105,000 in cash to purchase the plane. Leach, using the alias "Mr. Lear," registered the plane with the FAA in the name of one of Bradley's shell corporations, and delivered Trussell's next set of orders from Bradley: Trussell was to ferry the DC-4 to Phoenix, Arizona, with a former Lexington policeman named Steve Oliver, where the two men would be "type-rated" by the FAA as certified pilots of the multiengine aircraft.

Bradley remained in Savannah, where he made elaborate lists in his stenographer's notebook about the items needed for the haul: Two cases of strobe lights; twelve railroad flares; six gallons of deodorized disinfectant; two portable lamps; three hundred cardboard boxes; heavy-duty trash bags; two cases of survival food.

He then dispatched three Bryson employees to Dothan, Alabama, instructing them to drive in two separate vehicles. The trunks of both cars carried the necessary supplies for the drug run—the flares, boxes, etc. When they arrived in Dothan they located the DC-4, which had been flown from Arizona by Trussell and Oliver, and loaded it with the provisions. The next day, on January 10, Drew and Bradley arrived together in Dothan to oversee the situation. Bradley checked into a Ramada Inn to wait, while the two former Lexington cops—Drew Thornton and Steve Oliver—flew to South America to pick up a load of marijuana. They returned the following night, the plane so heavy with its twenty-thousand-pound load that it barely flew above the ground, grazing a shrimp boat off the Georgia coast and nearly causing it to capsize. Finally, it landed safely at Lexington's Blue Grass Airport. On the ground a short time, Thornton and Oliver departed while another pilot waited for the off-load crew to remove the ten tons of pot. In less than an hour, the plane was unloaded and flown by different pilots from Lexington to the Louisville airport where it was parked and abandoned by its crew.

Years later, it would become apparent that Drew's buddy Harold Brown at the DEA had told the Lexington police not to get involved.

Arousing the suspicion of airport employees, the unmarked plane prompted queries to the DEA, which was forced to respond. Reluctantly boarding the vacant aircraft, DEA agents found marijuana residue, a sleeping bag, a five-hundred-gallon fuel tank, and a magazine with an address label for "Gary Scott"—a Savannah pilot known to belong to the international drug-smuggling conspiracy that the DEA knew as the Company.

Parked near the DC-4 was a black pickup truck carrying two Bryson employees. The two men readily admitted to the DEA they had been instructed to travel from Savannah to Louisville, meet the DC-4 and unload all boxes and equipment on the airplane, vacuum its interior, lock it, and return to Georgia. Each man had been promised one thousand dollars for the task.

Much of the evidence at the scene suggested the involvement of Bradley Bryant: The plane was registered to a company owned by Bradley; the ground crew in Lexington had been identified as Bradley's employees; the truck in Louisville belonged to Bryson International; Bradley was the subscriber to a phone number found in the possession of one of the Bryson employees. Yet the DEA never pursued criminal charges against Bradley Bryant, or anyone in Bradley's organization, even though they seized the aircraft.

Johnny Trussell figured he must have passed muster on the DC-4 incident, for two weeks later he was assigned a more substantive and financially rewarding endeavor. Bradley gave Trussell seventy thousand dollars in cash to purchase a Queen Air aircraft in North Carolina and to fly it to a small airport near Houston, Texas. Bradley had told him to make numerous takeoffs and landings from the airstrip over a period of three days to determine if he attracted any heat—or law enforcement surveillance.

"Once you feel clear," Bradley told Trussell, "then call Dan Chandler in Vegas. Chandler will take it from there."

Bradley provided Trussell with two phone numbers for Chandler —the unpublished number at his home on the Las Vegas Country Club, and his direct line at Caesars Palace. When Trussell felt certain he was not being watched by any cops or curious airport personnel, he transferred his belongings from one hotel to another. Checking into the Houston Airport Ramada Inn, he placed his call to Chandler.

Chandler directed Trussell to stay at his hotel, not to make any additional phone calls, and to wait for another individual whom Chandler did not identify.

"A day or so later, a man arrived at the hotel and told me he was the man I was waiting for," Trussell later told police. Trussell claimed never to know the identity of the man. The man drove Trussell to Houston, where Trussell was told to wait to be contacted by a man using the name "John Wayne" who would "set up the drug deal." Trussell waited at the Houston motel for several hours before a towering redhead who called himself "John Wayne" appeared. Wayne directed Trussell to fly them in the Queen Air to a remote ranch Wayne apparently owned near the U.S.-Mexican border.

"This is where you can reach me if you need to," "John Wayne" said, handing Trussell a business card. With that, "Wayne" was gone, leaving Trussell with three Mexican men unknown to him.

After stripping the seats from the aircraft and equipping it with radar detection devices and a "bladder," or extra fuel tank, Trussell and the three men flew to the interior of Mexico. Greeted at the jungle landing strip by several armed Mexicans, Trussell waited as the Mexicans loaded the plane with twelve hundred pounds of marijuana. He left his passengers at the dirt airfield, and returned solo. Hugging the ground to avoid detection by American radar, Trussell flew the plane in an electronic blind spot along the border. He landed safely back at the ranch in Sonora, Texas, where the pot was immediately unloaded and hauled off in camper pickup trucks by three men Trussell had never seen before.

When Trussell was unable to start the plane to return to Georgia, he called Bradley for directions. Bradley told him to burn the plane and leave it in Texas. Trussell balked, afraid such a fire would attract too much attention. Bradley, who hated his judgments to be challenged by his underlings, reluctantly agreed to send Trussell the necessary spare parts and a mechanic. However, when Trussell returned to Georgia, Bradley withheld twenty thousand dollars from Trussell's compensation, so angered was he by Trussell's insubordination.

In addition to worrying about Trussell and the Queen Air deal, Bradley was waiting to hear from his cousin, Larry Bryant, about whether he had obtained the military equipment he had promised Bradley. Stationed at Nellis Air Force Base in Las Vegas, Larry Bryant possessed a national security clearance to work on classified radar systems, and had offered to provide Bradley with sophisticated electronic detection equipment from the government's top-secret China Lake.

Bradley was especially anxious to receive several Starlight night-vision scopes and an IFF Radar, called the "Green Box." The Green Box, nicknamed "friend or foe," is a classified device that U.S. military aircraft use for communicating with other military installations in friendly countries. Such an instrument would allow Bradley's drug-smuggling aircraft to enter and leave numerous Central and South American countries, his planes sending a signal that they were friendly, without resorting to radio communication.

Larry and an eccentric Las Vegas weapons expert named Alvin Snapper were also under contract to Bradley to come up with various types of electronic mechanisms. Bradley hoped to have all the items in his possession by the time of his upcoming run scheduled in the next few weeks.

Bradley was waiting for the money to filter back to him from his distributors to whom he had fronted the Queen Air load. When the money arrived, he needed to go to Vegas to pay off some of the investors in his business. He hired Harold Foran, a pilot who owned a Lear Jet, to fly him and a bodyguard to Vegas from Savannah. "When we arrived at the airport, Bryant deplaned, went into the terminal, and exchanged briefcases with two thugs," Foran said. "Bryant then turned around and reboarded the plane, without spending any time in Vegas. On the return trip, Bryant remarked that he had 'made a lot of money on this trip.'" Foran considered the remark strange, since Bradley rarely discussed business transactions with anyone except Drew Thornton.

■

Lance Alworth was a San Diego businessman who owned a chain of self-storage warehouses and health spas when he first met Bradley. The baby-faced, Arkansas native had retired from professional football, having played with the Dallas Cowboys and San Diego Chargers. He was somewhat under fire at the time, following revelations by the FBI the previous summer that he had a financial relationship with Allen Glick

—the former owner of the Stardust Hotel in Las Vegas. Glick's pent-house suite at the Stardust had been raided by FBI agents searching for documents linking Glick to the Chicago mob. Among items found were documents tying Glick to various sports figures, including Alworth and Al Davis—the owner of the Oakland Raiders. Concerned about any blatant conflict between sports figures and sports bookmakers, the FBI had widened its investigation of organized crime and casino skimming to include possible game-fixing.

In September 1979, Alworth asked his friend Al Davis to get him some seats at the heavyweight boxing championship to be held at Caesars Palace. "No problem," Davis told Alworth. His friend Dan Chandler would be happy to accommodate Alworth. When the time came for the Friday night fight between Larry Holmes and Earnie Shavers, Chandler had arranged for Alworth to be seated next to Bradley Bryant. The two men were acquainted from previous meetings in Vegas.

Bradley had been told he could trust Alworth, so it was without hesitation that Bradley initiated a conversation about drugs. Alworth would later tell federal agents that Bradley tried to persuade him to invest more than a quarter million dollars in a drug-smuggling venture. Bradley told Alworth that he performed contract assignments for the CIA, and, in turn, the CIA allowed him to smuggle drugs. Bradley's system sounded foolproof, the way he presented it. To Alworth, the risks seemed minimal compared with the return: He could double his money in the span of a few weeks. Alworth admitted his interest in the prospect, and the men arranged follow-up meetings.

Drew Thornton saw Lance Alworth as one more potential blight on what he feared was becoming a loose, undisciplined organization. Vulnerable because he was an FBI target, Alworth didn't seem an appropriate candidate as a financier. In fact, Drew didn't think much of the whole Vegas crowd—Dan Chandler included.

"We don't need them," Drew was saying more and more frequently to Bradley, referring to Dan Chandler, Jimmy Chagra, Lance Alworth, and others.

Bradley was also throwing too much money around the 1790. Savannah was a small town, and Drew didn't think they had it wired the way they did Lexington. He complained that the six-hundred-dollar tips, bottles of Dom Pérignon every night, open talk about guns and travels, hints about the CIA—was attracting unnecessary attention. Drew was becoming increasingly alienated by Bradley's ostentatious style. Drew remained close to his own inner circle: Bill Canan, Henry Vance, Rex Hall, Mike Kelly and Jay Silvestro. But Bradley was branching out and endangering them all, bringing new players into the fold every day.

One of those characters was a retired U.S. Army Intelligence officer named Jim Atwood, who owned a forty-acre island near Savannah. An importer of World War II relics and weapons, Atwood was the author of *The Daggers and Edged Weapons of Hitler's Germany.* One of Chris Jurgenson's oldest friends, Atwood was a regular in the 1790 bar and restaurant. He had served a tour of duty with the U.S. Marines shortly after World War II, before joining the FBI in Washington, D.C. He left the FBI in 1950, enlisting in the Army, and received his training at Fort Campbell, Kentucky. Like Drew Thornton, Atwood became a paratrooper.

A shadowy spook around Savannah, Atwood was known primarily for his purchases of large vessels that had been forfeited to the U.S. Government as evidence in drug and income tax evasion cases. He also owned or controlled several companies used for international gun deals, and was a manufacturer of lightweight SM-90 submachine guns—a hand-held weapon popular among gunrunners and drug smugglers.

When Atwood met Bradley and Drew, he was under investigation by the IRS for criminal tax evasion, and by ATF for arms sales to Central America. Federal law enforcement officials speculated that his weapons activities were condoned by the CIA, making Atwood a difficult target for investigation by other agencies.

Bradley and Atwood had an instant affinity for each other. "We have a mutual admiration society," Atwood said. "He's a man's man."

Drew was skeptical. He told Jan Fisher he suspected Atwood was a CIA operative whose loyalties were unclear, and not someone they should trust.

A frequent visitor to Guatemala, where he owned a residence, Atwood was engaged in several enterprises in that country, including selling salt-damaged British sports cars; establishing factories to manufacture knives and prefabricated houses; and exporting canned hams from the United States to Guatemala. He also held government contracts—along with the father of Gary Scott, the Georgian who had been on the drug-laden DC-4 in Kentucky—for mosquito-control spraying. For that reason, it was necessary for Atwood to spend most of his time in Guatemala, and he wondered if Bradley would be interested in renting his Savannah island residence, named Torshima. Attracted to the seclusion and security of the Japanese-styled home, Bradley agreed to move from Jurgenson's to Atwood's.

When Bradley learned that Atwood was helping the Guatemalan government bring legalized gambling into that country, Bradley suggested to Atwood that such a gambling enterprise would greatly interest his friend Dan Chandler. In the spring of 1979, Bradley arranged a meeting between himself, Chandler, Atwood, and several high-level Guatemalan officials to discuss the opening of casinos.

But a cold-blooded act in Texas shattered their grandiose plans, and sent the Company running for cover.

CHAPTER

SIX

The telephone rang in Drew Thornton's hotel room on the evening of May 29, 1979.

"The judge has been hit," Bradley told him.

Drew felt his stomach sink, his face drain. Like Bradley, he was scared. He knew they were all in deep trouble.

"Come to an emergency summit meeting in Savannah," Bradley said. Then Drew heard a click and the phone was dead.

U.S. District Judge John Wood had emerged into San Antonio's steamy air that morning. His eyes squinted from the diffused sunlight as he headed for his station wagon. Scheduled that day to preside over the trial of Jimmy Chagra, who had been indicted two months earlier on drug-trafficking charges, Wood had made it clear he intended to put Chagra away for life.

As he reached for the car door he felt the shot that ripped open his spine. Collapsing on the pavement, blood spurting from his back, he was barely conscious when his wife reached his side.

The sixty-three-year-old jurist was dead on arrival at a nearby hospital, a .243-caliber bullet, probably fired from a high-powered hunting rifle, lodged in the upper part of his chest.

John Wood, nicknamed "Maximum John" for his notoriously stiff sentencing of drug dealers, became the first federal judge to be assassinated in this century. The judge with the heaviest narcotics caseload in the country would never hand down a harsh sentence again.

Wood's brutal murder underscored the characteristic lawlessness that federal agents in Texas were blaming on drugs. The mesquite and piñon-covered flatlands of this tough river town, home of the Alamo, have been the scene of vigilante tactics since the Mexicans first clashed with the Indians and settlers. For a law-and-order judge such as Wood to run into trouble in this kind of place was not out of context. Historically, a volley of smuggling activity has pervaded the U.S.-Mexican border—undocumented workers, weapons, spare parts, vehicles, drugs, electronic equipment. The smuggling profession is bequeathed to the offspring of Chicano and Lebanese clans on both sides. Through an interrelated network of distant cousins, cherished friends, and nepotistic alliances, cartels are formed.

Wood's murder was but one of an emerging macabre pattern of violence associated with the enterprise—only fourteen blocks away and six months earlier, the car of assistant U.S. attorney James Kerr had been ambushed. That Wood and Kerr should fall prey to the drug underworld was no surprise to court observers. Both were waging a much-publicized war against the Chagra narcotics organization.

By 1979, the government's case against Jimmy Chagra—four counts of importing marijuana and cocaine from Colombia—was ready to go. Chagra was arrested and Maximum John Wood had set bond at a million dollars. Chagra was incredulous. Wearing prison denims and slippers to his bond-reduction hearing, he listened disbelievingly as a federal magistrate refused to lower the bail. It wasn't until he brought in a million dollars' worth of his wife's diamonds and jewels that the judge reluctantly agreed to lower the bail to four hundred thousand dollars. But the tension in the court had only begun to escalate. Wood vowed that despite the reduction, the slippery criminal would not escape his wrath. Chagra's lawyers retaliated by attacking his objectivity and his close friendship with prosecutor Kerr. When Wood declared that he, not a new "impartial" judge, would hear the case, the matter was closed.

Whatever hopes for a fair trial Jimmy Chagra nurtured vanished as his May 29 trial date approached. "It's a stacked deck," Jimmy complained to family members.

Within hours of Judge Wood's death, the FBI zeroed in on Chagra as the number-one suspect.

Though Bradley had a solid alibi for his own physical whereabouts at the time of the murder, he feared he would somehow be tied to the crime. He immediately dispatched Jan Fisher to El Paso to locate three individuals who were DEA informants in the case against Jimmy

Chagra. Fisher knew Bradley had sent him on this mission at Chagra's behest, and he couldn't help wondering what type of retribution Chagra planned to take against the snitches. Fisher assumed that Chagra was somehow involved in Wood's death because Fisher knew that Wood's bias against Chagra had been the topic of numerous discussions among Jimmy Chagra, Bradley Bryant, and Dan Chandler. Though Fisher knew that Bradley had not killed Judge Wood—Fisher had placed a phone call to Bradley at a Denver hotel room within moments of the shooting—he felt certain Bradley knew who was responsible for the death.

At the Savannah strategy meeting, Bradley flew into a rage. Employees heard him screaming and hollering and slamming his fist during the rambunctious argument he was waging with Drew. Drew, with characteristic cool, reminded Bradley how he had warned him to disassociate from Chagra. "I'm a cop, remember? I know what's going to happen next. They're going to be all over us, every move we make. Jimmy Chagra is a tactless ass who's going to drag you down with him."

Bradley was tired of placating Drew, of constantly defending his decisions, of pointing out the necessity of associating with people such as Chagra. "The heat will be on Jimmy Chagra, not on us," Bradley yelled.

Incredulous at Drew's shortsightedness, Bradley was already salivating at the chance to control Jimmy's entire organization.

"Who wants it!" Drew responded.

"Drew got up and walked out," one employee remembered. "Didn't say a word to anyone. Just walked out. Left town for good."

A few minutes later Bradley summoned his employees into his inner sanctum. "From this point forward you will not talk to Andrew Thornton. You will not deal with him. No one in this building is to have anything to do with Andrew Thornton ever again."

Bradley immediately plotted his takeover of the Chagra drug network, anxious to take advantage of Chagra's sudden, and potentially terminal, paralysis as a kingpin. He also set about to eliminate Drew Thornton as a competitor in the drug trade. He dispatched Johnny Trussell to Mississippi to search for a remote airfield that was accessible to a highway, had little air traffic activity, and would be capable of accommodating large aircraft. He traded the Queen Air that Trussell had used a few months earlier to bring a load into Texas for a Twin Beech whose seats had already been removed. When Trussell returned from Mississippi and recommended using the airport located in tiny Starkville, Bradley told Trussell to prepare the plane for the smuggling trip to Bogotá, Colombia, and back to Starkville. Trussell installed three steel fuel tanks, special radar equipment, and the other specialized items necessary for such a venture.

While awaiting completion of the details for the trip, Bradley made plans to move his operational headquarters to Tampa, Florida. Having filed for bankruptcy in Savannah for his International Harvester truck dealership called Bryson International, Bradley was anxious to skip out of town before the Feds decided to take a closer look at the financial shenanigans associated with Bryson International.

Bradley had been living at Torshima—Colonel Atwood's secluded island—for several months, having surrounded it with a twelve-foot fence and installed a half-dozen phone lines. But he had had a disagreement with Atwood, apparently over the cost of renting the island, and in June Bradley ordered Trussell and Jan Fisher to move his weapons from Torshima to Tampa. Among the items moved were several AR-7s, a Walther PPK pistol, two Colt .38-caliber pistols, a Mini 14 rifle, a gold-flecked shotgun, and a revolver with a gold trigger. Trussell was particularly interested in a carton of electronic dart guns, called Tasers; when he commented about the weapons to Bradley, Bradley presented him with one as a gift—a gesture that would later become significant to federal authorities.

Trussell and Fisher loaded the items into a Lincoln Continental, and Bradley's bodyguard—Roger Barnard—drove the car to Tampa.

A few nights later, Fisher received a phone call from Colonel Atwood. Furious, Atwood claimed Bradley had stolen his guns. Atwood threatened Fisher with prosecution if the weapons were not returned. A few hours later, Atwood filed charges with the Savannah police, who issued warrants for the arrests of Fisher and Trussell.

Angry that Bradley would place him in such a compromised position, and intimidated by threats of criminal prosecution, Fisher succumbed to Atwood—an act that Fisher knew would infuriate Bradley, especially coupled with Fisher's previous insubordination at the 1790. That same day, Bradley summoned Johnny Trussell and Don

Leach to Tampa to finalize plans for a flight to Santa Marta, Colombia, where they would rendezvous with Bradley.

The trip went off without a hitch, and after a circuitous flight path, the three men met as planned at the northern Colombian coastal town in mid-July 1979. Bradley, accompanied by three Colombians invoked Jimmy Chagra's name incessantly, creating the distinct impression that he was Chagra's emissary. Bradley told Trussell that the Colombian participants in the dope operation were high-level government officials, including a senator named Orlando López.

Trussell examined the airfield the group planned to use for the operation—a dirt runway camouflaged by debris and trees, located thirty miles northeast of Santa Marta on the edge of a stream and the shore of the Caribbean. Not satisfied, he selected an alternate airport situated on a fruit farm south of Santa Marta.

When their plans were completed, Bradley and Trussell departed for the United States, leaving Leach behind as collateral for a debt owed by Bradley for a previous load of marijuana—a tactic systematically used by Jimmy Chagra. Leach had been told by Bradley that his assignment in Colombia was to examine that country's security procedures, in order to secure a hideout for Jimmy Chagra, who planned to skip out on his four-hundred-thousand-dollar bail if convicted on drug charges.

■

The muggy air hung in abeyance for days on end during the 1979 heat wave. Ralph Ross was accustomed to the suffocating Kentucky summers, the smell of sour mash stubbornly clinging to the atmosphere, no breezes daring to blow it away. He had endured the familiar stickiness, odor, and haze for forty-six years like an annual visit to the dentist.

He left the windows down on his pickup truck, waiting for the air conditioner to take effect. He felt his shirt already sticking to the seat. A perfectionist, he carefully draped his suit coat across the seat next to him. Checking his hair in the rearview mirror to make sure it hadn't been blown out of kilter by the fan, he rolled up the window and shifted into gear.

As he pulled out of the driveway of his Lawrenceburg home he felt a mixture of relief and remorse. His marriage was falling apart before his eyes—something that probably should have happened ten or fifteen years earlier. He and his wife were in a stalemate and he knew his days at the house he had built for his family were numbered.

His state police career had always been a strain on the marriage. But in more recent years, the nights away from home, the drinking, the danger, the secrets he kept, had culminated in irreconcilable distances between himself and his wife. After years of arguing, they had finally fallen into a snare of silence, neither possessing the necessary energy for battle. Their tacit agreement to stay together "for the kids' sake" seemed suddenly shot full of holes. Their two girls, Connie and Christie, had graduated from high school and were starting lives of their own.

"Shoulda left a long time ago," Ralph said to himself, reminded of his encroaching age by the sight of his thinning gray hair in the mirror. Yet something drew him home every night, like an old loyal dog.

He turned his thoughts to less resolved matters: Drew Thornton and Bradley Bryant. Ralph was on his way to Louisville to meet with FBI agents who planned to open a widespread investigation of corruption in Lexington, using the federal racketeering statute nicknamed RICO.

By summertime 1979 Ralph had heard numerous references to a narcotics and paramilitary group called the Company. DEA reports that had been provided him identified the "incorporation" date of the Company as early 1976. According to those reports, the group was founded at a tiny Italian restaurant in Alton, Illinois, by two Vietnam veterans who had met with considerable success bringing marijuana into Georgia via Colombia and the Bahamas.

Somehow, between 1976 and 1978, the smuggling group had mushroomed to include a stable of attorneys, a slush fund for bail and dirty tricks, a fleet of airplanes, and numerous landing strips.

Bradley Bryant, Ralph was told by the DEA, was the "East Coast kingpin" of the group. How Bradley had gotten connected with the organization was not clear. But Ralph knew one thing for sure: If Bradley was in charge of East Coast operations, then Drew Thornton was certain to be his first lieutenant.

What other Lexingtonians were also involved?

Faced with a lack of resources and jurisdictional authority, and working under the direction of a governor with close personal ties to the suspects, Ralph's efforts to infiltrate the Lexington organization seemed doomed from the start. A review of Governor Julian Carroll's official phone records reflected hundreds of phone calls from the governor's office to the residences of Drew Thornton, Henry Vance, and Bradley Bryant every month since 1977. Governor Carroll, a good ole boy from Paducah, would be leaving office in a few months, and the future of state law enforcement would remain a mystery until after the primary elections in September. Ralph knew that the general election probably wouldn't matter—Kentucky's governors are always picked in the Democratic primaries. Unable to succeed themselves, gubernatorial candidates line up years in advance to begin bickering over who can deliver which counties and who can raise the most money.

Rumor had it that a dark horse was going to lead the pack, a high-rolling gambler and millionaire named John Young Brown, Jr., who had been the last to enter the race. Brown and his beauty queen wife Phyllis George had awed the voters with their movie-star friends, flying in and out of mountain towns in a flashy helicopter, vowing to run the state as a business.

If Brown were to be elected, the Kentucky State Police would be his tool, leaving the only possibility of serious law enforcement in the hands of the FBI, which Ralph referred to as The Eye.

His relationship with The Eye dated back many years, to the mid-sixties. He had been trained by them, worked with them on hundreds of cases, and was respected by their technicians as among the best "sound men" around. They were his drinking buddies, traveling partners, and yarn-telling friends. Like Ralph, most of the agents were old-fashioned law-and-order cops who made sure they got the job done without taking themselves too seriously along the way.

Situating himself at the conference table in the FBI's Louisville offices, he told them what he knew and what he suspected, hoping to initiate a generalized probe.

"I think the focus should be on Jimmy Lambert," Ralph told them, referring to the Lexington nightclub owner and former Kentucky Fried Chicken franchisee. "We've had him under surveillance and we know he was in close contact during the spring and summer of 1979 with both Drew Thornton and Bradley Bryant. Politicians and Lexington police officers spend a lot of time at his house and at the Library Lounge, where he gives them free booze and who knows what else." Ralph was convinced that the Library Lounge was the center of the prostitution, drugs, and gambling ring operating in Lexington.

"Meanwhile," Ralph said, "police in Mississippi notified us this week that Bradley Bryant's organization planned to smuggle a load of marijuana and cocaine into Starkville, Mississippi, but something went haywire. I think Customs down there may have ended up with a couple of snitches in the group," Ralph told the FBI, unknowingly referring to Trussell, Leach, and Fisher, who had recently fallen out with Bradley. "Maybe Bradley's about to get taken down by them."

Ralph continued, outlining the evidence in the disappearance of Melanie Flynn and the murder-for-hire of Ray Ryan. "Drew Thornton and the Lexington police are in the middle of both of those," he said.

"While we're on the subject of Melanie Flynn," one of the agents said to Ralph, "there's someone you need to talk to."

The agent went on to tell Ralph about a young woman named Mary Shasta. "She's a Christian psychic who thinks she knows what happened to Melanie. We've interviewed her and think she's credible, but don't really have the jurisdiction to open a case. Why don't you take it from here?"

Ralph wrote down the woman's name and telephone number in his childish scrawl and agreed to get in touch with her.

■

Jan Fisher had heard through the grapevine that Bradley was going to kill him because he had sided with Colonel Atwood in the dispute between the two men. So it was with trepidation that Fisher answered a phone call from Bradley on July 31, 1979. Fisher listened with skepticism to Bradley's apologies and attempts to downplay their spat. Bradley blamed his short fuse on the pressures associated with the Wood murder, the Bryson bankruptcy, the falling out with Atwood, and intensifying animosity between him and Drew Thornton. If Fisher would accept his apology, Bradley would give him an opportunity to make a sizable amount of money.

He told Fisher to meet him at the Memphis airport the next day —the first of August—to conduct surveillance. Fisher was met in Memphis by Bradley and a Lebanese weight lifter and bodyguard named Turk Paz. Immediately upon arrival, Paz grabbed Fisher by the arm, loaded him into the backseat of a car, and set out on the hundred-mile drive from Memphis to Starkville, Mississippi. Using aliases to check into a Ramada Inn in Starkville, they forced Fisher to stay alone in a room with Paz. After a few hours, he was summoned to Bradley's room.

Entering the motel room, Paz gripping his right arm, Fisher was relieved to see Johnny Trussell, whom he considered to be reasonable and a friend. He noticed Bradley was particularly sullen and preoccupied with two cartons—a blue suitcase and a black box.

"You and Johnny are taking a trip," Bradley said to Fisher.

"Where to?" Fisher was nervous, the earlier death threat combined with Paz's bullying didn't bode well.

"Don't ask any questions," Bradley replied. "Pack your passport, driver's license, and one change of clothes."

Fisher glanced around and was disturbed when Trussell lowered his eyes. He had faith in Trussell and didn't really believe any harm would come to him as long as Trussell was there. He opted to stay calm, silently formulating an escape plan. But less than an hour later, Fisher found himself being shoved onto the Twin Beech airplane that was equipped with extra fuel tanks, a radar receiver, a single-band radio, and survival gear. Trussell took his place in the pilot's seat, and motioned to Fisher to sit beside him. He watched as Bradley handed the mysterious cartons to Trussell and noted how Trussell acknowledged their significance. Relieved when Bradley and Turk Paz deplaned, Fisher turned to Trussell for an explanation.

Once airborne, Trussell explained that he was under instructions from Bradley to fly to Santa Marta, Colombia, to retrieve Don Leach, who was being held hostage by the Colombians, and return to Starkville with sixteen hundred pounds of marijuana. Before Fisher had a chance to bemoan the fact that he was allergic to marijuana and feared a severe attack if confined with a planeload of pot, Trussell replaced those anxieties with an even worse scenario.

"I'm supposed to throw you into the ocean," Trussell told Fisher. "Brad hasn't forgiven you for returning those guns to Atwood."

Fisher glanced at Trussell, wondering incredulously if the plans for his demise would be pursued.

"Don't worry," Trussell said. "We're going to rescue Leach and get the hell out of Colombia. I'll deal with Brad later on. This plane isn't capable of carrying a ton of dope. Besides, we were all under surveillance in Mississippi and the cops will be waiting for us when we return to Starkville."

Fisher asked about the contents of the two cartons.

"You don't need to concern yourself with those." Trussell knew one of the boxes contained an ultrasophisticated radar device that Larry Bryant had apparently stolen from an F-4 jet fighter at a U.S. military base. The other contained a starlight night-vision scope that Larry Bryant had gotten from the China Lake Naval Base. Trussell was under strict instructions not to discuss the contents with anyone, under any circumstances. As an ex-cop, he knew the seriousness of transporting stolen military equipment to foreign countries, and was not about to incriminate himself, even to Jan Fisher.

"That one is full of money," Trussell lied, pointing to the suitcase. "We're supposed to give it to the Colombians in exchange for Leach."

Early the next morning, the Twin Beech began its gradual descent over the Caribbean. Both men were exhausted from flying all night.

"You know how to swim?" Trussell asked Fisher.

"Why?" Fisher asked, eyeing Trussell apprehensively.

"Because we're going into the water."

Before Fisher had time to figure out what was going on, Trussell had dropped the plane so its wingtips nearly grazed the sea.

"I'm going to beach it," Trussell said, noticing Fisher's nervousness. "I'll tell Brad we developed engine problems and were forced down."

Certain tacit rules exist in the drug world that provide freedom from liability. A smuggler escapes financial responsibility for an ill-fated venture only if he is busted, his plane crashes, or if he is forced by circumstances to abandon his aircraft to avoid apprehension. Without the presence of one of the excuses accepted industry-wide, a smuggler whose undertaking sours often faces death at the hands of his accomplices.

Intentionally or not, the airplane slid under Trussell's guidance onto the shoreline, coming to a standstill partially immersed in water. Fisher watched Trussell unload both cartons, holding them aloft as he waded neck-deep to dry land. Fisher dove into the shallow water and followed Trussell.

Once ashore, Trussell guided Fisher to a dirt road. He had accurately calculated his location and grasped his bearings. They were within walking distance of the farmhouse where Bradley had left Leach two weeks earlier. When a native driving a pickup truck offered a ride to the unlikely hitchhikers—two soaking-wet gringos carrying suitcases —Trussell gratefully directed him to the hostage hideout. But upon arrival at the remote farm they were greeted by three Colombians whose identities they didn't learn until later.

"Neither one of us spoke any Spanish," Fisher recounted. "So we explained our situation the best we could . . . about the crashed airplane." The Colombians put Trussell and Fisher under guard and dispatched scouts to check out the Twin Beech.

After being held in captivity for two days, Trussell and Fisher were finally transported to Santa Marta where they were reunited with Leach. Robbed of their jewelry and passports, they were given eight hours to contact Bradley Bryant to notify him of the unfortunate turn of events. If they were unsuccessful, they were told, all of them would be killed.

Leach told Trussell and Fisher that Bradley's Colombian associates had placed Leach under "house arrest" as soon as Bradley left the country and that Senator López had received a phone call from Bradley the day before the Twin Beech was scheduled to arrive. Leach had been told that Trussell would land at 4 A.M., and that the senator had bribed Army personnel who would have been on duty at that time. Leach was taken to the airstrip, located on Senator López's farm, to await the plane's arrival. He assisted the Colombians in lighting smudge pots to illuminate the field. The Colombians waited impatiently and angrily for the plane that did not arrive.

When informed about the plane crash by his captors, Leach had

been led to believe that Trussell and Fisher were both dead. Although
he had been treated well, Leach expected he would spend the rest of his
life in Colombia unless Bradley repaid a substantial debt. Bradley's
growing reputation for reneging did not inspire Leach's confidence.
Leach's prospects suddenly brightened when Trussell and Fisher arrived upon the scene. He assumed Trussell and Fisher were bringing
payment for his release. However, the Colombians didn't seem satisfied
with the suitcase and added Trussell and Fisher to Leach's captivity.
Unable to reach Bradley, the three reviewed their options, and agreed
upon a scheme to win their freedom.

     "We felt like Brad had written us off," Fisher complained. "So
we started negotiating with the senator, telling him we had a DC-9
parked on a runway in Florida." The Colombian official was interested
in having the three Americans run Colombian gold marijuana from
South America to the United States. He had lost faith in the abilities of
Bradley and Jimmy Chagra to direct a successful smuggling organization, and was hoping to create a new export operation. Trussell, Leach,
and Fisher assured the Colombian that if their passports were returned
to them they would retrieve the DC-9 in Florida and fly back to Santa
Marta the next day to load it with dope. They boasted of their own
alleged connections, convincing the senator that business could continue as usual without Bradley or Chagra. The Colombians provided
them each with a one-way ticket by commercial airline back to Miami,
extracting vows that they would return immediately to retrieve the load
of drugs that was already waiting. Why the Colombians were dissatisfied with the military equipment as payment for Bradley's delinquent
debt would remain unclear.

     Once back on American soil, the three men made arrangements
to return to their homes in Savannah and Tampa. Each had decided to
sever their ties with Bradley Bryant—decisions that would eventually
contribute to Bradley's downfall.

■

Bradley was unaware of the extent to which Drew and his former associates intended to betray him. He knew that Drew was undermining him

and vowing retaliation for the hundred thousand dollars Bradley owed him. But he still felt invulnerable.

Using the alias "Bradley Wilson," Bradley rented a self-storage unit at the U-Store-It warehouses located on New Circle Road in Lexington. He then ordered two of his employees to drive a car loaded with weapons from Tampa to Lexington, to be stored in the warehouse.

Bradley's cousin Larry was en route to a planned rendezvous with the eccentric Alvin Snapper. Snapper's inventions included the breakfast drink Tang and the IBM typewriter ball. He and Larry Bryant had become partners in an electronics security firm following their meeting a few years earlier at a convention of antique weapons collectors. Bryant had taken an instant liking to Snapper—who, coincidentally, was a Kentucky native—and was impressed by Snapper's ownership of the world's largest private collection of automatic weapons.

As Larry maneuvered his Ranchero into Snapper's curved driveway, he managed to hide the mini-truck behind a World War II tank that was parked in front of the garage. He was greeted at the Spanish-style stucco house by his cagey partner. Peeking out from behind the front door, Snapper motioned to Bryant to enter.

A few minutes later the garage door opened, and the two men began loading five starlight night-vision scopes and one low-light-level television camera into the bed of Larry Bryant's vehicle. Across the street, unbeknown to Bryant and Snapper, FBI agents were photographing their activity.

Larry Bryant then traveled to the isolated China Lake Naval Base. Located in California's Mojave Desert, China Lake is the Navy's supersecret test center where exotic weapons and electronics systems are developed. Air space is restricted from the ground to infinity for the eighteen hundred square miles of desert owned by the base, and state-of-the-art measures are taken to prevent access to the area where classified missile and air-warfare maneuvers occur. Yet Larry Bryant was able to penetrate one of the government's most complex security systems in order to retrieve a remote-controlled helicopter, fifteen hundred rounds of .30-caliber M-1 tracer ammunition, and a radar receiver section from a sidewinder missile.

Awaiting word from Larry that the items he requested had been acquired, Bradley oversaw the hundreds of details for his next planned dope run. He spent the fall of 1979 traveling between Philadelphia, New York, Miami, Savannah, Atlanta, Lexington, Dallas, San Diego, Denver, and Las Vegas—staying at the top hotels, for which he paid with cash. He communicated with his friends, family, and associates by wire rather than telephone. He established an elaborate system for contacting subordinates, using portable pagers to relay messages directing accomplices to contact him by calling a series of numbers that had been coded for public pay phones in various cities.

He filled his daily diary and personal notebook with references to the upcoming operation, often using codes and abbreviations. "Meet D.C. [Dan Chandler] in Palm Springs," he wrote. "Obtain required maps." Under a heading called Work to Blue Fin—his nickname for an aircraft he had recently purchased that had blue-colored tail assemblies —he listed the numerous modification requirements: "Camera and monitor; green box; long and short range comms.; antennas; auto-pilot; ground power check; electronic installations; welding to cowl flap; seats removed and reupholstered; cover rear windows w/curtains? plus tint?" Under the heading "Misc. Support Equipment" he listed: "Telephone scramblers; bear cats; M-10s; 6 magazines for automatics; security; steel building; concrete pad [apparently for a helicopter landing associated with the operation]; M-79; 6 bug/frequency units; 3 vests; 5 lb. CO_2 fire extinguisher; raft; emergency rations; cooler loaded with ice; flight helmets; heavy duty plastic bags; tape; extension cord; axes (2); aviation oil; 12 volt battery in marine case; toilet; and heavy duty vacuum cleaner."

For Project Aqua, Bradley had rented a landing strip near the Chesapeake Bay in Maryland. His requirements for this operation were even more specific and military-like: "Block unrequired access roads; obtain fuel and wind sock; check property boundaries; hire contractor for installation of 6-foot chain link fence around property; radio and scanner installations; training of all personnel; field-testing under similar conditions; dry runs of entire operation; establish code and procedures for communications and response; registration of new trucks; install extra heavy duty suspension on all pick-up trucks ASAP; language work for Roger Barnard." He spent thousands of dollars on the airstrip location that he called Aqualand, including the installation of a remote telephone-answering service. Aqualand became his pet project

—its secluded location, airstrip, capability of docking large boats, and its proximity to both Washington, D.C., and Philadelphia, made it an ideal location as an off-loading point from which to distribute drugs to the East Coast.

Christmas was Bradley's favorite time of year for importing marijuana. It had come to be a tradition with him, as he found that police, like everyone else, were on relaxed work schedules. He believed the holidays resulted in unfocused attention by law enforcement in general, alleviating his increasing paranoia. Mostly, though, Bradley was sentimental, and he found it painful and sad to be away from his children during the Christmas season. His life in hotels was becoming boring and lonely—an emptiness that was exacerbated by his bitter divorce.

■

In the autumn of 1979, Ralph Ross received a copy of an FBI memorandum. The fifty-five-page document signaled the beginning of an investigation into *Illegal Gambling Practices, Prostitution, Murder, Extortion, and Narcotics* under RICO. Several subjects of the investigation, including Jimmy Lambert, Drew Thornton, and Bill Canan, were named in the memorandum.

At that time Ralph was not convinced that Bradley Bryant and Drew Thornton had split their organization. He thought that rumors of their break-up were brushfires thrown up as a smoke screen.

Yet insiders swear that following their tempestuous battle in Savannah Bradley and Drew never again spoke a word to each other. Those close to one or the other claim that beginning on that steamy summer day, the two childhood friends entered into a vicious competition that would eventually destroy them both. Lines were drawn, loyalties divided. Bradley, the master of finance and distribution, and Drew, the wizard of procurement and transportation, would build their own structures—each vowing to eliminate the other. Intimates of both contended that Drew was never able to collect his hundred-thousand-dollar debt from Bradley. At least not in cash.

The airplane crash in Santa Marta was a debacle that left the

Colombians disenfranchised and alienated many of Bradley's subordinates, some of whom chose to realign themselves with Drew.

Regardless of the relationship between the two smugglers, attempts to untangle the web became increasingly difficult. Some were Bradley's people, and some were Drew's. Still others were contract agents who worked for both sides, making it impossible to determine whether the two organizations were competing or were in cahoots.

Ralph ultimately decided that whether or not bad blood existed between the two men was inconsequential. He had been a cop long enough to know that such a falling out would eventually work to his advantage. Ralph was more interested in Drew than Bradley, mainly because of Drew's law enforcement background and continuing influence with the Lexington police.

He was satisfied that the FBI's RICO case, which targeted Jimmy Lambert and Drew Thornton, would at least chip away at the right prey. The Kentucky connections of Drew and Bradley had been so overlapped and intertwined as to be inseparable. The high-level financiers and distributors in Lexington remained the same, and Ralph's instincts told him that Jimmy Lambert was a common thread between both groups. With Lambert in the hands of the FBI, Ralph decided to begin surveillance on some of Bradley Bryant's and Drew Thornton's known Lexington associates and the locations they frequented.

■

On Christmas Eve 1979, Bradley flew to Atlanta to meet with Johnny Trussell. Trussell had broken off relations with Bradley after the Colombian fiasco, and resented the fact that he still had not been paid any of his fifty thousand dollars. But Bradley had a hard sell.

"We have a new organization," Bradley told Trussell. "It's tighter. Better people. Drew's out and some new people are in. But you don't need to know who they are. It'll work this time. I have five contracts to fulfill, and I really need you as a pilot."

Bradley bragged about his ground crews, his off-loaders, his transportation personnel, his electronic equipment, his Maryland airstrip, his new airplanes, his network of wholesalers.

"We have three tiers," Bradley said. "The transporters, like you, who are responsible for bringing the load into the country. The personnel who take care of finding the landing strips, aircraft maintenance, purchasing and storing heavy trucks for unloading the planes. And, third, the distributors. Everyone will get rich. All you have to worry about is flying it in. Can you fly a Herky Bird?" Bradley asked.

Trussell nodded yes, then asked: "When do I get paid?"

"When the deal is done," Bradley replied.

That's what Trussell didn't like about the organization—waiting for the profits to trickle down after the Colombians were paid and all the pot had been sold in the United States. Bradley's credit with Trussell had lost some credibility.

Trussell wanted his money up front.

Bradley agreed to a small advance of twenty-five hundred dollars, which he counted out for Trussell in one-hundred-dollar bills, and Trussell reluctantly acquiesced.

Bradley gave Trussell instructions to meet someone on December 27 in Atlanta—"someone you'll know," Bradley said, refusing to identify the individual—"and fly him wherever he tells you to."

Bradley flew that day from Georgia back to Philadelphia. Upon his arrival, he called Don Leach. Like Trussell, Leach had avoided Bradley since August, after being held hostage in Colombia. Though Leach had disassociated himself from Bradley, he thought it prudent to remain on amicable terms.

"I need a gun permit," Bradley told him. "Can you help me out?"

Leach acquiesced. "Meet me at Winstons," Leach told him, referring to the Valley Forge, Pennsylvania, restaurant where Leach was working as a bouncer. "I'll get you a permit from the Tredyffrin Police Department."

"Do you know where I can get a silencer?" Bradley asked, pushing his luck.

"No," Leach replied.

At the same time, one of Bradley's employees, a Savannah pilot named Gary Scott, knocked on the door of a Bulloch County, Georgia, farmhouse.

"Are you interested in renting one of your pastures for a day?" Scott asked the farmer. "I'll make it worth your while."

"What do you mean?" the farmer asked.

"I'll give you fifty thousand bucks if I can land a plane here next week, on January 2. It'll only be on the ground a little while."

"Don't see why not," the farmer replied.

The farmer watched from the doorway as Scott drove his white Corvette down the dirt road. As soon as the sports car was out of sight, he called the local sheriff.

CHAPTER
SEVEN

"I was visiting some friends in Lexington one night a few weeks ago," Mary Shasta began, speaking with deliberate calm.

Ralph Ross had arranged to meet with the psychic who claimed to have knowledge about Melanie Flynn's disappearance shortly after learning of her existence from the FBI.

"So it was sometime in August 1979, right?" Ralph interrupted.

"Yes. About the middle, I believe."

"Anyway," she continued, "we were watching the news on television and suddenly two men appeared on the screen. I recognized them as the men who had been appearing in my dreams for the past two years . . . dreams I was having about the disappearance of Melanie Flynn."

"Who were the men?"

"I had never seen them before," she said, "except in my dreams. I was very shaken when I saw them on television, but I tried to nonchalantly ask my friends who they were. She was told by her friends that one was a former Lexington policeman named Andrew Thornton.

"Did you know Melanie Flynn?" Ralph asked her.

"No. I read about her disappearance in the newspaper, and I suddenly began dreaming about her frequently. She was often with those two men in my dreams. But I didn't know who the men were until I saw them on television."

"Did you tell anyone about your dreams?"

"Just my husband, family, and some close friends," Shasta answered. "Until now, two years later. After I recognized the two men from my dreams on television, I decided to go to the FBI. I had a friend in the FBI—a man who goes to my church. And I decided I should tell him about my dreams."

"Let's talk about the dreams," Ralph said. "When did they begin?"

"In January 1977. Right after Melanie disappeared. The same dream continued every two or three weeks, until May 1977. Then, in June 1977, the dream changed."

"Describe the dreams to me."

"I envisioned a petite, young woman underwater, her hair floating like seaweed. I knew it was Melanie Flynn because I had seen a picture of her in the paper. That's all I saw . . . the same image, from January until May. In early June 1977, I envisioned Melanie seated, her right leg crossed over her left. She was in a large bar area of a dimly lit, but very plush, nightclub. She was wearing a black satin jumpsuit, backless. She was laughing and puffing on a cigarette, which she held in her right hand, between her upper index and middle fingers. Her body was partially turned, with her right elbow resting on the back of a chair. That dream ended with a vision of Melanie underwater again.

"A few weeks later," Shasta continued, "I dreamed that Melanie and I were together in a large apartment. She stepped out of the shower, and I noticed she was smoothly tanned all over her body. Her wet hair fell just above her collarbone and was slightly wavy. She was petite, yet very well built, her body firm and muscular. She had large brown eyes, a small turned-up nose, full lips, a sexy and mischievous smile that showed nice teeth.

"In the dream, I was trying desperately to convince Melanie to leave the apartment and accompany me . . . that I would take her someplace where she would be safe. Melanie was hesitant and confused at first, truly not knowing whether or not to trust anyone.

"During this discussion, we were interrupted by a tall man who entered through the bedroom door. He stood about six-two, and had dark curly hair and a mustache. He was also a well-toned, muscular person. The man seemed angry and suspicious of Melanie and me. We told him that Melanie was helping me pack my belongings, but he apparently didn't believe us. He started toward Melanie, cursing.

"A sandy-haired man restrained him long enough for Melanie and I to escape through the bathroom window. We ran across a large, dry yard around the corner of the building, and entered a white station wagon."

"The next night in my dreams," Shasta continued, "I envisioned Melanie standing outside an apartment door. Snow covered the steps and a portion of the breezeway. She was wearing a pant-length white coat made of real or imitation sheepskin. Then, during July, August, September, October, November, and December 1977, I again simply dreamed about Melanie's nude body underwater, her hair floating around her."

The dreams abated for a while, coming less frequently and with less detail. Until January 1978, when she dreamed of a specific location.

"There was some type of a boardwalk, and at the end a large door that was painted black, with one square window. I couldn't see inside through the window, so I opened the door and walked in. To the left I saw a lounge where a large, fat man was tending bar. Several round tables and chairs were scattered throughout the bar. Past the bar was another doorway which looked the same as the doorway I had already entered. There by that door, several men were gathered around a large table. They were extremely tense and it seemed to be a frightening atmosphere."

The dreams stopped for six months, she told Ralph. Disturbed by the visions, Shasta decided to discuss the case with other professional and respected psychics. She was encouraged by her mentors to concentrate on the significance of her dreams in order to better understand their implications.

It wasn't until late June 1978 that the visions began again. "I saw Melanie's body wrapped in white cloth and dumped in a large utility bag. Again, the underwater images became prevalent in my dreams. In late August 1978, I envisioned a small-featured woman with short red hair. She picked up a framed photograph of Melanie. The woman was focusing on Melanie's face and upper torso. The woman was teary-eyed and obviously grieving for Melanie.

"Four months later, in mid-December, I saw the same tall, dark

curly haired man who had appeared before. He was threatening Melanie, and she was backing up against a steel girder. The beam had large
bolts in it, reminding me of an old bridge. Melanie's hands were grasping the girder so tightly that her knuckles were white. The ring finger
on her left hand appeared slightly larger than her other fingers."

On January 3, 1979, Melanie appeared to Shasta in a vision.
"She referred to me as 'kid' and repeatedly expressed how very cold
she felt . . . almost freezing. She was surrounded by swirling, muddy
water." A week later, Shasta envisioned some divers in a lake who were
searching for Melanie. The wet suits were constantly being torn by
cone-shaped obstacles. The divers were concerned that rising water
would make the body bag surface. Later the same evening, Shasta saw
Melanie stuffing a white three-by-five index card into some hidden location in a bedroom. On the card were written the letters "Z, C, and B"
and some numbers that Shasta could not recall upon waking.

"On January 17," she told Ralph, "I saw a petite young woman
slumped across the back seat of a car with red interior. The woman was
wearing black shoes and a silky black blouse with a small print. She
was lying horizontally across the seat. Then, on January 23, I saw the
chunky sandy-haired man standing with the tall dark-haired man atop a
rocky area. There was no foliage, and the rock was covered with ice and
snow. The dark man was wearing a black and white tie, and the blond
man was wearing jeans, a black turtleneck sweater, and tan corduroy
jacket. Each was especially concerned about saving his own skin."

Two days later, Shasta dreamed about an underwater rock cliff.
"The cliff had jagged shelving and appeared at first glance to be two
separate rock formations, although it was really only one. I couldn't
distinguish the depth of the formation, but it seemed to form a deep
horseshoe cavern midway into the section. A steel bar or rod had been
placed across the shelving. A chain was wrapped around the bar and
extended several feet down. Attached to the chain was a large canvas
bag with brass ring seals. A body wrapped in cloth was inside the bag,
which was totally encased in water. Fragments of hair were floating in
the bag, and two gold earrings were in the bottom of the bag."

In February, Shasta told Ralph, she envisioned Melanie grasping the shoulders of the dark-haired man. "She was shaking him, and

was shouting and crying, telling him how desperately she wanted to live."

The dreams were frequent from that time forward. Sometimes Melanie would appear to her, vaguely, during which times Melanie displayed varying emotions such as fright, frustration, anger, spite, and determination. Shasta also sensed a fierce competition between the dark-haired and light-haired men. "They competed for women, and in many other ways as well," she told Ralph. There was no dispute, however, that the dark man—the man she eventually came to believe was Andrew Thornton—wielded the most power.

"On July 1, 1979, I envisioned a large gathering of people. They were proceeding up a large stairway. In a hallway, people were lined up as if waiting to be seated in a classroom. Through a doorway was an auditorium that had been converted into an elegant funeral home. Outside, the weather was that of early winter."

That was to be Mary Shasta's last dream. But its intensity affected her more than the others, for it was at that time that she first perceived an occult overtone. Her dreams about Melanie Flynn, she told Ralph, had propelled her further into religious faith. She found herself delving into the study of cults, devil-worshiping, and the spiritual struggle between good and evil, becoming increasingly convinced that her psychic powers had led her dangerously into a world of evil—a world that could only be counteracted by devotion to God.

But as Shasta sat with Ralph Ross in September 1979, matter-of-factly relating her series of visions, she was clearly overwhelmed and frightened by the murky world into which she felt she had been thrust. She drew a diagram on a piece of paper in Ralph's notebook. The crude drawing showed a body bag hanging between two rocky ledges. She then told Ralph she believed the crevass where the body was hanging was located somewhere in Herrington Lake—a man-made lake fifteen miles southwest of Lexington.

Ralph arranged for himself, Shasta, and several of his investigators to take a state police boat onto Herrington Lake. Shasta guided the police officers to a picturesque setting amid cliffs and rolling hills. When they neared the stone abutments of an old covered bridge that had been torn down, Shasta told them to stop the boat. "It's here," she said, when they had almost reached Camp Nelson.

Ralph cocked one eyebrow as he looked at her. "Are you sure?" he asked.

When Shasta nodded yes, Ralph said: "This is where Melanie's purse was found."

■

"Isn't Drew Thornton's farm right around here?" Ralph asked the detective who had researched Jessamine County land records in order to locate the seventy-acre parcel that Drew, Canan, and another Lexington policeman named Danny Murphy had purchased the year before.

Sure enough, Mary Shasta had unknowingly directed them to the back boundary of Triad—the fertile and wooded riverbank farm where Drew and Bradley had stockpiled the Company's weapons.

For days, Ralph Ross's state police divers searched the Kentucky River and Lake Herrington for Melanie Flynn's body, to no avail.

Disappointed, Ralph thanked Mary Shasta for her time and assistance, and asked that she contact him if the dreams persisted. But he was not prone to placing much stock in matters of the supernatural or spiritual even though he found Shasta to be remarkably credible and her deductions uncanny. He contemplated the possibility she raised that Drew was involved in the occult. Ralph had little knowledge or experience relating to such matters, and saw nothing in Drew's personality to suggest such a fascination except for Drew's obsession with the martial arts. But then again, Ralph knew that a lot of cops and soldiers studied karate and other oriental fighting techniques.

Coincidentally, Ralph had suddenly been receiving complaints about suspicious activity on Triad. Neighbors had reported to state police that a cult of devil worshipers frequented the remote property, and that the constant firing of automatic weapons could be heard. Dozens of people wearing military camouflage uniforms were seen rappelling from the back cliffs of Triad.

Ralph had dispatched one of his investigators to the Recorder of Deeds in Nicholasville—the county seat—while sending another detective to the location to take a look.

"The private road to Triad is blocked by a locked gate," the

detective wrote in his case report to Ralph. "A sign on the fence surrounding the property reads: NOTICE—TRESPASSING ON THIS PROPERTY
MAY BE HAZARDOUS TO YOUR HEALTH." The word Triad was painted on
a sign at the entrance to the farm; a horseshoe-shaped symbol under
the letter "i" depicted the devil's pitchfork, the state policeman
noted.

Other federal agencies had also been enticed by rumors
of arms-stockpiling and mercenary training at Triad. U.S. Customs
agents in New York, who were monitoring the activities of Saudi arms
dealer Adnan Khashoggi, briefly entertained the possibility that Triad
was a subsidiary of Khashoggi's Triad America Corporation. The fact
that Khashoggi was frequenting Lexington added fuel to the speculation.

Ralph knew that the FBI in Lexington had received reports that
foreign "dark-skinned" soldiers of unknown nationality—possibly Libyan or Nicaraguan—were being trained at Triad in guerrilla warfare
techniques. Some of the reports suggested that Triad was CIA-sponsored. Ralph was also aware that ATF had conducted an investigation
into activities at Triad that had concluded that those attending the
"camp" were "survivalists who on occasion dress in military fatigues
and play war games—i.e., shoot at each other with plastic bullets containing red blood-like dye, parachute from airplanes, firearms training,
etc." Triad evidently offered training in self-defense, advanced first aid,
radiation detection, and the perfection of individual survival skills. ATF
investigators found that trainees rappeled off the back cliffs of the farm
down to the Kentucky riverbank, while avoiding automatic fire. But
ATF found "no information indicating any connection between above-
described activity and foreign/domestic terrorism, guerrilla warfare,
and other activity possibly in violation of neutrality laws."

Then, an unidentified man called the state police. A few days
earlier he had seen a white twin-engine airplane gliding low over Triad.
"I heard the engines start as the plane came out of a glide. Then duffel
bags dropped out of the plane and the plane turned northeast toward
Lexington. A few days later, a single-engine Piper, silver with red
stripes, flew low over the same route, also dropping its cargo onto the
Triad property."

The description and tail number of one of the aircraft matched that of a Piper Navajo that had been temporarily seized off the coast of South America. That plane, flown by Bill Canan and another former Lexington police officer named Steve Oliver, was identified by U.S. Customs the previous month, August 1979, as ferrying handguns to the remote Dutch Antilles Island of Aruba.

Canan and Oliver had flown the aircraft from Fort Lauderdale, Florida, to Aruba and somehow aroused the suspicion of Dutch officials. The plane departed Aruba, but then returned a week later, piloted by Oliver and Lexington policeman Danny Murphy. Having coordinated with U.S. officials, Aruba Customs agents decided to search the plane upon its second arrival, they found that all of the passenger seats had been removed, and extra fuel tanks had been installed. Found on board the aircraft were a .38-caliber Smith & Wesson with ninety-nine rounds of ammunition, and a 9-millimeter Walther PPK with twenty rounds of ammunition.

During questioning, Oliver and Murphy flaunted their police credentials and claimed they were in Aruba on official law enforcement business. Although Dutch and U.S. Customs agents suspected the Kentucky men were involved in some type of gun trafficking that violated neutrality laws, they had no real evidence. They ultimately decided against detaining the men, while seizing the aircraft and notifying Ralph Ross at the Kentucky State Police.

Oliver and Murphy caught the first possible commercial flight back to the United States. A month later, an associate of Drew's—a Lexington lawyer and pilot named Randy Reinhardt—traveled to Aruba to retrieve the plane. Reinhardt told authorities he represented Aero Sport, Inc., the company that owned the airplane. He flew the plane back to the States, stopping briefly in the Dominican Republic.

"The plane was illegally detained," Reinhardt would say when questioned by the media. He would refuse to identify the actual owner of the plane, or discuss the matter further, and no charges were ever filed. But the plane was sighted frequently landing and taking off from the Triad property.

U.S. Senate investigators somehow got wind of the mysteries swirling around Triad. On the heels of these incidents, the Senate Committee on Security and Terrorism asked the state police and FBI about the possibility that Triad was in fact a full-scale "terrorism school."

Ralph decided to send in a team of undercover agents to sneak onto the property. His men found evidence that Triad was indeed a paramilitary training ground, but there were no maneuvers underway at the time the state police infiltrated. The physical layout was consistent with a military training ground. Most of the acreage had been carefully groomed, but in the middle of the manicured area was a clump of trees, within which were situated rows of barracks. Ralph dispatched a state police airplane to obtain aerial photographs of the property. The pictures showed the tire tracks of large vehicles, possibly tanks, heading toward the barracks area.

The day after the state police plane conducted its surveillance, Ralph received a phone call from Lexington Police Sergeant John Bizzack. Bizzack told Ralph he was conveying a message from the owners of the property—Drew Thornton, Bill Canan, and Danny Murphy: If the state police flew over Triad again, the plane would be shot down.

Ralph blinked in disbelief. The Lexington police had no jurisdiction over the Jessamine County property.

Following the surveillance of Triad and the reports from U.S. Customs of the trip to Aruba, all indications suggested to Ralph that Bradley and Drew were trafficking as heavily in arms as in dope. The paramilitary interests of the group, the soldier-of-fortune aura they emulated, and their military and police training in weapons, led Ralph to believe they were committed to munitions as the currency of both the present and the future. Drugs might be no more than a sidelight to their *real* business—that of funneling guns to foreign governments and right-wing rebels.

Was it possible that Melanie Flynn had posed an even greater threat to the organization than Ralph previously considered? Had Melanie been privy to the sources for their weapons? Had she known the identity of the military insiders who provided them with guns, ammo, and explosives?

Did her knowledge of the secret operations of Triad prove fatal for her and leave her floating lifelessly in a body bag on the shore of the mysterious property, as the psychic believed?

Convinced that Bizzack, as lead investigator on the Melanie Flynn case, had less than total commitment to solving Melanie's disappearance, Ralph decided against sharing with him the psychic's revelations.

CHAPTER
EIGHT

Bradley Bryant slid three pieces of luggage onto the scale at the Delta Airlines ticket counter, checking them through to Atlanta. With his free hand, he kept a tight grip on the handle of his aluminum attaché case. The ticket agent remarked on Bradley's cowboy hat.

"Pierce," Bradley said, when the agent asked his name.

As he turned to leave, Bradley must have sensed he was being watched. Within moments, Bryant felt both his arms being grabbed. "Philadelphia police," his captors said.

In what police believed to be a routine drug-smuggling investigation, they seized Bradley's luggage from the conveyor belt, the attaché case at his side, and handcuffed him. While he rode in the backseat of a police vehicle to headquarters, back-up narcotics officers were raiding Suite 608 at the Sheraton Airport Inn. Bradley, his cousin, Larry Bryant, and one of his bodyguards, Roger Dale Barnard, had been staying in the suite for the past week.

As it turned out, they stayed one day too long.

Hotel maids had grown suspicious when they noticed marijuana smoke wafting out from under the door. The three men had refused maid service, tipping chambermaids a hundred dollars to stay out of their rooms. Each day, an individual who identified himself as "Doug Clark" paid for the rooms in cash with one-hundred-dollar bills. Finally, on January 3, 1980, the hotel manager decided it was time to call the police.

Assuming the search of the Bryants and the suite of rooms would probably net marijuana, and possibly cocaine, police were surprised to find no illicit drugs.

What they *did* find puzzled them.

In Bradley's luggage at the time of his arrest were semi-automatic weapons that had been threaded for silencers; commando daggers; disguises; and a dozen fraudulent Kentucky drivers licenses. There were also telephone numbers for the CIA and other contacts in various parts of the world, stolen Texas license plates, and mysterious ledgers with references such as: "$10,000 to the Mayor." Follow-up investigation revealed that Bradley planned to travel from Philadelphia to Denver, where he had reservations at the Fairmont Hotel, to attend a fundraiser for a mayoral candidate in that city.

They also found confidential pamphlets including *Ten Lethal or Incapacitating Drugs Stored by the CIA* and *The Top-Secret Registry of U.S. Government Radio Frequencies.* A complete airline schedule for Europe and the Middle East as well as Russian, Spanish, and English dictionaries were also in his luggage.

Bradley's notebook contained the names and addresses of several former and current Lexington policemen—including Triad owners Drew Thornton, Bill Canan, and Danny Murphy—and references to planned missions named Blue Fin and Aqua. Investigators also found what they believed to be an assassination kit, raising suspicions that Bradley was involved in something other than a standard drug operation. Since Senator Edward Kennedy had been scheduled to speak in Philadelphia, the Secret Service was alerted to take extraordinary precautions.

In the attaché case Bradley so carefully guarded—a tiger decal on both sides—police seized $22,800 in cash, a Walther PPK semi-automatic pistol, a two-shot Deringer, a telephone scrambler, a passport, five different wallets, and pistol permits issued in Georgia and Nevada. The cash was later traced to the Federal Reserve in San Francisco, and had been part of a bulk shipment delivered to Caesars Palace in Las Vegas.

In the Sheraton suite, police found four more attaché cases containing weapons, silencers, scramblers, shoulder holsters, and numerous rounds of ammunition, including "velet," a rare type of ammunition that detonates on contact with a target. A variety of sophisticated electronic devices capable of intercepting, identifying, and monitoring law enforcement frequencies were of particular interest to the cops. The only articles of clothing found in the suite and in Bradley's luggage were ten blue sweatshirts, two black ski masks, and three flight suits, all of which were brand new.

A sheet of Caesars Palace stationary found in an unmarked envelope in Bradley's possession contained the home address of a Las Vegas resident named "George Haddad," a physical description of him, his place of employment, the license number and description of his car, and details about Haddad's girlfriend and their social habits. Three candid photographs of Haddad were in the same envelope.

When Philadelphia police contacted other investigative agencies about the identity of Haddad, they were told he was an "intelligence agent" who did work for both the U.S. and Libya. Haddad denied his involvement with the intelligence community and claimed not to know Bradley Bryant. "Frankly, I was petrified," Haddad said, seemingly incredulous that he was an apparent target for a contract murder. "I was questioned by police and I didn't know what to say. I didn't know anything about Bradley Bryant or why my name would be associated with him. He even had pictures of me. I'm a simple working man, in the hotel business . . . not the gun business, and I've never even *been* to Las Vegas."

Haddad said police told him that Bradley was in the midst of a weapons deal with a foreigner, and that the transaction was scheduled to take place in Fort Worth, Texas. Bradley apparently planned to retain Haddad as a translator for the deal, although Haddad denied any knowledge of such a venture. "I'm Lebanese and I speak the Arabic language." Haddad swore it was a case of mistaken identity. "But like I said, I'm just a simple living human being and I was petrified when I heard my name associated with that group," he said, referring to the Company.

Documents in Bradley's possession that were seized by Philadelphia Police included manuals describing the production of counterfeit drivers' licenses, passports, and birth certificates.

Always when operating in the field and on assignment, false identification should be used, one document read. *It is always best to assume the actual identity of a totally foreign and innocent party. This can be done by researching deaths of infants and obtaining identification in the dead babies' names.*

Other materials stated that *"our* people should be collecting obituary pages in newspapers from areas where they may be on assignment." It was unclear to police who *our* people were.

Realizing they had inadvertently busted a member of a large-scale weapons network, the Philadelphia police solicited the help of ATF. ATF systematically inventoried the electronic equipment seized, fascinated by its sophistication and similarity to government-issued instruments used to locate covert transmitters from body wires or room bugs; mini-scopes used to repair electronic equipment; telephone scramblers to be used so telephone conversations could not be monitored by outside parties; devices used to match transmitters with antennas; microphones; transceivers to communicate with mobile or base operations; and an electronic language calculator containing capsules that convert English to Spanish, German, and French.

Philadelphia officials were seduced by the case. "The case reeked to me of international espionage," said Frank Scafidi, the Philadelphia Police Department's chief of detectives.

"It was an exercise in the bizarre," said then-assistant U.S. Attorney Roberto Rivera-Soto.

When ATF agents interviewed the three Kentucky natives, the suspects divulged little information.

Larry Bryant revealed he had recently retired from the Air Force after twenty years of service "specializing in defeating Russian radar systems." At first he said that he and Bradley were involved in a clandestine CIA attempt to steal a sophisticated Soviet radar unit from Libya. He later retreated from that story, claiming he would discuss the matter only with an electronics expert.

Barnard, the bodyguard and muscleman who was described as Bradley's "silent shadow," revealed nothing substantive.

Bradley was the most secretive of all.

"We're good guys, not bad guys," was the only thing Bradley would say.

■

Ralph Ross was one of the first police officers in Kentucky to learn about the Philadelphia arrests. ATF agents briefed him on Bryant's activities and on the items seized. In turn, Ralph gave them information on Bryant's background and on his associates.

"We know about Chandler," one agent said to Ralph. "He offered to post seventy-five thousand dollars' bail for Bradley. What else do you have on him?"

"He worked for John Y. Brown at Kentucky Fried Chicken in public relations until Brown sold the company," Ralph answered. "Chandler left Kentucky when he was charged with federal income tax evasion. The story goes that his friend Brown got him set up in Las Vegas. He still owes half a million dollars in back taxes."

Ralph was told that Chandler was currently living in Las Vegas with a woman named Dolores Dandrea—the daughter of convicted New Jersey organized crime figure, Carmine Dandrea. Their interest clearly piqued by the Chandler-Caesars-Bryant connection, the federal agents broached the next topic.

"What do you know about Jimmy Chagra?"

"Never heard of him," Ralph replied.

"He's the prime suspect in the murder of a federal judge in Texas," Ralph was informed. "He was convicted a few months ago on drug charges and Bradley Bryant helped him skip the country to avoid sentencing."

Ralph was not familiar with the specifics of the Judge Wood murder. But he *did* know that FBI Director William Webster had declared it the "crime of the century." Numerous FBI teletypes had come across Ralph's desk in the past six months, imploring cops everywhere to be on the lookout for the Wood assassin. Ralph had hastily scanned the teletypes, never imagining his Lexington group would be at the nucleus of the conspiracy.

"An analysis of telephone calls placed from Bradley's suite at the Sheraton is incomplete," Ralph was told, "but it's producing some good leads."

Many of Bradley's calls were made to Johnny Trussell, Don Leach, Jan Fisher, and Dan Chandler, which came as no surprise. Several calls were also made to Jimmy Chagra's Las Vegas attorney Oscar Goodman, and to a New York attorney by the name of Phil Ryan. Other individuals called by Bradley included a lieutenant in the Michael Thevis organized crime and pornography organization; a subject of an ATF gun-smuggling investigation; a suspected drug smuggler from El Paso; and former NFL player Lance Alworth.

"What about Mike Kelly?" they asked. "Bryant made sixteen calls to Kelly in Lexington."

"He's a fat kid who runs around with that bunch," Ralph answered. Ralph went on to tell the feds that Kelly's old man owned a wholesale pharmaceutical company in Lexington that was once accused by the DEA of failing to account for a hundred thousand Valium tablets; that Mike had a federal firearms license and was reputed to be an electronics expert; and that state police suspected him of manufacturing M-10 automatic pistols. Mike bought gun parts, Ralph told them, and then threaded them for silencers or turned them into automatic weapons. Mike also owned a farm over on the Kentucky River—close to Triad—that state police suspected was also being used for mercenary activity.

"What about Larry Bryant? Anything on him?"

Ralph replied that state police files revealed no biographical information on Bradley's cousin, except that he was a graduate of Millersburg Military Institute near Lexington.

"We don't know much more," Ralph was told by an ATF agent. "He's a master sergeant with the Air Force, attached to the Tactical Fighter Weapons Center Range Group at Nellis Air Force Base in Las Vegas. He had a national security clearance. He has no arrest record, but is currently under investigation by the Naval Investigation Service for the theft of nine Starlight nightscopes from China Lake Naval Base in California. The FBI investigated him in 1978 in connection with a missing range tank. The tank turned up in Southern California and nothing came of the case. Then, last fall, the FBI saw Larry Bryant driving a truck that belonged to a Texas drug dealer.

"We've looked for connections between the Bryants and Ed Wilson and Frank Terpil," the ATF agent continued, referring to two ex-CIA operatives who were under investigation in Washington, D.C., for conspiring to ship explosives, firearms, and night-vision equipment to Libyan strongman Muammar Qaddafi. "So far, we haven't found any connection. One witness has told us that a man matching the description of Frank Terpil was seen entering Bradley's room at the Sheraton. But we haven't been able to confirm that information."

Among the documents seized during the search of the Sheraton was a lease agreement for storage space in Lexington.

"We've had that warehouse under surveillance," Ralph said, referring to unit number 95 at the U-Store-It complex on New Circle Road. "I guess you'll be executing a search warrant there."

"We're just waiting for probable cause," the ATF agent responded.

■

At 4:30 A.M. on Valentine's Day, February 14, 1980, fifteen federal and local police officers raided the warehouse. Discovering an arsenal of weapons worth a quarter of a million dollars, ATF and FBI agents had a field day tracing the ownership of the guns.

Included in the cache of arms was a Soviet-made machine gun, a .50-caliber anti-aircraft gun, a 20-mm anti-tank gun, two fully automatic M-2 carbines, twenty-one "Taser" stun guns, and several handguns. Two suitcases contained numerous exotic knives, a can of tear gas, ankle and belt holsters, three cocaine test kits, several boxes of ammunition, a range-finder, and a bulletproof vest. Preliminary investigation indicated the Tasers belonged to Mike Kelly, while a .22-caliber "Explorer" survival rifle was registered to Drew Thornton.

But four items immediately overshadowed the significance of all others—three automatic weapons of the type used in the attempted assassination of Assistant U.S. Attorney James Kerr in Texas, and one of the Starlight nightscopes stolen from China Lake.

A few hours later, Bradley Bryant was arrested without incident at his father's Lexington home, and charged with one count of Criminal Possession of a Destructive Device. He was out on bond at the time, awaiting trial in Philadelphia on the firearms charges stemming from the Sheraton raid.

"It's no secret that I've always had a big gun collection," Bradley told his hometown newspaper following his arrest. He dismissed his mysterious behavior, explaining his necessity to maintain a low profile due to his ongoing divorce proceedings, coupled with his ownership of a private security firm.

Bradley contended that he had not violated any weapons laws in either Philadelphia or Lexington. "Everything seized in Philadelphia was wholly consistent with running a protection service. All that electronic surveillance equipment can be purchased commercially; so can the guns," Bradley told the *Lexington Herald.* The government disputed Bryant's excuse claiming that he was unable to produce evidence that EP Ltd. had any legitimate clients.

Larry Bryant, who was facing indictment in Philadelphia but had so far escaped criminal charges in Lexington, was asked by federal agents to explain how a nightscope from China Lake ended up in the Lexington warehouse.

He claimed that several nightscopes had been retrieved from China Lake to be traded to Libya for a Soviet radar system the Libyans had purchased from the Russians. The U.S. Government wanted to examine the Russian system, according to Larry Bryant's scenario, in order to duplicate it. All of the China Lake employees implicated in the disappearance of the items were top-secret specialists in long-range, surface-to-air radar systems, as was Larry Bryant.

Larry Bryant contended that the covert operation was going to save the U.S. Government millions of dollars in research and development costs. "We're good guys; we work for Uncle Sam," said one of the employees later indicted for pilfering the equipment.

Some federal agents believed that explanation. Or parts of it.

"The possibility that the Bryants were involved in a CIA operation was very reasonable and logical to us at the time," said one ATF agent assigned to the case who begged anonymity. "You have to understand how the CIA operates," he explained. "It's really very simple. None of this cloak-and dagger stuff. The CIA's typical method of operation is to hire private contractors, and then to disavow any knowledge of their activities. For example: Let's say there is some foreign equipment overseas that the CIA wants to examine. They make that desire known throughout the intelligence underground, as well as the price they are willing to pay for the desired item. The CIA handles these transactions in cash, with no strings attached. The agency doesn't care who gets the equipment, or how they get it. If the private contractors are retrieving a piece of Russian radar equipment, for instance, and they have leftover space in their airplane on the return trip—if they want to bring back a load of dope, that's their business. There is no agreement signed. When the private contractor walks into Langley, or Nellis Air Force Base, or China Lake carrying a piece of equipment the CIA desperately wants, the CIA will pay the price. No questions asked. Does that mean he works for the CIA? If a contractor gets busted along the way, bringing a load of dope into the country, he can't expect the CIA to intervene. At least not overtly. If the contractor keeps his mouth shut, he may be helped behind the scenes. But if he claims to be working for the CIA, you can be sure they'll leave him singing in the wind."

Ralph Ross refused to believe that any genuine ties existed between the Bryants and the CIA—or any other intelligence agency. "That's all in their imaginations," Ralph told his colleagues. "They've been watching too much TV." But Ralph couldn't help being flabbergasted by the sophistication and magnitude of the Company. How did a couple of hometown boys get the wherewithal to mastermind what the DEA was calling the largest gun-for-drugs conspiracy in the United States?

The Philadelphia and Lexington incidents spawned peripherally related investigations by a dozen law enforcement and intelligence agencies.

The $22,800 cash found in Bradley's possession, and traced back to Caesars Palace, coincided with a DEA probe in Las Vegas of the laundering of drug money through Caesars—specifically by high-rolling drug dealer Jimmy Chagra. The fact that Dan Chandler's name surfaced in connection with Bradley further raised the eyebrows of DEA agents. As Casino Host at Caesars, Chandler extended credit to casino customers, including Chagra. When evidence suggested that Chandler had introduced Bradley Bryant to Jimmy Chagra, Chandler became a target of the federal investigation. Disturbed by the heat on one of their executives, Caesars officials transferred Chandler to Lake Tahoe in early 1981.

ATF was convinced that the Lexington warehouse was but one of as many as fifteen cryptic stashes of weapons in the country. In fact, ATF agents learned that Bradley had recently solicited Lance Alworth's help in renting a San Diego warehouse for the purpose of hiding guns. Working hand in hand with U.S. Customs, which was pursuing reports that Bradley had been in the process of fulfilling a contract to supply five hundred thousand receivers for automatic weapons to South America, Treasury agents were determined to locate the hordes.

Defense and Treasury Department investigators intensified their probe of the China Lake thefts, searching for links to ex-spies Wilson and Terpil. Like the Bryants, Wilson and Terpil had recruited China Lake employees to build bombs destined for Libya, and had sponsored repeated thefts from China Lake. Larry Barcella, assistant U.S. attorney in Washington, D.C., was on the brink of seeking a federal indictment for Wilson and Terpil for their role in supplying weapons and terrorist training to Qaddafi. Interviewed by ATF agents about the matter, Barcella said he had no evidence a connection existed between the Wilson/Terpil network and Bradley Bryant. Although there was a great deal of suspicion that some of the items Bradley Bryant had in his possession in Philadelphia were bound for Libya, coupled with the insistence by the Philadelphia police that Terpil had visited Bryant at the Sheraton prior to Bryant's arrest, Barcella was unable to prove that a relationship existed.

Despite the magnitude of the various gun- and drug-related investigations, there could be no doubt that Bradley Bryant's perceived knowledge about the assassination of Judge Wood took precedence over all other probes. When the relationship between Bradley and Jimmy Chagra—the main suspect in Wood's murder—came to light, federal agents decided that Bradley was the smoking gun they needed.

CHAPTER

NINE

On May 8, 1980, a strategy session was held at the Department of Justice in Washington to "discuss all intelligence aspects regarding the individuals arrested in Philadelphia and additional associates who have been determined to be members of . . . *the Company.*" Headed by Philadelphia U.S. Attorney Peter Vaira, the meeting was attended by U.S. attorneys and DEA, FBI, U.S. Customs, and ATF agents from Pennsylvania, Kentucky, Georgia, and Texas.

A government report distributed to those attending the meeting included an overview of the Company as it operated at that time:

"The organization referred to by its members as the Company *is a well-financed operation structured along corporate lines, with each employee having a specific function and title and answering to a superior. Quantities of money are set aside by the organization for specific functions, i.e., bonds, aircraft purchases, etc. . . . Each prospective member of the organization undergoes a screening process to include a polygraph examination prior to his position: Pilots for the large aircraft receive $100,000 per trip; and drivers/ground crew earn $10,000 plus one pound of marijuana for the initial trip, and $20,000 plus one pound for the second venture.*

Corporations are established as fronts to cover the organization's illicit activities and are responsible for the purchase, sale and registration of vehicles and aircraft. In addition, remotely located farms, warehouses and airports open to use by the public are purchased to land drug-laden aircraft as well as to store drug cargoes prior to distribution.

Maintaining a fleet of aircraft ranging in size from small single-engine planes to large four-engine variety, the organization is constantly replacing the older, well-utilized planes with newer ones, paying cash in the majority of cases. Some of the older, repeatedly used planes are sent out of the organization's operating area for storage, rather than chancing law enforcement attention to their activities. A team of mechanics is employed to care for the aircraft and wheeled vehicles, seeing to it that they are in top mechanical condition and ready for use at a moment's notice.

Larger aircraft, such as DC4, DC6, and DC7, are utilized when the cargoes are large, and the smaller planes, usually Cessna 404 Titans, are used when the cargo requirement is smaller. When Titans are utilized, they are sometimes flown back-to-back, one landing approximately 20 minutes behind the other. Each smuggling venture is well-planned, with a primary and one or two alternate landing sites, and, in many cases, the aircraft undergo an electronic sweeping prior to their deployment to South America or to one of several Caribbean territories. In many cases, members of the group selected for participation in a smuggling venture attend planning meetings, usually at hotels, several days prior to the actual operation.

Several hours prior to the arrival of the aircraft, a team of ground support personnel, ranging in number from 8 to 20, arrives at the airstrip with several wheeled vehicles, including tractor-trailers and 2 1/2 ton dump trucks. Electronics equipment, to include scanners, air-to-ground radios, and CBs are used to monitor law enforcement activity in the area and to permit communications between the air and ground crews. Upon arrival of the plane, ground crewmen use flashlights to illuminate the strip. The plane usually lands in the early morning hours, and is off-loaded by means of a human conveyor system; typically, a plane is completely off-loaded in less than one hour. The drugs are loaded onto the large vehicles and transported to several storage facilities and distribution points.

When members are arrested, a staff of attorneys, some of whom are actively engaged in the organization's activities, are sent in for legal representation and to effect the members' early release on bond. Subsequent to their release, each arrestee undergoes another polygraph examination to determine if he is cooperating with any law enforcement agencies.

Ralph did not attend the meeting, but was apprised of the FBI's desperation to ensnare Bradley Bryant. They felt he was the key to the Judge Wood murder case, which was costing the government millions of dollars and still remained unsolved.

The Justice Department had made the murder of Judge Wood the number one priority in the country. They learned that Bradley

Bryant had actually been offered the contract to kill the judge, but had turned it down. When they found out that Bradley had actually introduced Jimmy Chagra to the hit man who killed the judge, their directive was to make a case against Bradley Bryant on any charges possible. The point was to hold him and put enough pressure on him so he would break the Wood case for them.

That same month, Bradley would stand trial on firearms charges in Lexington stemming from the raid on the U-Store-It warehouse. Called "a case even a dog could try" by a federal prosecutor in Philadelphia, the Lexington jury trial was considered a charade by law enforcement. Having interviewed several renowned criminal attorneys, dangling thousands of dollars in legal fees before their eyes, Bradley had followed the recommendation of Dan Chandler, and had settled on Las Vegas lawyer Oscar Goodman. Famous for his often successful defense of organized crime figures—including Mafia boss Meyer Lansky, Stardust Hotel owner Allen Glick, Kansas City crime boss Nicholas Civella, drug kingpin Jimmy Chagra, and Chicago mobster Frank "Lefty" Rosenthal—the forty-year-old Goodman had earned a reputation as an outspoken critic of federal law enforcement tactics.

Bradley's instincts had paid off. The attempt by Lexington's U.S. attorney, Joe Famularo, to convince a local jury that one of their hometown boys had gone bad fell on deaf ears. Nothing wrong with having a bunch of guns, the jury apparently felt. Kentuckians have always felt strongly about their right to bear arms. In short order, Goodman's high-powered legal machinations and brilliant courtroom demeanor won Bradley's acquittal, inciting the federal judge to tell reporters he was "flabbergasted" by the verdict.

Still facing some minor weapons charges in Philadelphia—charges Oscar Goodman could certainly help him to overcome—Bradley must have breathed a sigh of relief. His problems behind him, Bradley seemed anxious to get back to business. But he apparently had no idea how tenacious his trackers would be.

Claiming a government vendetta, Bradley publicly blamed his mushrooming legal problems on Jimmy Chagra. "Chagra thought someone was trying to kill his whole family," Bradley was quoted as saying. "So he came to me. I was in the business of providing first-class protection to people who had a real problem . . . I had absolutely nothing to do with the federal judge, and I certainly did not spirit Jimmy Chagra out of the country," he said. "Apparently someone thinks Chagra was involved in the judge's death and that maybe I know something about where Chagra might be—but I don't."

Ralph noticed Drew Thornton's conspicuous absence during Bradley's trial, and assumed Drew was busy running the Company in Bradley's stead.

Not to be confused with the commonly used nickname for the CIA—or perhaps purposely named to create such confusion—the Company had emerged as a paramilitary narcotics organization comprised of mercenaries, lawyers, bankers, smugglers, arms merchants, pilots, polygraphers, renegade CIA agents, and assassins.

Confidential documents in Ralph's possession identified Bradley as the East Coast kingpin of a loosely organized group of three hundred members involved in drug smuggling, gunrunning, and international mercenary missions. Ralph thought that information dovetailed with rumors about stockpiled weapons and the training of Libyan terrorists at Drew Thornton's Triad farm.

Reading a classified report he had received from ATF, Ralph used a yellow marker to highlight a synopsis of the Company's illegal activities:

. . . the smuggling and domestic trafficking of narcotics and dangerous drugs; the infiltration and hidden control of gambling casinos domestically and internationally; the trafficking and smuggling of firearms and military hardware; the acquisition and diversion of large amounts of currency; contract assassinations; arson for profit; business scams; and the corruption of public officials in the U.S. and abroad . . . Bryant's associates include organized crime leaders and attorneys; members of international drug organizations; paramilitary groups; those associated with the distribution and control of pornography; management level personnel of large casino operations; former and current law enforcement officers; and prominent political figures . . . traditional La Cosa Nostra crime families are involved with the Company for purposes of mutual benefit.

A classified report issued by the El Paso Intelligence Center (EPIC), further revealed that the Company was a widely diversified corporation with small suborganizations, the heads of which took orders and answered to a group of superiors. Each prospective member of the organization had undergone a screening process, including a polygraph examination, prior to his employment. The EPIC report indicated that the Company, which had $75 million banked, had a board of directors, divisions of securities, real estate, and distribution, a fleet of aircraft, at least nine airports owned or used by the group in the United States, a battery of attorneys across the country, and foreign bases in Colombia and the Caribbean.

Ralph began to wonder if such a complex organization, with access to secret military weapons and sophisticated CIA apparatus, could really operate without government collusion at some level. But it was hard for him to believe that his own government would stoop so low as to sanction the activities of Bradley Bryant and Drew Thornton. As long as the CIA continued to deny any connection to the Company, Ralph felt he must assume no relationship existed.

Law enforcement agencies from outside Kentucky started to flood Ralph with inquiries.

In November 1980, a federal indictment was handed down in what the government contended at that time was the largest guns-for-drugs conspiracy ever uncovered in the history of the United States. The culmination of a fourteen-state undercover investigation conducted by six federal agencies, which hinted for the first time publicly of ties between drug smugglers and the intelligence community, netted eleven individuals—including a Lexington polygraph expert.

Operation Gateway, as it was called by its DEA creators in St. Louis, Missouri, detailed the inception of the Company which grew to a net worth of a billion dollars, and which had headquarters on the East Coast, in the Southern states, and in the Midwest. According to the indictment, "members of the enterprise would be furnished false means of identification so as to conceal their true identities and hinder police investigation of their illegal activities. Such false identification included false birth certificates and drivers' licenses. Further, the defendants would employ the services of skilled electronics experts who would employ counter-intelligence equipment to identify and remove electronic tracking devices from aircraft used in smuggling operations . . . these co-conspirators derived a gross income in excess of $55 million . . . the co-conspirators obtained sensitive and confidential documents and materials of the U.S. Drug Enforcement Administration in order to maintain an active counter-intelligence network and aid in the identification of law enforcement personnel and informants . . . and obtained the secret and classified radio frequencies utilized by the U.S. Drug Enforcement Administration, the FBI, U.S. Customs, and other law enforcement activities during the pendency of a smuggling operation."

Robert Snyder, a nationally known polygrapher who had performed lie detector tests for the Lexington police, was charged with ordering the murder of two informants—one named "Big Red" from the St. Louis, Illinois, area and another named William Wade Hampton from Georgia. Snyder, who Ralph knew had been associated with Bradley Bryant and Drew Thornton since Snyder's employment with the Lexington Police Department, immediately went into hiding.

■

Whatever hopes Ralph had of a leisurely Christmas vacation were quickly dashed.

On Sunday morning, December 21, 1980, at 12:30 A.M., Ralph was awakened by a ringing phone.

"Sergeant Ross?"

Ralph listened as one of his detectives told him a DC-3 was in the process of smuggling marijuana into an airport at Murray, a small town in western Kentucky. "Drew Thornton's on board and might be the pilot."

"Did you arrest him?" Ralph asked.

"No. He won't let us search the plane. We don't have a warrant."

Earlier that night, at about 9 P.M., the airplane had landed at the municipal airport in Murray. The airport manager called the state police to report the suspicious plane that hadn't used its lights, or radioed ahead to the airport requesting that the runway be illuminated. By the time the detective had arrived at the airport, the plane had already taken off—its crew apparently spooked by something. An hour and a half later, at 10:30 P.M., the airport manager again called the state police. The same DC-3 was returning, again landing in total darkness.

The plane was still parked at the airport when the detective arrived the second time. He blocked the runway with his car, and waited for the occupants—Drew and two men from Savannah—to disembark.

"The pilot told us the plane had engine trouble. They had called a wrecker service to come tow the plane," the detective told Ralph. Drew refused to sign a consent form allowing the state police to search the plane. While the plane was being hooked up to the tow truck, its three crew members jumped on board and remained there for several minutes. When deplaning, the three unloaded what appeared to be personal luggage, and Drew Thornton placed heavy locks on both cargo doors.

"We think Harold Brown might have something to do with this," the detective told Ralph, referring to the head of the DEA's regional office in Louisville. The detective said Brown had been sighted by a witness in the vicinity of the airport when the plane came in.

Ralph instructed the state troopers to glean as much information as possible from the three men. "Get a search warrant and put them all under surveillance," Ralph said. "And stake out the airplane. Set up a roadblock on the Blue Grass Parkway, because they'll probably rent a car or be picked up, and head back to Lexington. Get the dog ready just in case," Ralph said, referring to the German shepherd trained to sniff out drugs.

"What is the plane's tail number?" Ralph asked.

"N625E."

"I'll check with the FAA for the ownership and registration," Ralph said.

"Thornton told us the plane is owned by Air Transport Systems . . . whoever they are."

Ralph hung up, tossing and turning for the next several hours. Just as he was about to doze off, the phone rang again. This time it was 6 A.M.

"A couple of hours ago, we followed Drew and his buddies to a Holiday Inn in Murray," his detective said. "They rented two rooms, and Drew made one phone call from the lobby pay phone. At 3:45 A.M. a red Dodge van that is registered to Drew Thornton, and which was driven by an unidentified white male, came to the Holiday Inn. Drew loaded the van with three suitcases and an overnight bag and all three men got on board. They headed east on the Western Kentucky Parkway, and we assumed they were going to Lexington. We had a roadblock set up, but when they reached Elizabethtown they turned north toward Louisville instead. The van was obviously equipped with an extra fuel tank. I also think they were monitoring our radios."

Ralph sighed, wishing he had more thoroughly considered the options available to Drew. "Where are they now?"

"They've all checked into one room at the Executive Inn West in Louisville. Drew keeps leaving the room to make phone calls from the pay phone in the lobby."

"Just keep on top of them," Ralph said. "Don't lose track of them. Get the maids at the Holiday Inn in Murray to search the rooms for anything left behind."

"By the way, Sergeant Ross," the detective continued, "headquarters got a report from the Winchester police. It seems the same plane was spotted at eight-thirty Saturday night flying over Interstate 64 near Paris, where Drew's parents live. Smoke was pouring out of the aircraft and witnesses thought it was about to crash. But apparently it continued on to land at Murray."

"Keep me posted," Ralph said.

Ralph decided he might as well go into the office, even though it was Sunday, and just four days before Christmas. Waiting, he heard nothing from the detectives until nearly 6 P.M. And then it wasn't good news.

"We lost them," Ralph was told.

"What happened?"

"Around noon they left the hotel and drove to the airport. They parked the van and went to the Delta ticket counter to check the flight schedule. Then they went into the restaurant. We think they split up, using the restaurant and restrooms for cover, and maybe using disguises, and then all met up again back at the van. We didn't have enough men to cover the ticket counter, the restaurant, and the parking lot. When we got back to the van, it was gone."

"Any flights scheduled from Louisville to Lexington?" Ralph asked.

"Yeah. One arrived at 6 P.M., but none of them were on it. We also had Customs check the flights heading to Georgia. They just got away."

By the time the detectives' paperwork was turned in to Ralph, a day or two later, one item stuck out like a sore thumb.

"On Saturday, December 20, 1980, at approximately 11 A.M. before any of this came about, I received a call from Harold Brown," the detective's report stated. "Harold told me he was at the Holiday Inn in Gilbertsville, Kentucky. He said he had some information for me that might lead to something and that he would get back with me. After the DC-3 situation started later that night, I called his room at approximately 11:30 P.M. but received no answer."

The detective's statement indicated he had no more contact with Brown until two days after the incident. "Brown called me a couple of times on Monday, December 22. He told me that the DC-3 landing was what he was down in Gilbertsville checking on. He said that he had an informant who told him that a DC-3 would be landing in the west Kentucky area to refuel. Harold said he was present at the Kentucky Dam Airport when the DC-3 landed there. This had to be between the time the plane first landed in Murray and its second landing in Murray. He told me that his informant locked himself in a room at the airport and that he [Brown] waved the plane off and told them that they would have to go to Paducah to get fuel."

It was clear to Ralph that his detective was suspicious of Brown's motives. "I asked Harold Brown on December 22 if he knew Mr. Thornton. Mr. Brown told me that he used to work with Thornton when Thornton was a police officer in Lexington. He also told me that he was investigated about a year and a half ago in reference to Thornton, and was cleared of any wrongdoing. I asked if he now had anything to do with Mr. Thornton and he told me that he did not."

Ralph made a note to himself to attempt to ascertain which agency previously investigated Harold Brown and Drew Thornton. He wondered if it was Brown's own agency—the DEA—trying to weed out a bad apple.

By the time the state police finally got a court order to board the plane, on December 22, they found that all of the seats of the aircraft had been removed to make room for cargo. Plans to bring the drug-sniffing dog on board were futile, as the entire plane had been doused with STP Motor Oil before the plane was abandoned.

"The empty cans were still on board," the detective said. "They had to have done this when they boarded the plane while it was being towed."

The DC-3 incident was as close as Ralph had come to actually catching Harold Brown with his paws in the middle of a drug deal. Was Drew a covert DEA agent, as was hinted by Brown whenever the subject of their relationship arose? Was he an informant for Brown? Ralph didn't think so. He considered it highly unlikely that Drew was infiltrating drug rings on behalf of Brown or the DEA—hence, the lack of significant DEA arrests in Kentucky. Did Brown refuse to believe that his friend and former colleague, Drew Thornton, had become a drug smuggler? Possible, Ralph decided, but very improbable since such an attitude would require extraordinary naïveté on the part of Brown. Did Brown decide to turn his back on Drew's activities, out of loyalty to an old friend, asking nothing in return? Doubtful.

What did that leave?

Harold and Drew are partners, Ralph concluded. If Drew worked as an informant for the DEA, Ralph decided, he only snitched on his competitors in the drug business.

The bottom line, Ralph thought, is that what had been identified by several federal agencies as the country's largest narcotics, paramilitary, and weapons organization was masterminded by a nucleus of Kentucky men. For Harold Brown—the chief narcotics officer in the state, who had virtually unlimited resources available to him—to have failed to dismantle the group suggested nothing less than complicity.

By May of 1981, it seemed to Ralph that every law enforcement agency in the country had an interest in the "Lexington Connection"—everyone except the Lexington Police Department, which was mysteriously silent about the sudden national notoriety of its native sons.

Ralph was briefed by an assistant U.S. attorney in Fresno, California, about an upcoming indictment of Bradley and Larry Bryant on charges of embezzling and receiving stolen government property. The Bryants had been the subjects of a Naval Intelligence investigation into the theft of ten rifle scopes designed for night use, a low-light television camera, and a remote-control helicopter from China Lake Naval Base.

Navy documents revealed the two Bryants had been under investigation since September 1979—about the time the FBI in Las Vegas surreptitiously watched Larry Bryant transfer the nightscopes from a garage of the eccentric inventor Alvin Snapper to the bed of Larry's mini-truck. Ralph recalled the events of 1979, jotting down a crude chronology: The year had started off with the DC-4 loaded with ten tons of dope that flew into Lexington; that was followed by Judge Wood's assassination in May; then the ill-fated drug venture in August that involved an airstrip in Starkville, Mississippi; that same month, some of the Lexington cops had been detained in Aruba on gunrunning suspicions, and the mercenary activity on *Triad* was in high gear; Bradley and Larry had been busted in Philadelphia with weapons and exotic spy paraphernalia.

Ralph had spent most of 1979 preoccupied with the gubernatorial election of John Y. Brown, Jr. He speculated about what might have escaped his attention during that time. What Ralph did not yet know was that at least one of the stolen military devices had been used as currency in a South American drug deal.

Actually, there was a lot Ralph didn't know. But he felt he was on the verge of discovery.

The internal Naval Intelligence documents read like a spy thriller. But the Navy's files, when coupled with Ralph's information, began to shed light on an even more bizarre world that had not yet been explored by novelists.

The Navy's investigation had begun when the Starlight nightscopes were noticed missing from the China Lake weapons department. During an internal inquiry, a China Lake employee admitted he had stolen the scopes from the Department of Defense Surplus Property System, and had given them to Larry Bryant to be used in a classified project. The removal of the nightscopes was part of a complex, CIA-sponsored plan to trade U.S. military equipment in Libya for Soviet military equipment to be analyzed by American experts, the employee said in a statement that matched Larry Bryant's earlier statement.

At the time, Larry Bryant was a highly regarded electronics technician who at China Lake had participated in classified projects "of mutual interest to the Navy and the Air Force."

Faced with criminal prosecution, the China Lake employee was convinced by the Navy it would be in his best interest to cooperate with the government's probe: In the fall of 1979, the witness set about to lure Bradley and Larry into the government's trap by eliciting incriminating statements from them. Interviewed by Naval Intelligence in May 1980, one of the witnesses told federal authorities that the Bryants "had attempted to involve him in a business deal involving the acquisition of a hotel in Guatemala which would be a security retreat for dignitaries."

Another of the witnesses, a China Lake employee involved in "Special Projects," said that Larry Bryant had asked him on several occasions to procure government property from the Naval Weapons Center at China Lake. The employee assumed the requests were for official purposes, given Larry's Air Force status and top-security clearance. "Once he [Larry Bryant] called and asked [me] to get ahold of an AN/ALR-45 radar warning receiver." Then, in September 1979, "he [Larry Bryant] said he was involved in an *acquisition program* involving a foreign country . . . that he was working for a country which had a contact in Libya, and that he was looking for an early warning-type radar known as Tall King." The witness told authorities that Larry and Bradley had also tried to interest him in a "Guatemala Hotel deal that would be used as a 'refuge' for the Shah of Iran."

The Navy's investigation had progressed splendidly, resulting in a tidy indictment of the Bryants and three Californians. An August 1981 trial was scheduled, and the Navy seemed anxious to prosecute its misfits outside the uncomfortable glare of publicity.

The fact that some of the stolen military hardware was traded in South America for drugs was a delicate matter. Neither the Navy, the Air Force, nor the CIA seemed particularly interested in either pursuing or publicizing that avenue. But the departments of Justice, State, and Treasury were not so willing to ignore the implications of military arms and technology being illegally exported as currency for drugs, Soviet radar equipment, or anything else.

The FBI, Customs, DEA, ATF, and myriad state and local police forces, were all pushing for further investigation, prompting the U.S. attorney in Philadelphia, who was prosecuting the Bryants on gun charges, to make a formal request for an interagency investigative force.

That request was denied by the Criminal Division of the Justice Department.

"We banged our head against the wall for months trying to get some coordination," said an assistant U.S. attorney in Philadelphia. "Some kind of task force should have been organized. Instead, we had a bunch of assistant United States attorneys fumbling around the country because they didn't know what each other was doing."

While the Defense Department may have preferred to have the Bryants quietly convicted and sentenced, too many other federal agencies, encumbered by their own jurisdictions and agendas, refused to allow that to happen.

The FBI was still hot on the trail of Bradley for his knowledge about the contract murder of Judge Wood, and saw the China Lake indictments as a great opportunity to squeeze him into cooperation.

U.S. Customs in Louisiana had opened a criminal case against Bradley's former employees—Johnny Trussell and Jan Fisher—for illegally exporting the Starlight nightscope and Green Box radar unit to Colombia.

Ralph's Special Operations team within the Kentucky State Police was anxious to reopen the drug importation case of the DC-4 that had unloaded 20,000 pounds of pot at Lexington's Blue Grass Airport, before being abandoned an hour later in Louisville—apparently with the collusion of DEA regional chief Harold Brown.

ATF agents were still pursuing leads generated by the weapons found during the raid of the Sheraton in Philadelphia and the U-Store-It warehouse in Lexington, including guerrilla warfare activities at Triad.

The Georgia State Bureau of Investigation was actively pursuing Drew Thornton on a drug-importation case in Savannah.

DEA agents in Florida were just weeks away from arresting an associate of Bradley and Drew—Mike Kelly of Lexington—for importing several tons of marijuana into the west coast of Florida.

The IRS in Kentucky had opened tax evasion cases against several of Bradley's associates, but was precluded by law from sharing its information with any other agency.

The DEA had an informant—one of the former China Lake employees—who was in the middle of a drug deal with Bradley. The "sting" was expected any day, and Bradley, who had been released on bond on the China Lake charges, operated with seeming obliviousness to his predicament.

Bradley's far-flung activities came to an abrupt halt on May 18, 1981, when he sold 804 pounds of high-grade marijuana to an undercover DEA agent near Chicago.

Federal agents posing as drug purchasers handed Bradley $240,000 in cash in Room 141 of the Holiday Inn in Elgin, Illinois. Wearing a three-piece suit and an open-collar shirt, Bradley counted the money. He then ordered his accomplices to transfer the marijuana from a van rented by him to a second van that had, unbeknown to Bradley, been rented by the DEA.

While awaiting the return of his subordinates, who had been arrested as soon as they transferred the pot from one vehicle to the other, Bradley told undercover agents he would be able to deliver another 20,000 pounds of pot in a couple of months.

Shortly after making that statement, Bradley was read his Miranda rights: Anything he said could be used against him in a court of law.

Federal agents determined that the marijuana had been stored at a farmhouse near Elgin, Illinois, and was part of a bulk shipment of pot that had been off-loaded at an airstrip several months earlier near Tampa, Florida.

Not coincidentally, Bradley's partner in the deal—Robert Walker—had become a government informant. The fifty-nine-year-old Florida man who operated the Pasco County airport had long been considered a kingpin in a huge narcotics organization, and had recently opened a bank in the Bahamas to launder his "narco-dollars." But shortly after his indictment on money laundering charges he decided to make a deal with the feds.

But before he had the opportunity to testify against Bradley or any other associates, he mysteriously disappeared.

Coincidentally, at almost the exact same moment that Bradley was being arrested in Illinois, Walker's badly decomposed body was being retrieved from a Florida swamp. He had been strangled by a cord, in apparent retaliation for having become a government snitch.

As it turned out, Walker was but the first in a trail of dead bodies that would litter Ralph Ross's life during the next several months.

■

In July 1981 Ralph stretched out in the bulkhead of a commercial airplane bound for Fresno. He had carefully folded his brown suit jacket and placed it in the vacant seat next to him. As soon as the jet was airborne, Ralph opened his leather briefcase and retrieved a file labeled "Mike Kelly."

The first page identified Mike's legal name as Wallace McClure Kelly. The thirty-three-year-old, 350-pound, bearded son of a Lexington pharmaceutical businessman had been a Boy Scout who liked hot-rod cars and music. He attended Henry Clay High School in the mid-1960s and, though slightly younger, counted Drew Thornton, Henry Vance, and Bradley Bryant among his boyhood friends.

His wife, Bonnie Lynn Gee, was the oldest of twelve children who had been raised in an eastern Kentucky "holler" near Tick Ridge. The peroxide-blonde began her life with Mike Kelly in 1974, at the impressionable age of twenty-two, after he rescued her from a motorcycle gang that was holding her against her will.

Kelly had been arrested a few weeks earlier by Florida authorities, and Customs agents and Florida police followed up with a raid of Kelly's Lexington home on June 29, 1981. Kelly was charged (though later acquitted) with attempting to smuggle seventeen tons of marijuana into the west coast of Florida in early June.

The pot had been loaded onto a seventy-two-foot shrimp boat which was scheduled to rendezvous with a ground crew waiting at a Charlotte County, Florida, marina. Parked at the marina were four refrigerated tractor trailers. Ready to haul the dope north, the trucks had *PRODUCE* emblazoned across their panels.

All the smugglers connected to the deal had abandoned the boat and vehicles moments before the feds arrived, apparently tipped off to the impending bust. But Florida authorities located Kelly at a local dirt airstrip where he was waiting to be picked up by a private airplane. Kelly provided the cops with identification, but they had lacked the evidence to arrest him at the time. Further investigation showed that two radios found aboard the shrimp boat belonged to Kelly, and eventually Florida police were successful in building a criminal case against the overweight Lexingtonian.

Ralph flipped through a stack of ATF documents that showed Kelly had been a federally licensed firearms and ammunitions dealer since 1971—when he was only twenty-three years old. Through a company called Diversified Equipment, Inc., which listed a Lexington address, Kelly sold shotguns, rifles, handguns, and ammo, and manufactured alarm systems. On his license application, Kelly claimed he obtained all of his weapons from Phillip Gall & Sons—the infamous Lexington gun wholesaler and retailer.

In 1975, however, a routine inspection by ATF had turned up numerous violations. Like his father—the owner of a wholesale drug company who had been charged for failing to maintain appropriate records of narcotics sales—Mike risked his license by failing to keep track of weapons transactions, as required by law.

He had explained to the feds that he stored his inventory at his remote Jessamine County farm because he was afraid the guns would be stolen from his Lexington office. It was therefore difficult, he explained, to remember specific details about his guns. Unimpressed by Kelly's excuse and lax record-keeping system, and suspicious of his high rate of reported stolen weapons, the ATF had recommended Kelly's license be revoked in 1976. Kelly had somehow managed to bring his company back into compliance, however, compelling ATF to drop its charges.

Ralph pulled a notebook from his briefcase and began listing the events that had initially brought Mike Kelly to his attention:

▪ *During an inspection by the DEA of inventory at the W. Kelly Company in 1977, the feds found evidence of drug diversion—specifically, the disappearance of forty-three thousand doses of Valium.*

▪ *Kelly had been identified by police as one of the off-loaders of the marijuana from Bradley Bryant's DC-4 at Lexington's Blue Grass Airport in January 1979.*

▪ *Kelly, for the past several years, had used his expertise in electronics to install burglar alarm systems in Lexington commercial properties; to build broadcast antennas; to sell sophisticated radio equipment to drug dealers and police officers; and to sell rifles, shotguns, and handguns throughout central and eastern Kentucky. He had admitted that Bradley was one of his "clients" for electronic equipment—as were several Kentucky judges, Kelly had been quick to point out.*

▪ Bradley had made sixteen long-distance phone calls to Kelly from the Sheraton in Philadelphia prior to Bradley's arrest.

▪ Electronic dart guns seized from Bradley's Lexington warehouse belonged to Kelly.

▪ Intelligence information had long suggested that Mike was an expert at manufacturing M-10 machine pistols, and Kelly and Henry Vance made silencer parts and converted semi-automatic weapons into fully automatic weapons; Kelly also made false Kentucky driver's licenses for members of drug organizations.

By the time the jetliner touched down in California, Ralph had reviewed all the files in his possession regarding Bradley Bryant, Larry Bryant, Andrew Thornton, Bill Canan, Mike Kelly, Harold Brown, and Dan Chandler. He felt thoroughly prepared to convince Assistant U.S. Attorney Brian Leighton, as well as the federal grand jury, that sufficient evidence existed to indict each of those individuals, along with two more former Lexington cops—Jack Hillard and Steve Oliver—for, at the very least, their participation in the importation of ten tons of pot into the Lexington Blue Grass Airport.

Upon his arrival in Fresno, Ralph was told by Leighton that the first China Lake indictment against Bradley and Larry Bryant had been replaced by a superseding indictment. The original indictment, handed down in March 1981, dealt only with the theft of military equipment from China Lake. The superseding indictment, filed a few months later, had been expanded to include charges of conspiracy and intent to distribute narcotics. That twenty-page federal indictment detailed various overt drug-smuggling acts, including: The DC-4 flight into Lexington; the Queen Air trip from Texas to Mexico and back; and the jaunt from Starkville, Mississippi, to Colombia that had been thwarted.

Although the number of defendants had increased from five to eighteen, neither Drew Thornton, Mike Kelly, Harold Brown, nor Bill Canan were named. Ralph was determined to rectify those omissions. He also believed that Dan Chandler, who had been named as an unindicted co-conspirator, should have been questioned about his role in the importation of twelve hundred pounds of pot from Mexico onto a ranch near Sonora, Texas. Chandler had been the person Johnny Trussell contacted, at Bradley Bryant's behest, and Chandler had arranged meetings at which drug deals were discussed.

After testifying before the grand jury, and meeting with other cops from various state, local, and federal law enforcement agencies, Ralph felt confident that a *second* superseding indictment would be handed down within weeks.

Ralph returned to Kentucky feeling a sense of completion, as though years of loose ends had been gathered into a tidy ball. Bradley, Drew, Canan, and Harold Brown would be out of his hair for a while. Now he would be free to focus on nightclub owner Jimmy Lambert, who, so far, had managed to float in and out of the shadows, protected by his social status, political connections, and wealth. Ralph marveled at how Lambert kept his hands so clean.

The summer of 1981 proved to be relatively quiet. Lexington's big operators seemed to have taken a hiatus from smuggling. The Fresno grand jury was taking much longer than anticipated. The simmering scenarios of the summer proved to be the bizarre deaths of low-level players in the Company—individuals who had either "flipped" to become government witnesses, or were suspected by the conspirators of being susceptible to government pressure.

Homicide investigators in Florida and Georgia continued to seek clues in the strangulation murder of Robert Walker, who had been named in one of the early China Lake indictments, and had then agreed to testify against Bradley Bryant.

In Lexington, in the middle of a hot, muggy afternoon, the bodies of Danny Sheppard and Cindy Baker were found. They had both been stabbed several times in the heart, and left in the bathtub of their home. The shower was running and the bathroom walls were drenched with blood. The two were known drug couriers, and had been identified by Ralph's undercover men as regulars at Lambert's house on Old Dobbin Road.

Like Walker, Sheppard and Baker had become government informants against Company members just prior to their deaths. Apparently the Company had impeccable sources within both local and federal law enforcement agencies in order for them to learn the identities of snitches so quickly.

Ralph rolled his eyes as he read Lexington policeman John Bizzack's account of the investigation that was published in the *Lexington Herald.* Calling the incident a "bizarre Romeo and Juliet suicide and homicide," Bizzack decided to close the case without further ado.

Bizzack explained that he had "re-created" the scene and examined the thrusts of the weapons, and had concluded that Cindy first stabbed Danny in the heart. Danny lived just long enough to be able to pull the knife from his chest and plunge it into his girlfriend's heart.

Once again, Ralph's hands were tied by jurisdictional limitations. Frustrated, he observed from the sidelines as the Lexington police seemingly blundered their way through the grisly probe, conveniently drawing a neat conclusion. He watched angrily as the Lexington newspaper provided a forum for the police, never challenging the "official story." He tried to "leak" tantalizing tidbits to individual news reporters, hinting that the state police, as well as the medical examiner, found the murder/suicide explanation to be factually and physically implausible. But his attempts to incite any investigative initiative fell on deaf ears.

Ralph thought about Bradley and Drew: In 1970, they had been clean-cut sons, devoted husbands, natural-born leaders. Ten years later, they were suspected of running a behemoth dope and gun-smuggling syndicate that boasted millions of dollars' worth of boats, planes, trucks, warehouses, and landing strips—all hidden in a labyrinth of offshore corporations.

By 1981, Bradley and Drew were under investigation in Pennsylvania, California, Georgia, Mississippi, and Florida.

Only in Kentucky were they always guaranteed sanctuary.

Ralph was determined to change that. As head of the new all-encompassing Special Investigations Unit of the Kentucky State Police, he considered the Company his domain.

Ironic though it would later seem, Ralph's opportunity to dismantle the international crime network based in Lexington came under the patronage of the new governor of Kentucky—John Young Brown, Jr.

PART

BOOK
THREE

ONE

HIGH
AMBITIONS

"Nobody had heard very much about John Y. Brown before he ran for governor," Ralph Ross remembered. "Suddenly he and his wife Phyllis George were running a wild campaign, flying a helicopter in and out of them hollers of eastern Kentucky, and spending millions of dollars on TV ads. They dazzled everybody with flashy clothes and jewelry and celebrities. Before you knew it, he was elected."

John Young Brown, Jr., was five years old in 1939 when his father, John Young Brown, Sr., suffered the first in what would be a series of defeats at the hands of the Kentucky Democratic political machine. Accusing then-Governor "Happy" Chandler of fixing the governor's race in favor of Chandler's hand-picked successor, Brown began what would be a lifelong feud between the two men. Until 1939, Brown Sr. had been a tenacious young politician who clawed his way through the world of Kentucky's legendary rough-and-tumble politics. A fiery underdog, he had managed to serve two terms in the state legislature, and one in the U.S. Congress. But the tide would turn and Brown Sr. would eventually be pounded by Chandler's political muscle. By the time of his death, Brown Sr. had run for governor once, the U.S. Senate seven times, and the State House twenty times. He was elected to the state legislature only six of those times.

By all accounts, young "Johnny" took it hard when his daddy lost his bid for governor. As did all little kids, Johnny thought his daddy was the smartest, strongest, most courageous man alive. He watched in awe as his father took his licks, yet continually got up and went back into the ring. He listened as his daddy extolled the values of competition, hard work, manliness, ambition, resourcefulness, and education. The firstborn son, Johnny felt an enormous weight on his shoulders from an early age—to surpass the standards set by his larger-than-life father. He was expected to carry his father's torch, to avenge his father's defeats.

Pressured to excel, Johnny horrified his parents by refusing to walk before he was eighteen months old. Alleviating his parents' fears that he was mentally retarded, medical specialists suggested that Johnny was merely lazy. When Johnny finally decided it was time to walk, he was suddenly like a hog on ice—skating through the family's fashionable Lexington home.

The shadow of Brown Sr. was at once intimidating and comforting to Johnny. Johnny would come to yearn for his own style, to escape his father's legendary status as a college football star and renowned criminal attorney. Yet he would use it as a safety net when it suited his purposes.

Johnny received good grades at Lexington's Lafayette High School, spending most of his free time winning golf tournaments for the school team. He frequented the local country clubs, and socialized with the sons and debutantes of Lexington's finer families. He was yanked out of Lafayette by his father because the public school had no football team, and was enrolled in the Kentucky Military Institute in Louisville, which Brown Sr. hoped would make Johnny a man. Much to his father's chagrin, Johnny did not excel on KMI's football team, or in any other athletic endeavors besides golf. Fearing his father considered him a failure, Johnny vowed to prove himself in other ways. Legend has it that after one of his routine verbal jousts with his dad, Johnny exclaimed, "One of these days, I'm not going to be known as your son. You're going to be known as my father!"

Whether or not the statement was ever made has become a moot point. It has been so widely reported throughout Kentucky as to be considered factual—a fact over which John Young Brown, Sr., busted with pride in his twilight years.

John Y. —as he came to be called after outgrowing the nickname Johnny—had a natural inclination toward sales and gambling.

He spent his summers during high school selling vacuum cleaners door to door in Lexington, and wagered his earnings on anything that moved. When he entered the University of Kentucky in the fall of 1952, his private stashes of money impressed coeds and attracted male friends. He quickly fell into a crowd of partiers and gamblers, joining the wealthiest fraternity and hanging out with athletes.

In the early fifties, the University of Kentucky campus had a country club atmosphere in the stereotypical Southern tradition. Johnny and his friends spent their spring and autumn afternoons at the idyllic Keeneland racetrack, drinking mint juleps from mock silver cups.

Adolph Rupp had been lured to Kentucky by Governor Chandler, who sat on the Board of Regents, to coach the Kentucky basketball team into national prominence. Awash in a point-shaving scandal, the ball club had nonetheless become the benchmark of Kentucky's notoriety and status. Chandler's son Dan played on the team—a slot that many contended was a patronage position.

Dan Chandler and John Y. Brown, Jr., became close buddies, sharing an interest in sports and betting, despite, or maybe because of, their fathers' deep-seated hatred for each other. Chandler and John Y., along with a Henderson, Kentucky, native named Jimmy Lambert, held regular poker nights that continued until dawn. John Y.'s uncanny card sense, high-stakes mentality, and ability to bluff earned him a reputation as a serious gambler—an image that would haunt him in future years.

The University of Kentucky was not known for its stringent academic standards and John Y. took a minimum course load, selling Encyclopedia Britannica in his spare time. "John Y. was a tremendous promoter," said a former student at Eastern Kentucky University in Richmond. "He'd recruit students from Eastern Kentucky University and other campuses in the state to sell encyclopedias for him. He'd tell us to buy the local newspapers to read the birth announcements so we could try to sell encyclopedias to the parents of the newborns. He would hang out at the old Palms nightclub in Lexington, flashing a bankroll and throwing money around." By 1956 he was Britannica's district manager, netting nearly twenty thousand dollars a year. "What kind of education do you have in your home for your children?" John Y. would ask parents in rural Kentucky areas. "They got to feeling guilty," he would later tell the *Washington Post*. "It's amazing . . . I sold most of 'em in the mountains and those people who didn't have the financial means were the most receptive."

Many weekends, John Y. and his buddies drove the eighty-mile stretch north to the plush casinos and speakeasies of northern Kentucky. He loved the lifestyle of the ritzy joints, the dance revues and chorus girls, the dice and card tables, the numbers rackets and slots. He enjoyed the fancy showrooms which boasted big-name acts such as Sophie Tucker and Tony Martin. "Those were the days," one old-time gambler recalled wistfully. "Prostitutes were a buck, and people dressed up to come into the places. Even Governor Chandler—once he came to the casino without a coat and tie and the bosses wouldn't let him in dressed that way."

Newport and Covington, on the banks of the Ohio River, were meccas to John Y. He frequented the Beverly Hills Country Club, the Latin Quarter, the Red Rooster, the Merchants Club, the Primrose Club, the Glenn Rendezvous, and Jack's Shack. He loved the Little Club—the downstairs hideaway at Jimmy Brink's Lookout House—anxious for the day when he could afford the stakes of that most prestigious of clubs. That was where the *real* money changed hands; where players like "Sleep Out" Louie Levinson and Ray Ryan dropped hundreds of thousands of dollars. " 'Sleep Out' could come to a joint at closing time, and we'd always keep it open," remembered one of the dealers at the Little Club. Some say "Sleep Out" was so-named for his much-revered ability to sleep between poker hands; others say he was nicknamed for his notorious failure to return home to bed every night.

The illegal casinos operated openly in those days, controlled by organized crime syndicates from Detroit, Miami, Cleveland, and New York. Individuals such as Moe Dalitz, "Niggy" Devine, Morris Kleinman, Sleep Out's brother Eddie Levinson, and the Lansky brothers—Meyer and Jack—were the men commonly referred to as the "juice" or "muscle" in the joints.

John Y. got to know the working men—the dealers and pit bosses and shift bosses—men who would relocate in Las Vegas when illegal gamblers were finally run out of northern Kentucky. In the early 1950s, the Estes Kefauver congressional committee's revelations temporarily halted gambling, but before long the joints were back operating at full scale. "Except when the grand jury was in session," remembered a casino employee. "We all went to Florida every year while the grand jury was meeting. We'd take bail money in our pockets, and just stay down there in the sun till the coast was clear."

It wasn't until 1960—when a Cleveland Browns football player named George Ratterman was elected as a reform sheriff in Newport, Kentucky—that the illegal gambling that had operated since the Prohibition era came to a final standstill.

More than fifty gambling figures—most of whom were Kentucky natives—moved to Las Vegas where gambling was legal and the bosses were the same. "All you had to say when you landed in Vegas was that you were from Kentucky, and you had a new job that day," said a dealer who was chased out of Newport.

■

Rumors about John Y.'s gambling started flying as soon as he entered the governor's race. In a state known for beautiful horses and fast women, combined with the history of speakeasies and moonshine in northern Kentucky, gambling isn't really frowned upon by most voters. John Y.'s Republican opponent tried to make gambling an issue, but nobody seemed to care much. Except some of the voters in Kentucky's dry counties.

After John Y. won the primary election, Ralph Ross decided to build a dossier on him. Surprisingly, the state police didn't have any information on Brown because he had kept a low profile. He had spent most of his adult life in Tennessee, Florida, and Nevada, jetting in and out of Kentucky for parties. Ralph read all the news accounts available and talked to sources in order to find out what kind of man was going to be his next boss. The fact-gathering started out to be pretty routine. But then, Ralph thought that what his investigators began turning up was "right interesting"—especially in light of the fact that Brown was destined to be the next governor. Ralph saw patterns in John Y.'s behavior that dated back to his formative years.

By his senior year in college, John Y. Brown was already talking about someday running for the U.S. Senate. He entered the University of Kentucky law school, with a vision of parlaying a high-visibility law practice into a life as a potentate. After a brief hiatus during which he was called to serve time at Fort Knox Army base in Kentucky, he was able to finish law school by 1961. While a student, in 1960, John Y. met Bob Strauss, who was spearheading fundraising efforts for the

Democratic National Committee. John F. Kennedy was running for president, and Strauss had encouraged Brown to become the chairman of Kennedy's campaign in Kentucky.

At the time, twenty-six-year-old John Y. was managing his father's bitterly fought bid for the U.S. Senate—a campaign that would become one of the most humiliating of Brown Sr.'s defeats. "To watch my father get beat by people less capable was frustrating," John Y. was quoted as saying. "And watching the political machine at work was distasteful too. I thought I could help change that . . . I had a lot of bitterness in 1960. I'd seen the races in 1939 and 1948 when he had them stolen in the aftermath of the count. I'm the kind of person who likes to be the underdog, who likes the challenge, because I've seen so much accomplished by those who had the drive and the desire to accomplish what they wanted."

A partner in his father's law firm, John Y. ran the company as his father continued his downhill battle with politics. John Y.'s mother had grown increasingly impatient with Brown Sr.'s political failures. While his parents were openly contemplating divorce, John Y. married a gracious brunette schoolteacher named Ellie Durall. A coal-miner's daughter, Ellie equaled John Y. in a passion for ambition and excellence. He considered her a perfect complement for his future in politics.

Through the law firm John Y. met one of his father's old friends and clients—a former bootlegger, insurance salesman, and rural restaurateur named Harland Sanders. The white-haired, crotchety old man who had had no formal education had been running Sanders' Cafe in Corbin, Kentucky, since 1929. Famous for its fried chicken, Sanders spent years refining his recipe. Finally, with the invention of the pressure cooker in 1939, he was able to fast-fry his chicken, which kept the moisture sealed in. His famous blend of eleven herbs and spices, attracted customers from miles around to visit his remodeled restaurant. Sanders fell on hard luck when his café was bypassed by a new highway junction. Forced to auction off his restaurant to pay his debts, Sanders loaded his pressure cooker and bag of spices into the back of his old Ford, collected his savings and $105-a-month Social Security check, and traversed Kentucky with the hopes of franchising his recipe.

Sanders signed up only five restaurants in the first two years, but by 1963 had managed to franchise more than six hundred restaurants. Kentucky Fried Chicken, as he called it, was a real mom-and-pop operation. His wife Claudia mixed and mailed the spices, while Sanders kept the books. Sanders' white goatee, white suit, and black bolo tie became a trademark for the honorary Kentucky Colonel, who netted three hundred thousand dollars that year. Since the franchise business was growing faster than he could manage alone, the seventy-three-year-old Colonel began searching for investors.

Tired of riding on his father's coattails at the law firm, John Y. saw Kentucky Fried Chicken as a potential gold mine. He felt that his sales aplomb and innate business sense suited him better than law, and he saw financial success as a perfect springboard into politics. To John Y., politics and sales were synonymous.

The seventy-three-year-old colonel was searching for investors since the franchise business was growing faster than he could manage alone. Colonel Sanders' apparently didn't envision a buyout, but in a deal orchestrated by John Y. in 1964, Colonel Sanders signed a contract turning over most of the business to John Y. and Jack Massey—a Tennessee millionaire and friend of John Y.'s. Massey put up $1.8 million, and John Y. borrowed $120,000 from a Louisville Bank to finance his stake. For that, John Y. and Massey acquired the franchise rights for most of the world, while Colonel Sanders retained ownership of all Canadian franchises.

Sanders was apparently disenchanted with the deal, which consisted of $2 million—paid over time at a 3 percent interest rate—and a lifetime annual salary of $40,000, which was later increased to $75,000 for advisory and publicity work. "I don't like some of the things John Y. done to me. Let the record speak for itself," Sanders told the *Washington Post,* refusing to elaborate. "He overpersuaded me to get out." Massey was also said to be left with a sour taste in his mouth, but has refused to discuss the partnership publicly.

At the helm of Kentucky Fried Chicken, John Y. gave lucrative jobs to several of his college buddies. He made Dan Chandler head of public relations, and put Jimmy Lambert in charge of the South American franchises. Two years after acquiring the company, John Y. and Massey decided to take the cash-only enterprise public. Following the initial offering of fifteen dollars per share, the trading of Kentucky Fried Chicken made John Y. a multimillionaire and the nation's most famous fast-food entrepreneur. Thirty-one individuals, mostly John Y.'s friends, became millionaires in the endeavor. He scheduled the board of directors meetings and Kentucky Fried Chicken conventions in Las Vegas, often at the Sahara Hotel, which gave him the opportunity to pursue his gambling interests as well.

John Y. had maintained his casino contacts from the northern Kentucky joints, and was treated like a king during his Vegas visits. He quickly earned a reputation on the Las Vegas Strip as a high-stakes dice and baccarat player, prompting a Las Vegas newspaper columnist to write that John Y. was "considered a hometown boy out here."

The buckets of money would make John Y. even more restless. Ellie stayed home with their three kids—John Y. III, Eleanor, and Sandra—becoming increasingly dissatisfied with John Y.'s workaholic, jet-setting lifestyle. The more time John Y. spent in Vegas, the more unstable his marriage became. Ellie felt uncomfortable in his crowd of high-rollers and ostentatious millionaires, preferring the role of the elegant, classy homebound wife.

The more time he spent at Caesar's—his home-away-from-home —the closer John Y. came to the casino's owners, Cliff and Stu Perlman. Through them he met other big players, such as Lee and Jimmy Chagra. He usually stayed in a plush suite Caesars provided for its VIP guests amid the Roman statues and indoor fountains. The Perlman brothers granted him an unlimited credit line, and the croupiers loved waiting on the boyish Southern gentleman they called "The Chicken Man."

"As the boys say along the Strip," the *Las Vegas Sun* reported about John Y., " 'There's a guy you can feel comfortable with.' He can walk into any joint with his buddy Jimmy the Greek or his local pal Dan Chandler—the Kentucky flash—and the welcome mat is out."

Bored with the day-to-day details of running a huge corporation, after seven years John Y. decided it was time to bail out. He had turned Kentucky Fried Chicken into the nation's largest commercial food organization—outranked only by the Army, Navy, and Department of Agriculture—whose annual sales exceeded $700 million. In 1971, at thirty-eight years old, John Y. reevaluated his life: His marriage was in shambles; he had become rich beyond his dreams, yet felt unchallenged intellectually; being a chicken magnate had provided him the financial freedom he had coveted, yet his incentive was waning; he had saturated the country with thousands of fried chicken franchises; and a recession was lurking in the stock market. In the spring of 1971, he jumped at the chance to merge Kentucky Fried Chicken with Heublein Inc. in a $288 million stock swap. John Y. walked away with $35 million worth of Heublein stock.

Less than a month later he paid $4 million for three hundred and fifty Lum's restaurants and franchise rights. What began in 1956 as a Miami Beach hot-dog stand had been parlayed by Clifford and Stuart Perlman into an international chain, enriching the brothers and enabling the weenie czars to purchase Caesars Palace in 1969 for $58 million.

Through a complicated series of financial transactions, John Y. made Jimmy Lambert president of two companies that bought the Lum's restaurants from Caesars World, Inc., then sold them to John Y. The machinations—which were further clouded by false press releases issued to newspapers—were scrutinized by Nevada gambling authorities, who wondered if John Y. was acquiring a "hidden interest" in Caesars. Speculation increased when John Y. insisted that his lackey, Dan Chandler, be given an executive position at Caesars, ostensibly threatening to take his gambling business to another casino if Caesars refused to employ Chandler.

Brown's friendship with the Perlmans went hand in hand with his high-stakes betting habits. Chandler had publicly taken credit for introducing John Y. to the Perlmans, and for arranging the Lums transactions between the two men. Because of the Perlmans' corporate ties with alleged lieutenants in the Lansky crime organization, the Perlmans were under investigation at the time by the New Jersey Casino Control Commission and the Securities and Exchange Commission (SEC). Meanwhile, Ralph had learned through the Bradley Bryant matter that Caesars Palace was under investigation by the DEA for allegedly allowing drug dealers such as Jimmy Chagra to launder narcotics profits through the casino.

The actual details of the Lums restaurants purchase by John Y. were contained in a quagmire of paper. Basically, between 1971 and 1977 Lums had sold the assets of at least three hundred and fifty restaurants to John Y. and Ted Strauss—the brother of Democratic

National Committee Chairman Robert Strauss—and Jimmy Lambert had somehow played a significant role in the corporate transactions. Because most of the sales, acquisitions, and mergers involved the exchange of shares of stock, rather than cash, even the professionals and government experts charged with understanding the web were stumped. Nevada and New Jersey gaming authorities, the SEC, as well as the Dade County Organized Crime Strike Force in Florida, had pored over the financial documents for different reasons. John Y. was sensitive about the Lum's transactions, refusing to discuss them during his campaign. He contended that his personal dealings were "nobody's business and have nothing to do with Brown as governor."

He divorced his wife, Ellie; bought and sold his share of the Boston Celtics basketball team; spent most of the 1970s living a playboy gambler's life, jetting between Miami and Las Vegas; and wooed and won the heart of a former Miss America-turned-sports reporter.

Married on St. Patrick's Day 1979 in Manhattan by Norman Vincent "The Power of Positive Thinking" Peale, the wedding of John Y. Brown and Phyllis George was a media extravaganza. Guests, including Walter Cronkite, Eunice Shriver, Milton Berle, and Bert Parks, heard Andy Williams croon "Just the Way You Are" to the blissful couple. On their honeymoon night, they romantically talked of their future together, making a joint decision that John Y. would jump into the Kentucky governor's race. The primary election was but two months away, but the newlyweds were undaunted: Between them, they had money, name recognition, charisma, energy, naïveté, and a born-again sense of righteous enthusiasm. Already, their sights were set higher— first governor, then senator, then . . . president?

Their first date had been two years earlier, in Los Angeles. Accompanied by sports commentator Howard Cosell and actor Warren Beatty, John Y. felt instant "chemistry" between himself and Phyllis George. But it was apparently one-sided, as Phyllis met and married Hollywood producer Robert Evans shortly thereafter—a disastrous marriage that ended in quick divorce. In January 1979, John Y. and Phyllis became reacquainted when she agreed to appear at a pro-celebrity tennis tournament at a glittery Florida resort John Y. owned.

"We were sitting out by the ocean," John Y. told the *Kentucky Post* newspaper. "We talked about everything. I couldn't believe she was so intelligent and interesting. Oh, I mean, we talked about our careers, how fortunate we'd been with me making money with Kentucky Fried Chicken and she winning the Miss America title. She was interested in politics. And of course I'd always been interested in politics. And we were both involved in sports. Why, I didn't know an old fellow my age could fall in love."

He proposed to her that night.

■

"The voters were star-struck," Ralph recalled. "They didn't know what hit 'em."

The glitzy campaign attracted the attention of the national media, prompting profiles of the political partners. "With his-and-her matching dimples, they are handsome enough to have inspired *The Candidate.* In public, at every opportunity, they snuggle, bill and coo, hold hands, cuddle, kiss," the *Washington Post* reported. "She sits in his lap at receptions and he says, 'I'm in LO-OVE.' When a taciturn man at a reception in Paducah grumbles, 'Y'all look like you're on a damn honeymoon,' George pats Brown on the cheek and says, 'We are.' "

Asked if their eyes were on the White House, John Y. told the *Washington Post:* "I would need a lot of experience before I could get into something like running for the presidency. But I certainly feel well-qualified, with my background."

The whirlwind campaign was devoid of specific issues. Draped in thousands of dollars' worth of clothes and diamonds, Phyllis announced to the voters she was "shocked" upon learning of corruption in Kentucky politics. John Y. vowed to clean up crooked government, and run the state like a business.

"Most governors don't have the background to manage," he told the *Wall Street Journal.* "I do. Perhaps the colonel said it best: Once a chicken man always a chicken man."

Former Governor Louie Nunn, John Y.'s Republican opponent, hired a private detective in Florida to conduct "opposition research" for the campaign. The investigator, a retired FBI agent, reported his findings to Nunn, who then leaked them to the press.

Nunn claimed to find "a lot of evidence of Brown's association with illegal bookmakers, drug dealers, and La Cosa Nostra (LCN) figures in Las Vegas and Miami," but Nunn had trouble conveying the significance of John Y.'s involvement with notorious criminals.

John Y. downplayed the magnitude of the charges, and the statewide media chose to focus upon his fast-lane lifestyle—criticism easily deflected in blueblooded horse country. A headline in the *Louisville Times* read—*JOHN Y. BROWN JR.: HIGH STAKES GAMBLER OR SOCIAL BETTOR?* Responding to reports that he had wagered more than a million dollars at the Paul Hornung Golf Tournament at the Riviera Hotel in Las Vegas in 1976, that he had bet more than half a million dollars in a poker game, and that he routinely bet twenty-five thousand dollars on sporting events, John Y. denied all charges. He claimed he had never been associated with bookmakers, that he had had no relationship with the Perlman brothers since his purchase of Lums in 1971, that he visited Las Vegas infrequently, and that he had never bet twenty-five thousand dollars on any sporting event.

At the height of the campaign, Nunn disseminated a report entitled "Operation Uncover," which questioned the credibility of a "multi-millionaire playboy who decided on his wedding night to run for Governor . . . whose high-rolling lifestyle places him far above the concerns of mere working people. We are not talking about social gambling and not pari-mutuel gambling, which pays taxes. What we *are* talking about is casino and bookie gambling which many times cheats Uncle Sam and the State out of taxes . . . John Young Brown, Jr. is representative of a very, very few people. He lives in another world. A world of jet airplanes, helicopters, yachts, roman palaces like Caesars, palatial privately-owned 'fun clubs' with rooms 'exotically decorated in harem motifs with waterbeds, whirlpools and sunken baths.' "

Targeting the Bible-thumping Baptist constituents of Kentucky's rural counties, Nunn blanketed the state with copies of his report.

John Y. dismissed the allegations as the whining of a desperate man. Aware of Kentuckians' traditional acceptance of wagering, John Y. admitted that as a young man he had done his fair share of low-stakes social betting—horse races and such—and that as a millionaire he had met a lot of exciting people whose backgrounds he didn't question. But that was all behind him, he assured the voters, who apparently believed him. Three million dollars and six months later, John Y. Brown, Jr., was elected governor of Kentucky.

The state police Intelligence detectives under Ralph's direction continued probing John Y.'s background even after he became governor. Ralph's preliminary fact-finding mission had merely whetted his appetite for more knowledge about the flamboyant playboy who was now king of the state.

Ralph's investigators uncovered four areas he thought worthy of closer scrutiny: John Y.'s 1977 purchase of a Florida tennis and yacht resort notorious for its previous ownership by major organized crime figures, which was frequented by Drew Thornton and Bradley Bryant; the conviction of one of John Y.'s trusted campaign employees on charges of importing ninety thousand pounds of marijuana into the United States; the appearance of John Y.'s name in the possession of Gil "The Brain" Beckley—a lay-off bookie and racketeer famous for accepting large sporting bets from the world's wealthiest wagerers; and John Y.'s close relationship with Caesars owners Cliff and Stu Perlman, who were under federal investigation for their business dealings with associates of organized crime boss Meyer Lansky.

Realizing that most of the information on John Y. seemed to be centered in Florida, Ralph decided to take a trip to Fort Lauderdale. He paid a visit to his friends in the FBI and the Florida Department of Law Enforcement (FDLE), who provided access to their investigative files. Ralph toured Le Club—the posh resort John Y. had owned located on the intracoastal waterway. Featuring waterbeds and suites of desire, tennis courts and yacht docks, thatched roofs and a gaudy discotheque, Le Club had apparently been John Y.'s center of social activity for the couple of years that he owned it. He had enlisted famous friends to sit on the board of directors, including actor Warren Beatty, singer Andy Williams, and former Green Bay Packer Paul "Golden Boy" Hornung. The mobster hideout had also become known as a place frequented by high-class prostitutes who catered to the jet set.

Police had long kept an eye on Le Club. Although it had changed hands several times, many of the same notorious individuals continued to visit while it was owned by John Y., including members of the Carlo Gambino and Lansky crime families. Police were convinced that John Y. had purchased Le Club in anticipation of legalized gambling in Florida, and when gambling was defeated in the state's 1978 election, John Y. sold the complex.

In 1979 Ralph considered Le Club significant, even though John Y. had sold it a year earlier, because its reputation and the notorious criminals who frequented the joint didn't vary, even with the change of ownership.

In effect, Le Club seemed to both Ralph and the Feds to be a regular meeting place for organized-crime figures—before, during, and after John Y.'s proprietorship.

Coupled with John Y.'s close relationship with the Perlmans, whose ties to the Lansky syndicate were under scrutiny, Ralph saw John Y.'s ownership of Le Club as further indication of his routine hobnobbing with mobsters.

He began to inform the FBI of his findings since it was really that federal agency that monitored relationships between public officials and criminal elements.

Ralph was especially interested in John Y.'s sixty-five-foot yacht, named *The Boat,* which he had kept docked at Le Club. The captain of *The Boat* was a Kentucky native named James Glenn Gibson, who had held a responsible position in John Y.'s campaign.

"Brown did everything he could to keep Gibson out of jail," a U.S. Customs agent later said, referring to Gibson's 1975 marijuana bust. The bust had been the largest marijuana seizure in the history of the DEA at that time. Indicted on federal charges of smuggling nearly fifty tons of marijuana from the Bahamas into Florida, Gibson was convicted and received a four-year sentence. But Brown exerted considerable political pressure to get Gibson's sentence reduced. Although Gibson's rap sheet indicated a history of robbery convictions dating as far back as 1951, Brown intervened with a federal judge, a congressman, and federal prison authorities to beg for leniency in Gibson's criminal case.

He implored Florida Representative Claude Pepper to pull the necessary strings to have Gibson transferred to a minimum security facility in Florida. He then dispatched a letter to U.S. Judge Charles Fulton, pleading that favoritism be shown Gibson because "no hard drugs" were involved in his arrest.

"I was aware of his pending sentence when I employed him [in 1976]," Brown wrote to the U.S. Parole Board. "During this period of time I had close personal contact with Jim. He was totally responsible for the operation and maintenance of *The Boat* (for me personally and also in connection with charter trips for Le Club.) In this capacity he was entrusted with substantial sums of cash, as well as unsupervised access to credit in my name . . . During vacation periods I also entrusted Jim with chaperoning my three children, ages 11 to 14, while they were visiting me in Florida . . . Upon his release it is my intention to employ him again." The letter, dated August 18, 1978, was written on Lum's, Inc., stationary. A few months later, Gibson was back in Kentucky, working on John Y.'s political campaign.

Ralph's investigators found that many of Gibson's codefendants in the marijuana load were identified by federal drug agents as members of the Company. Although Ralph didn't see any direct links between John Y. and Bradley Bryant or Drew Thornton, he felt the matter warranted further investigation. The last thing Ralph thought Kentucky needed was four more years of state police constraint by a governor who had personal relationships with the state's biggest crooks.

The basis for much of the controversy swirling around John Y.'s gambling associations began with Gil Beckley. When Beckley had been arrested in 1967 in Miami on illegal bookmaking charges, FBI agents raided his plush home and seized a little black book that read like a Who's Who of sports figures, entertainers, and gamblers. John Y. Brown's name surfaced along with celebrities such as Bob Hope, Frank Sinatra, Jimmy Hoffa, Paul Hornung, Rocky Marciano, Barron Hilton, and Jules Styne. The feds knew that Beckley's organization included a network of National Football League players.

After becoming a government witness, Beckley apparently met an untimely demise, though his body was never found. John Y.'s relationship with Beckley was but the tip of the iceberg where gambling was concerned. Through law enforcement sources and friends in Florida and Nevada, Ralph learned that Brown had been known to lose as much as half a million dollars at a Vegas baccarat table, betting twenty-five thousand dollars a hand.

Since the state police provided security for the governor and Cave Hill, Ralph learned a lot about what was going on: "That's how it became clear to us how closely John Y. was associated with bookies and drug dealers. We kept track of everyone who came and went. Brown's close relationship with Jimmy Lambert was immediately obvious. Lambert visited John Y.'s home weekly, sometimes daily. According to our logs, sometimes he'd even spend the night when Phyllis was out of town."

As governor, Brown put together a Cabinet comprised of wealthy and prominent businessmen who coined the phrase: "Kentucky and Company—The State That's Run Like a Business." The two men who controlled John Y.'s campaign, and who received two of the most powerful jobs in state government, were Larry Townsend and Frank Metts. Townsend became Secretary of Commerce, and Metts was appointed Secretary of Transportation.

Townsend, a forty-two-year-old insurance salesman and son of a minister, had served as a corporate officer of Lums, Inc. As state Commerce Commissioner, Townsend immediately initiated an extensive and expensive campaign to advertise Kentucky as a mecca for out-of-state developers. He opened Kentucky Commerce offices in New York, California, and Brussels, and quadrupled his department's advertising budget.

On the other hand, Metts, a former real estate developer known for his thrifty management style, cut his 9,300-person staff by 25 percent and vowed to seek the lowest bidder on state road projects, thereby challenging Kentucky's infamous history of patronage highway contracts.

To underscore his promises to clean up political corruption, John Y. began a nationwide search for a law-and-order man to head the state's law enforcement and regulatory agencies. If he was serious about a dark-horse presidential bid in 1984, John Y.'s confidants knew he would first have to overcome the scandalous rumors tying him to organized crime figures. What better way to counter criticism than to select a renowned law enforcement officer and organized crime expert to head the state police?

At the behest of a mutual friend, John Y. made overtures to Neil J. Welch. So tough that fellow agents nicknamed Welch "Jaws," the fifty-five-year-old, thirty-year veteran of the FBI was the reputed mastermind of Abscam—the two-year undercover probe in which six congressmen and one senator were videotaped accepting bribes.

Governor-elect Brown lured Welch to Kentucky by offering him the cabinet position of Secretary of Criminal Justice, and sweetening the pot by combining two salaries, one from the State Police and one from the Cabinet in order to offer him sixty-four thousand dollars a year. Welch would not only become the highest-paid official in state government, but also would be one of the few members of John Y.'s cabinet to receive a salary at all, since many of his inner circle—millionaires in their own right—"volunteered" their services for an annual salary of one dollar.

John Y. Brown considered Welch a prize catch. At a time when congressional Democrats were decrying Abscam and its most notable architect as overzealous, John Y. thought Welch's presence would elevate his administration above reproach. But what could be in it for Welch? If John Young Brown, Jr., fulfilled his presidential aspirations, would Neil Welch become director of the FBI? Or had Welch and the FBI bamboozled Brown—had the vulnerable politician unwittingly imbedded a fox in his henhouse?

From his fifth-floor office, in the spring of 1980 Ralph Ross had a view of most of Frankfort, Kentucky. He could see Main Street, the state capital's historic district, and, off in the distance, the rugged bluffs carved by the Kentucky River. To the south he could glimpse the majestic dome of the statehouse, a richly adorned structure built of the native limestone commonly called Kentucky marble. The General Assembly had convened for the first time since John Y. Brown had been inaugurated as governor, flooding the small town with politicians and lobbyists from the state's 120 counties.

Across the river a legislative committee peppered his new boss, Neil Welch, with questions about Welch's plans to use Abscam techniques in Kentucky law enforcement. Of concern to the legislators was Welch's proposed reorganization of the state police, which included the formation of a public integrity section and the purchase of a hundred thousand dollars' worth of electronic surveillance equipment.

Ralph was anxious to see how Welch would handle the heat. He knew how hostile it could get battling the power structure. He also knew this was just the beginning. If Welch was serious about his professed intention to dismantle the state's most sophisticated criminal organization—the Company—he'd better be prepared to play Kentucky hardball.

Welch had been on the job less than a week when he summoned Ralph and state police captain Don Powers. Welch had handpicked Ralph and Powers, following a recommendation from the FBI, to create a "Special Operations" unit. He addressed both men with questions such as, "What are the problems with the state police? What are the problems in Kentucky? What are the major criminal elements? What cases are ongoing? What types of resources do you need?"

Ralph and Powers responded without missing a beat. They told him that one of the more pressing criminal matters in Kentucky involved the group in Lexington—Drew Thornton, Bradley Bryant, and Jimmy Lambert. They told Welch about the Company, and what was required in order to tackle the outfit—primarily electronic equipment and manpower. They had been conducting surveillance for a long time, they told him, but the state police didn't possess the necessary sophisticated equipment and they had never been able to obtain approval from state police higher-ups to purchase it. The legislature had always dragged its feet, and the state police bureaucrats had thrown up obstacles at every turn.

So it came as no surprise when the state police hierarchy fought Welch's reorganization of the state police as a subsidiary of the Department of Criminal Justice. Particularly threatened by Welch was the state police commissioner, Marion "Butch" Campbell. Fearing a loss of control and authority, Campbell battled Welch every step of the way, lobbying behind the scenes against Welch's proposed budget.

But Welch sitting stonefaced before his critics in the legislature, coolly deflecting their barbs, eventually got his budget approved. He promised Ralph and Powers plenty of free rein and assigned them to select a group of men and begin training them, setting up their surveillance teams and putting them into operation, leaving Welch to fight off the political backstabbing.

Almost immediately, Welch referred to Ralph as his "right-hand man." Known in certain circles for his legendary abilities as a sound man, Ralph was a technician trained in the most sophisticated audio intelligence techniques available in the United States. Ralph and Powers, best friends since their rookie days, had always gotten their kicks from hounding the ubiquitous crooked politicians and hoodlums. Though both men laughed dozens of times during a day—their humor heightened by the vernacular and drawl of their version of the English language—both were like pit bulls with golden retriever veneers. Despite their aw-shucks, country affability, Ralph Ross and Don Powers were considered formidable adversaries by their targets.

John Y. Brown, through Neil Welch, had inadvertently created what became known throughout Kentucky as the God Squad—an apparatus that would eventually lead to the governor's downfall.

His fifty-member Special Operations team was far from ready, but the time had come to establish the priorities. He had recruited his officers and was in the process of training them in complex surveillance and undercover techniques. He had arranged for the purchase of vehicles, and ordered them equipped with "bird-dog" tracking devices. He intended to send some of his recruits through the National Intelligence Academy in Fort Lauderdale, whose curriculum included courses called "Surveillance City," "Wiretapping," "Microphone Links," "Listening Posts," "Optical Devices," "Entering Undetected," and "Countermeasures."

On Ralph's desk sat stacks of surveillance and intelligence reports, investigative files, witness interviews, photographs, and fingerprints dating as far back as 1970—what amounted to a decade of suspicions of a sinister netherworld.

Finally, it seemed, he had the wherewithal to accomplish his mandate.

■

Though Ralph's unit was a long way from ready, he put a few men undercover in Lexington right away to get a feel for what was going on. At the same time, he occupied himself with the task of interviewing men for the Special Operations team and traveling around the country buying electronic equipment. Ralph's men did two things right off the bat in Lexington: First they opened a "storefront" office so the Lexington police wouldn't know state police had entered their territory, staffing it with auditors and investigators; second, they rented two or three buildings under assumed names, and then headquartered the surveillance teams there. Ralph enrolled some of the guys in bartender schools, then placed them undercover in local saloons, and assigned a few more to drive taxicabs. He put scramblers on all their cars so the Lexington police wouldn't be able to monitor their movements.

The first thing Ralph ordered his men to do was to put Jimmy Lambert under surveillance. Bradley Bryant was never around town long enough to make surveillance worthwhile; and Drew was in and out all the time. It wasn't clear how active Henry Vance was, but he was working for the legislature in Frankfort so it was easy to keep an eye on him. Ralph decided that if they targeted Lambert, then all the other ducks would probably fall into a row. Not only was Lambert the governor's best friend, but he also had an almost inseparable relationship with socialite Anita Madden.

Known as a high-stakes gambler who would bet on horses and anything else that wiggled, Jimmy Lambert seemed oblivious to the constant observation. He backed his gray Cadillac in and out of his garage at all hours of the day and night, usually accompanied by various blond, long-legged women. Wearing cowboy boots and sunglasses, a gold chain around his neck, the governor's buddy and business partner acted as if he were a man without a care in the world.

Ralph had been curious about the flamboyant nightclub owner for several years, beginning in the mid-1970s when Lambert and John Y. Brown, Jr., shared the plush ranch-style residence on Lexington's Old Dobbin Road. John Y. had purchased the house following his divorce from Ellie, and had later sold it to Lambert for $130,000 when he married Phyllis George. While John Y. and Lambert occupied the residence, neighbors in the fancy subdivision whispered and speculated about the nonstop activity.

Most nights and weekends, Mercedes-Benzes and Cadillacs lined the circular driveway, overflowing onto the secluded street. Tracing the license plates, Ralph and his men found that Lambert's regular guests were politicians and gamblers, narcs and drug dealers, horsemen and lawyers, models and world poker champs, doctors and veterinarians, jockeys and trainers, and a slew of national sports figures and prostitutes.

Drew Thornton and Anita Madden appeared regularly, accompanied by an array of Lexington policemen, local bookies, heiresses, and coeds.

Neighbors told Ross's men that the Old Dobbin location was particularly lively during the evenings following University of Kentucky basketball games. That information, combined with reports that Lambert had spent thousands of dollars rewiring the house, sparked allegations that a full-scale, illegal gambling ring was operating—complete with hookers and drugs.

Pulling together his files during the summer of 1980, Ralph was able to compile an interesting dossier on James Purdy Lambert. Born October 26, 1938, in Henderson, Kentucky, Lambert was one of four sons of a grocer. He attended the business school at the University of Kentucky. After graduation, his college buddy, John Y. Brown, Jr., offered him a Kentucky Fried Chicken franchise in Newport News, Virginia. Lambert and John Y.'s father later opened a franchise together in Caracas, Venezuela. John Y. Brown, Sr., once told a Kentucky newspaper that Lambert had made a million dollars on his Virginia franchise, but that the South American venture went bust. " 'I wanted Jimmy because he knew how to run a place,' the elder Brown said. 'But after a brief spurt when the franchise expanded from one to four outlets, the deal went sour.' Because so many people in Venezuela are poor and hungry, Brown Sr. said, the stores were often robbed. 'Besides, Jimmy likes basketball, football and horse racing,' Brown Sr. continued. 'He didn't want to stay down there all year to control things. We folded and took our losses.' "

In 1971, John Y. used Lambert as the figurehead for his purchase of Lum's from the Perlmans, and Lambert apparently ended up with some Lum's hot-dog franchises. Lambert tried another business partnership with John Y.'s father, investing in an H. Salt Fish and Chips franchise. But when that deal also died on the vine, Lambert decided to switch horses. In August 1973, Lambert and another Kentucky businessman bought a shopping mall near the University of Kentucky campus, opening a Big Daddy's liquor store and the soon-to-become-infamous Library Lounge. The Library Lounge was inconspicuously located in the bland strip center. Windowless and cavernous, its heavy wooden doors gave no hint of its lively innards. The nightclub grossed half a million dollars in its first year of business.

Four years later, in 1977, Lambert, John Y., and former Green Bay Packer Paul Hornung entered into a venture together in Cincinnati —a nightclub similar to the Library Lounge, which they called Trumps. Installed at Trumps as manager was Phil Block—the nephew of former Kentucky governor Julian Carroll. The financial details of the partnership were vague. Trumps would eventually swirl with rumors of the murder of a waitress, and become the target of a drug and prostitute investigation by Ohio police. But by the time Trumps was awash with scandal, John Y. would deny involvement in the business.

Blights on the apparently successful career of Jimmy Lambert were interspersed throughout the dossier. The first incident to attract Ralph's attention had been in March 1974 when Lambert claimed to be the victim of a robbery and attempted kidnapping. Lambert reported to the Lexington police that at 2:30 A.M., as he was leaving the Library Lounge and carrying $180,000 in cash, three masked gunmen forced him into a car. After having been "hit over the head," and robbed of all the money, Lambert claimed to have fought and escaped his captors, even though all three were armed with .38-caliber handguns.

Conveniently, or coincidentally, Drew Thornton handled the investigation for the Lexington Police Department. Among other questions raised, wasn't $180,000 a lot of cash for a local barkeep to be carrying?

Then, in 1977, a state police detective filed a report with the agency: He had interviewed a Lexington undercover detective who had attended a party at the Old Dobbin residence, which had not yet been sold by John Y. to Lambert. Guests at the party were described by the detective as "suspected organized crime figures and illegal drug dealers." Hearsay, but useful, nonetheless.

Ralph's Organized Crime unit had determined that Lambert had ties to known Florida crime figures Meyer Lansky and Hymie Lazar. Lambert also traveled frequently between Lexington and Fort Lauderdale, where he stayed at John Y.'s Le Club.

From his desk drawer, Ralph retrieved the year-old FBI memorandum identifying Jimmy Lambert as one of the "subjects" of a RICO investigation: "Lambert presently has in his household a manual from the Audio Intelligence Device [AID] Corporation . . . and he has apparently expressed or shown interest in a telephone actuator, a receiver for such, a sub-miniature transmitter for the body which can be hidden easily on the person, a wall transmitter, an AC wall outlet, and a one-watt transmitter."

Since AID is not open to the public, but only to law enforcement officers who have completed training at its sister facility—the National Intelligence Academy (NIA)—Ralph concluded that someone on the Lexington police force had pirated a copy of the manual for Lambert.

The memorandum continued: "Lambert reportedly travels with bodyguards and has commented that he has Lexington Police [officers] on his payroll." Surveillance reports confirmed that police officers frequented both Trumps and the Library Lounge, "which is apparently the reason why Lambert has commented that he has complete protection from the City of Lexington, Kentucky."

In August 1978, according to the memorandum, a regional narcotics task force initiated a narcotics investigation of Trumps. Ohio police were investigating reports that Lambert was in the process of opening a discotheque in Cleveland to be called 23 Skiddoo, which would be financed by a Miami crime figure, and another disco to be located at Caesars Palace in Vegas.

"Telephone calls have been made from . . . the Library Lounge," the FBI report said, "to bookmakers in Miami, Florida, who have alleged ties to Meyer Lansky."

■

The blackened windows and heavy drapes in the plush house on Old Dobbin Road prevented state police detectives from watching the internal activity, so Ralph set about to infiltrate the Lambert "parties" with informants and snitches.

Ralph's informer told him that the governor was even closer to Lambert than previously believed. Since Ralph's men were watching the house they knew that John Y. visited Lambert regularly. Ralph chose not to dwell upon the relationship between Lambert and the governor, assuming that to do so would place Neil Welch, and the Special Operations team, in a delicate position with their boss. He kept Welch apprised of the day-to-day details of the Lambert investigation— purposely neglecting to mention John Y.—and received guidance and strategic input from Welch.

Ralph had spent his entire professional life working within systems—in both the military and law enforcement. Not only did he believe that a successful criminal investigation was comprised of compartments of stratified information, but he also understood the significance and necessity of maintaining appropriate channels.

Ralph always assumed that a Bureau agent of Neil Welch's caliber and reputation would have thoroughly investigated John Y. Brown's background before deciding to come to Kentucky. Ralph therefore had considered it imprudent to mention his suspicions about John Y. to Welch when Welch had first arrived upon the Kentucky scene. Ralph didn't believe that Welch had severed his ties with the Eye. "Deep down, I thought Welch had come to Kentucky to do a number on Brown."

CHAPTER
TWELVE

When beautiful Rebecca Moore left her Cincinnati apartment on December 16, 1980, she told her parents that Jimmy Lambert had invited her to a party he was hosting for Trumps waitresses to celebrate the sale of the nightclub.

"We never saw her again, and later found out there had been no party," Rebecca's mother tearfully recalled.

The twenty-four-year-old art student worked at the Cincinnati club owned by Lambert, Governor John Y. Brown, and Paul Hornung.

Ralph's surveillance team hadn't taken particular notice of the petite blonde entering the Old Dobbin house. To observers, the coed would have been but one of many attractive young women entering or leaving the cream-colored residence.

Normally, a Missing Persons Report filed with the Kentucky State Police would not have grabbed the attention of Ralph Ross. But when the missing person was a "pretty young thing" who had last been seen alive by Jimmy Lambert, Ralph could hardly contain his interest in the case. He pored over the available information, vague and disjointed though it was, searching for clues in the disappearance.

A reconstruction of events would determine that "Becky" drove her old Chevy Nova from Cincinnati to Lambert's house in Lexington. Sometime that day, she accompanied Lambert to Boonesboro, where Lambert owned a cabin located on the bank of the Kentucky River. The state police surveillance of Lambert did not include the cabin property, so the activities of Jimmy and Becky had gone undetected.

Dr. John Moore, a Cincinnati veterinarian, and his wife, Barbara, hired a private detective when Becky failed to return home. "She was due back on Friday, December 19, to help me with the last of the Christmas shopping," recalled Mrs. Moore.

Worried sick, the Moores finally retained investigator Peter Thielen on Christmas Eve. The sketchy report that Thielen provided the Moores a few days later raised more questions than it answered. Oddly, one of Thielen's first tasks was to contact Jimmy Lambert and Lambert's friends on the Lexington police force. Thielen apparently did not believe in subtlety or discretion, and seemed eager to tip his hand.

Leaving several phone messages for Lambert at Old Dobbin, Trumps, and the Library Lounge, Thielen received a call from the Lexington businessman.

"Lambert . . . explained that Becky finished finals on Wednesday and drove to his home on Old Dobbin," Thielen wrote in his report to the Moores. "She was 'strung out' from lack of sleep (awake three days) preparing for her finals. Upon leaving the home Becky asked if she would need her warm, dress coat. James said 'no' and they left the coat at the house . . . James and Becky left the house with her suitcase in the backseat. They first picked up a painting from a local artist paying $1,800 in cash. They went to dinner. Another $100 was spent . . . The night was spent at Lambert's cabin on Upper Amster Grove Road.

"Becky awoke the next morning (9:00 A.M.) and went for a walk alone. Lambert stayed in bed. He heard Becky return, take a shower and then leave again around 10:00 or 10:30. He did not get up until 2:00 that afternoon. All of Becky's belongings were left in the cabin, including her purse and wallet."

Lambert said he hadn't reported Becky's disappearance because he assumed she had intentionally wandered off—probably with the idea of running away to Florida. According to Lambert, Becky borrowed a black leather jacket from him, which had eleven hundred dollars in one-hundred-dollar bills in the pocket, when she went out to walk along the riverbank that morning. She said she wanted to find a cabin downriver from Lambert's that her father had once owned. Lambert noticed she took a sketch pad along, and assumed she was planning to draw. When she never came back, Lambert told the private eye, he decided that she had ripped him off—stealing his leather jacket and cash.

"On noon Friday, 12/19/80, Lambert returned to his Lexington residence with Becky's things. He moved her car from the side to the rear of the house," Thielen's report stated.

When Thielen asked Lambert for the name of a Lexington police officer who might assist Thielen in locating Becky, Lambert provided him with the names of John Bizzack and Drexel Neal—the same detectives who had unsuccessfully investigated the disappearance of Melanie Flynn.

Thielen called Sergeant Neal and told him of his plans to travel to Lexington to personally search for Becky and interview Lambert. Thielen then drove to Lexington to rendezvous with Neal at a Howard Johnson's restaurant. After providing Neal with all the information he possessed regarding Becky's disappearance, Thielen drove to Lambert's rustic, remote cabin on the Kentucky River.

He drove down a narrow dirt road until he reached the last house located at the dead end. Seeing no vehicles near the cabin, he assumed the house was vacant. When he walked up onto the front porch, Thielen noticed the front door was wide open. Apparently undaunted, Thielen made the decision to enter the cabin and search it for evidence of Becky.

Finding nothing, Thielen began to search the surrounding woods. While walking in the area, he was approached by a neighbor. Thielen showed the man a photograph of the slender, gray-eyed, blond beauty.

"Does this woman look familiar?" Thielen asked the neighbor.

The neighbor recognized the woman in the picture. "I heard my dog barking around 1:30 P.M. on Thursday, December 18," the man told Thielen. "When I went out on my front porch I saw a young woman wearing blue jeans, high boots, and a black leather coat, walking down the lane. She was carrying a book—it might have been a sketch pad. Her hair was braided and rolled on top of her head.

"I left to go shopping about that time," he continued. "When I returned I found my back door had been forced open with a chisel, and twelve hundred dollars' worth of guns and ammunition were missing."

Thielen thanked the man for the information and drove the half-mile distance to Halls-on-the-River—a restaurant and local hangout in the area.

Dropping a quarter in the pay phone slot, Thielen politely called

Lambert to inform him that his cabin was unlocked. Thielen volunteered to return to the site to secure the premises in order to save
Lambert the inconvenience of driving the twenty-mile distance.

That evening, December 29, Thielen reported Becky's disappearance to the Kentucky State Police. He then called Drexel Neal to
provide Neal with an update on his progress. Thielen told Sergeant
Neal that he had searched the area to no avail. Neal allayed Thielen's
fears that Becky was dead, contending that Becky was but one more
party girl who had voluntarily run off to Florida. Neal told Thielen he
had decided against opening a criminal investigation into the disappearance. Case closed. Just like Melanie Flynn.

Thielen drove back to Cincinnati late that same night, and a few
days later provided the Moores with a ten-page report that vaguely
outlined his daily activities and personal opinions.

Becky's parents were stung almost as much by Thielen's shallow
results and deferential attitude toward Jimmy Lambert as they were by
Lambert's seeming lack of concern for the whereabouts of their daughter.

PERSONAL OBSERVATIONS:

*Everything in this report is hearsay evidence. I can personally
verify little outside of my actions . . . I know Becky left Cincinnati and
drove to Lexington, presumably alone. If Lambert's story is true, I know she
made it to the River Cabin. I know she was seen walking in the area on
Thursday afternoon. I do know for sure that Becky is not hidden in Jim
Lambert's cabin anywhere. My search was quite thorough.*

*James Lambert has been most helpful to me. I have no reason to
question his honesty at this time, but I could be wrong. He has at all times
been courteous and has not refused to answer any question that I have
asked. He does seem concerned about Becky's welfare and safe return.*

*There are two obvious possibilities to the whereabouts of Becky.
First, the grim, that she is dead. The second and more probable, that she
did leave the cabin with the $1,100, knowing that she would not be pur-
sued by any police authority and has headed for a warmer climate to get
away from it all. Of course, a young woman as attractive as Becky could
get involved in anything under imposing conditions.*

It is not my purpose to paint a rosey or bleak picture. I only wish to relate all possibilities.

OPINION

I feel that Becky did leave the River Cabin area on her own free will. Where she is now, I have no hunch. I think she will return when she feels that she can deal with this escapade with her family. I feel Becky would and could do anything to maintain her existence, and is alive. Those are my gut feelings from my research into this situation.

Thielen provided no supporting documentation, but attached a substantial bill.

The Moores suspected foul play, and were not assuaged by Thielen's laid-back conclusions. To them, it seemed their investigator had been co-opted by Lambert's agents. Like Melanie Flynn's parents, they thought they knew their daughter better than anyone else did. Christmas was Becky's favorite time of the year. Barbara Moore would never believe that Becky would miss the holidays at home, voluntarily. But what else could they do? The police in Lexington were obviously not interested in finding Becky. Jimmy Lambert's blasé attitude was not encouraging. "What was a forty-two-year-old man doing with a twenty-four-year-old student?" Barbara Moore wondered.

"My husband and I both believe that Becky knew more about what was going on at Trumps than she should have known," her mother said. "Becky wasn't the type to go to the police and blow the whistle, so nobody really had to worry about her being a threat. She was just a college kid."

■

In January 1981, one of Ralph's detectives briefed him on the details of Rebecca Moore's disappearance and provided him with a copy of Thielen's report that they had obtained from the girl's family.

"Did Lambert ever report her missing?" Ralph asked.

He was told that not only had Lambert neglected to report the woman's disappearance, but the Lexington police, when contacted by Thielen, had declined to pursue the matter.

"Open a criminal investigation," Ralph said. "Get someone over right away to interview Jimmy Lambert."

Not surprisingly, Lambert was not cooperative with Ralph's investigators. He sat sullenly, as the detectives searched his secluded cabin after Rebecca Moore's car and personal belongings were found at his house.

Ralph assigned his underwater divers to search the river near Lambert's Boonesboro cabin, but the murky waters and sheer limestone cliffs made their search impossible.

Ralph felt a sense of *déjà vu*. Another nubile beauty, not much older than his own daughters, had vanished without a trace. He thought of Melanie Flynn, of the psychic who dreamed of Melanie's hair perpetually swirling in the muddy Kentucky River. He wondered if Rebecca, like Melanie, had been a potential whistleblower on the Lexington drug ring. Had she threatened to expose them? Or did she slip and fall off a cliff, making the similarity of her disappearance to that of Melanie Flynn's purely coincidental? How many more girls would be drawn to the fast-lane lifestyle of Lexington's elite, unaware of the hidden dangers? How many more drug-celebrity-gambling groupies had already fallen prey?

BODY IN RIVER IDENTIFIED AS MISSING ART STUDENT

The newspaper's headline glared up at Ralph from the top of his desk. *A badly decomposed body found Friday in the Kentucky River has been identified as Rebecca Anne Moore, a twenty-four-year-old Cincinnati art student who has been missing since December,* said the first paragraph of the story.

"Too bad her body was found on the Fayette County line," Ralph commented to his partner, Don Powers, knowing the location of the corpse meant the Lexington police would have jurisdiction in the investigation.

When the once-striking blonde washed ashore on June 5, 1981, rumors quickly flooded Lexington that the body of Melanie Flynn had finally turned up. But the comparison of dental records proved the dead woman to be Rebecca Moore instead.

Since the local media had succumbed to pressure from Lambert, deciding not to report Becky's disappearance six months earlier, a public mini-stir was created when her remains were found. The body—which was little more than a skeleton with a small amount of flesh on the torso—had been ravaged by the cold river water since December 18, 1980. That was the day Jimmy Lambert claimed she had left his Boonesboro house to go for a walk. Five miles downriver from Lambert's cabin, Becky's torso became snagged on debris on the bank of the river, attracting the attention of passersby.

The coroner in Lexington, Chester Hager, quickly ruled out foul play, and determined the death to be the result of "accidental drowning."

Ralph called the detective he had originally assigned to investigate Becky's disappearance.

"Don't pay any mind to what the county coroner says," Ralph told him. "Get the autopsy report from the state medical examiner."

When he received a copy of the postmortem examination, Ralph honed in on one section: "There is extensive body decomposition and maggot infestation. Examination reveals absence of the left hand, right foot, and right forearm."

Overruling Chester Hager, State Medical Examiner George Nichols opined that "no anatomic cause of death"—including accidental drowning—could be determined, given the massive deterioration of the cadaver.

On the possibility that Becky's foot was missing was because it had been "weighted" by something heavy enough to hold the body underwater, Ralph ordered the five-mile stretch of river between Lambert's cabin and the location where Becky's body had surfaced searched by state police divers.

He dispatched three detectives to Boonesboro to retrace the route that Lambert claimed Rebecca had taken from his cabin. They reported back to Ralph:

Assuming she tried to walk along the riverbank, she would have encountered approximately a half mile of steep earthen embankment followed by a half mile of sheer limestone cliffs. It appears to be impossible to

travel by foot on the bank of the river in this area. Had Rebecca Moore
fallen in the river at the area of the cliffs, her body would have traveled
approximately eight river miles to where it was recovered.

The detectives, who were also scuba divers, decided that such a
search would not only be futile, but would be exceedingly dangerous
due to the geology of the area.

Despite his investigators' decision to abandon the search for
Becky's body parts, Ralph felt optimistic about the prospects of the
probe. He finally had a full-fledged homicide case on his hands—something much more tangible than Melanie Flynn would ever prove to be.
Even more significant, Jimmy Lambert was smack dab in the middle of
the case—at the very least, the primary witness; at the most, the suspect. Ralph arranged for Lambert to be given a lie detector test. That
assignment faced innumerable political obstacles, creating an increasingly tense atmosphere between the governor and his elite police force.
Finally succumbing to the examination, Lambert reacted "negatively"
to a couple of questions, according to test administrators. A few days
later, Welch approached Ralph and asked for a copy of Lambert's test
results. Governor John Y. Brown had asked Welch to obtain a copy,
Welch told Ralph.

Ralph assigned the Lambert investigation a case number, and
euphemistically titled it "Confidential Investigation"—its true nature
concealed from those outside Ralph's team. Every day, beginning January 3, 1981, at least five undercover detectives, dressed in plain
clothes, wove in and out of traffic behind cars driven by Jimmy Lambert, Drew Thornton, Bill Canan, and others.

Each officer detailed his precise movements and observations,
submitting reports every few days. Ralph studied them, poring over
every line for clues, piecing together the significance of the items.

INVESTIGATION: Surveillance was continued on James P. Lambert,
805 Old Dobbin Road. Surveillance report for January 8, 1981:

0800 hours: Surveillance was set up on Lambert's residence. A gray
Cadillac, KY DYK-124 was parked in front of the residence.
0900 to 1315 hours: No activity.

1315 hours: The Cadillac, operated by a white female with brown hair departed from the residence.

1325 hours: A brown station wagon parked in front of the residence. Operator unknown.

1330 hours: James Lambert departed from the residence in another Cadillac.

1340 hours: Lambert's vehicle arrived and parked in the 800 block of Euclid Avenue. He exited the vehicle.

1342 hours: Lambert entered the Bank of Commerce.

1350 hours: Lambert exited the bank.

1353 hours: Lambert entered the Mid-State Disco Lounge.

1400 hours: Lambert departed the Disco Lounge.

1405 hours: Lambert returned to his vehicle and drove east.

1410 hours: Lambert's vehicle arrived and parked in front of the Library Disco Lounge. After exiting the vehicle, he entered the Lounge.

1420 hours: A Lexington Metro cruiser was observed parked at Lambert's rear garage. License number of the cruiser was LA1-827, Kentucky official.

1440 hours: Lambert returned to the vehicle. The vehicle departed heading north on Woodland Avenue.

1450 hours: Lambert arrived at his residence.

1744 hours: White Nova pulled into drive. Parked in front of residence. White female, dark shoulder-length hair goes to front door.

1802 hours: White and red Cadillac with Florida tags parked at residence.

1829 hours: White and red Cadillac leaves residence, travels north on Tates Creek Pike.

1841 hours: White and red Cadillac parks in front of Hyatt Regency. White male, 6'1", brown hair, short beard, late 30s, checks in.

1941 hours: Returns to Cadillac with envelope in hand.

1949 hours: Parks west of the Little Inn Restaurant, enters. In the restaurant the subject met with two white males. One, 6'1", dark hair, brown coat, clean-cut, driving 1977 Mercedes, personalized plate. Entered restaurant carrying a folder. Second white male, hunch-backed, late 40s, driving a black Oldsmobile.

2220 hours: Mercedes left the Little Inn.

2223 hours: Oldsmobile left the Little Inn.

*2240 hours: Subject leaves the Little Inn with a white female, 5'3",
possibly a waitress. They sit in a Mustang in the parking lot.*

*2320 hours: Subject exits Mustang, gets into Cadillac and returns to
Hyatt.*

2328 hours: Subject enters Hyatt.

2400 hours: End of day.

0100 hours: Surveillance terminated.

Request registration checks on all vehicles referred to.

Attached to each report would be a computer printout detailing
the ownership and registration of the cars. No editorial comments or
indication of personal opinions on the matter were added.

By May 1981, Ralph had nearly fifty people working full-time
on Jimmy Lambert, and part-time on Drew Thornton. The more elusive
of the two, Drew proved to be difficult to track. His reputation was that
of a transporter *par excellence.* Drew piloted planes into the country,
turned them over to the ground crews and distributors, and walked
away clean. What happened after his plane landed was someone else's
problem and responsibility. Drew varied his patterns and never stayed
long at one location. Sometimes he would spend several days at the
condominium of his friend Henry Vance; other times he would alternate
between his parents' farm in Paris and Triad in Jessamine County; or at
the apartment of his girlfriend, Rebecca Sharp, or the home of his
former girlfriend, Sally Sharp—who was Rebecca's aunt. Most of the
time, though, Drew was not to be found in the Lexington area, spending
weeks at a time in Miami, the Virgin Islands, New Orleans, Honduras,
Costa Rica, and Detroit. Some reports indicated that Drew was a regular
cocaine user, while others claimed he never touched the stuff. Regardless of his personal habits, Drew confided in few, and those whom Drew
allowed into his inner circle were loyal to the point of devotion, encir-
cling him against hostile forces. The more Jimmy Lambert and Bradley
Bryant moved into the limelight, the more Drew seemed to recede into
the background. Ralph considered Drew's ability to maintain insulation
despite his hands-on involvement an art.

Jimmy Lambert, on the other hand, was practically an open
book. He operated with total abandon and flamboyance, as if any sug-

gestion of vulnerability was an insulting absurdity. Partying was second nature to him, and the wild cavorting at Old Dobbin Road was hardly a secret to Lexington's campus, sports, police, and society crowds. Keeping track of Jimmy Lambert's daily activities had become a form of vicarious living for many of the investigators. Models and actresses were daily fare at Old Dobbin Road, providing the troopers with light-hearted relief from the tedious and boring task of physical surveillance.

Not once had Bradley Bryant turned up at Jimmy Lambert's house during the months of Ralph's investigation. Ralph assumed Bradley's conspicuous absence during the spring of 1981 merely meant that Bradley was running the Company's drug operation from another locale.

As Ralph drove his pickup through Frankfort's wide streets, he was oblivious to the playful lights that emanated from the windows of the Victorian homes. The country Western radio station he always listened to was playing a mournful honky-tonk tune, with which Ralph sang along. He considered popping into Beans for a bourbon or two, but decided to head home when he saw the bar's parking lot was empty. No point in boozing it up alone at some depressing saloon. He could just as easily contemplate the Company while lounging on his motel-room bed.

Ralph felt a momentum building, as though he were being catapulted forward. For a decade, from 1970 until 1980, he had plodded along, carefully monitoring and analyzing the activities of Drew Thornton's group. Once or twice a year, an event had occurred that attracted his attention: Drew sold pot on the University of Kentucky campus and stole evidence from the Lexington police narcotics unit; Melanie Flynn disappeared; Bradley's house burned down; Ray Ryan's car blew up; Bradley was busted in Philly, his warehouse raided in Lexington. Plenty of time went by between incidents, affording Ralph the luxury of stalking his prey in the orderly, disciplined fashion that was his nature.

But now everything accelerated. The assassination of Judge Wood seemed to mark a turning point—as if May 1979 was the beginning of a new game, and Ralph wasn't sure of the rules or how to keep score. To kill a judge was pretty brazen . . . prosecutors, witnesses, cops, and reporters were off-limits to more traditional crooks. Ralph wondered what else was considered fair game to this new breed of criminal. Suddenly, dramatic events occurred with more frequency. The governor's best friend was under surveillance; jets owned by Bradley Bryant were bringing tons of dope from South America to Lexington; a top-secret military base in California was missing nightscopes and radar equipment; the CIA's involvement was being bandied about as if the "Agency" routinely used thugs and smugglers to perform its dirty work; Drew Thornton's remote farm, Triad, whose air traffic and rifle range was once nothing more than an irritation to neighbors, had segued overnight into a suspected haven for terrorists and Central American soldiers; DEA agent Harold Brown was boldly flexing his muscles, blatantly associating with Drew and meddling with other investigative agencies; and now, another girl was missing and presumed dead.

Dirty cops were hard to catch. Dirty spies even harder.

■

Already, another summer was approaching Kentucky with its full range of sweltering temperatures and humidity, ticks and chiggers, and tornado watches and warnings. Every year springtime quickly faded into a steamy summer that would last well into September. Spring epitomized the best of Kentucky, those few precious weeks when the tulips, redbuds, and azaleas adorned every household, rich and poor alike; when the silky foals stood shakily on a bluegrass carpet, nursing from their famous mothers; when the April rains were followed by azure skies and puffy white clouds. But all too inevitably, the new greenery would turn a heavy, mossy color and the fluffy clouds would meld into a stifling haze.

Ralph figured the summer of 1981 would take a lot of reckoning. His divorce now a foregone conclusion, he had stored his meager belongings, packed up his clothing, guns, and favorite photographs of his daughters—Connie and Christie—and taken up residence in a modest Frankfort motel. Melancholy about his personal life, Ralph felt blessed by a demanding professional schedule that precluded excessive brooding. The times he felt blue were usually after-hours, when the Kentucky bourbon stopped performing its magic.

The demands of his new position with Neil Welch in the Department of Criminal Justice—commanding nearly fifty men in a blanket

operation with unlimited resources and technology—had been the proverbial straw that broke the camel's back. What semblance of a marriage remained had rapidly disintegrated before his eyes.

Confident he had placed the Rebecca Moore investigation in
competent hands, one of the first things on his agenda was to convince
the federal grand jury in California to widen its scope. Ralph saw the
China Lake indictment as a vital opportunity to bust the whole conspiracy—not just Bradley Bryant.

He was not alone in this belief. U.S. Customs agents had become zealous in their pursuit of some of the Kentucky players they
suspected of gunrunning, and were increasingly suspicious of the lack
of cooperation they received from both the DEA in Kentucky and the
Lexington police. Finally, Ralph's long-held belief that DEA's Harold
Brown had been corrupted was gaining recognition. The problem with
tackling a dirty cop, Ralph knew from experience, is the bureaucratic
sensitivity. Law enforcement agencies don't like to have their reputa-
tions tarnished, and will traditionally go to great lengths to avoid a
public scandal. As a result, the internal affairs department of any police
organization is intensely political, and transfers are routinely used as a
disciplinary measure. Among the ranks, such subtle transfers are recognized as demotions, while providing the agency with systematic evasion
of the public's inquisitive eye.

Twice, DEA inspectors from Washington interviewed Ralph
about the extent of his knowledge of the compromising of Harold
Brown. He thought they were fishing to find out how much he knew.
Ralph gave them all the evidence the state police had accumulated that
was detrimental to Brown. He told them he suspected Brown's involvement with the DC-3 that Drew had flown into Calloway County, Kentucky, and that Brown was an active participant in that attempted smuggling venture. Ralph provided them with memoranda outlining
intelligence information and suspicions that Harold Brown and Andrew
Thornton were partners in the drug business; he provided them with
copies of surveillance reports that showed a long-standing relationship
between Brown, Thornton, and Henry Vance. He briefed them on the
mercenary-training activities at Triad, and told them that he knew Harold Brown frequented the farm.

Shortly after the DEA inspectors left the second time, Ralph was contacted by another DEA agent, who was supposedly interested in making a case against the Kentucky conspirators—Harold Brown included. Ralph assured the agent the state police would cooperate with him in any way necessary. The agent claimed to be working with the federal grand jury in Fresno, California, that had indicted Bradley and Larry Bryant for the China Lake thefts. He told Ralph he had personally been investigating Bradley Bryant since Bradley's 1980 arrest in Philadelphia. He also claimed to be responsible for Bradley's more recent arrest in Chicago, and said the Fresno grand jury wanted to expand its investigation to include Drew Thornton, Harold Brown, Bill Canan, Mike Kelly, Dan Chandler, and several other men from central Kentucky. The agent told Ralph the DEA had several *snitches* working for them who were "spilling their guts" about Drew and Bradley.

The flaw in the agent's commitment, Ralph believed, lay in the close relationship that developed between him and the Lexington Police Department. Ralph knew that just because Thornton, Steve Oliver, Jack Hillard, Rex Hall, and others had left the Lexington police to pursue drug-smuggling activities didn't mean the department was clean. Each of the officers, except Bill Canan, had left of their own volition, and not because of any scrutiny or reprimands by their agency. As far as Ralph was concerned, the Lexington Police Department had never investigated itself, as warranted; he knew from personal experience that security and integrity breaches flourished, and that the Company had high-level sources within the department.

Ralph was slightly perplexed as to why a federal grand jury in California would have the impetus to explore drug-smuggling activities two thousand miles away. He was not yet aware of the extent of the connections between the theft of military equipment from China Lake and the Company. He knew about the one nightscope that had turned up in Bradley Bryant's Lexington storage facility, as well as the nightscope and radar unit that were taken to Colombia by three of Bradley's associates. But he didn't know that Naval Intelligence considered Lexington's drug smugglers to be a potential threat to national security.

Regardless, Ralph was relieved that some prosecutor somewhere was prepared to pursue the "scroungy rascals." Ralph had become convinced by the summer of 1981 that no state or federal prosecutor in Kentucky had the courage or independence to tackle the

Lexington gang. Neither the state nor federal prosecutors had expressed much interest in empaneling a grand jury to hear evidence against the drug smugglers, despite repeated briefings by the state police about the seriousness of the allegations. Nor had they been inspired to subpoena witnesses in the Melanie Flynn or Rebecca Moore matters. The political stakes were becoming too high: Dan Chandler was the son of an enormously popular former governor; and Drew Thornton, Bradley Bryant, Henry Vance, and Mike Kelly were the well-bred sons of prominent, respected families. The recent Lexington trial of Bradley had made clear that Lexington juries did not respond favorably to accusations against its elite.

Within weeks of the DEA agent's appearance upon the Kentucky scene, Ralph was contacted by Brian Leighton—the assistant U.S. attorney in Fresno in charge of the China Lake case. Leighton asked Ralph to forward copies of all state police reports and memos relating to the group, and asked if he would testify before his grand jury. Ralph agreed, and the next thing he knew he was hit with a subpoena.

■

That long, oppressive summer had crept up on Ralph, consuming his energies and thrusting him into autumn before he knew what hit him. At least the continued demands upon his time precluded him from contemplating his abominable personal situation. He moved from the Frankfort motel into a brand-new apartment complex in Lexington called Kirklevington. Located near a busy intersection on New Circle Road—the main beltway around the city—Ralph conveniently situated himself within a five-minute drive of Jimmy Lambert's home, Drew Thornton's frequent residence, Henry Vance's townhouse, Bill Canan's apartment, Mike Kelly's house, and the Lansdowne Shopping Center, where "the group" conducted most of their meetings.

At this time, Ralph had a problem with one of his detectives—a seemingly innocuous man by the name of Terry C. Barnes—and immediately took steps to have Barnes removed from the team.

But overall, his job had been eased by the enforcement actions of others. Finally, in late September, the federal grand jury in Fresno had handed down a second superseding indictment—or the third indictment in six months—which charged Drew Thornton, Steve Oliver, and Mike Kelly with conspiring to import and distribute marijuana. Disappointed that Harold Brown had not been included in the weighty criminal indictment, Ralph was at least relieved that Brown was forced to resign from the DEA.

Meanwhile, Bradley Bryant had been indicted on separate federal fraud charges in connection with his shenanigans with the International Harvester truck dealership in Savannah. Already incarcerated in Illinois for selling pot to undercover DEA agents, Bradley awaited trial for the China Lake thefts. Bradley was being "encouraged" by the FBI to identify the hit man in the Wood assassination. Bradley, Ralph could safely say, was out of the picture. Mike Kelly was also now facing trial in both Florida and California.

One big loose end was Drew Thornton. Drew hadn't been spotted in Lexington for several months—ever since his federal indictment in Fresno on marijuana-smuggling charges. The presumption was that Drew had fled to avoid prosecution.

Ralph figured Drew would turn up sooner rather than later. Customs intelligence information indicated Drew was operating pretty heavily out of New Orleans; the odds seemed good that it was just a matter of time before he would slip up.

Having recently been sworn in as an arm to a newly empaneled special, federal grand jury mandated to investigate political corruption, Ralph was expected by Welch to expand his functions. The Justice Department in Washington had dispatched a team of special prosecutors and FBI agents to Kentucky; these agents operated outside the control of the local U.S. attorney's office, reporting directly to the Public Integrity Section of Justice.

Neil Welch had offered the feds the full cooperation of Ralph Ross and the Special Operations division of the Kentucky State Police. In fact, Ralph learned that Welch had "strategized" in Washington with those directing the wide-scale probe even prior to Welch's accepting a position in Governor John Y. Brown's cabinet. Tight-lipped about their ordinance, the D.C. attorneys, though green with naïveté, sent shock waves through Lexington and the state capital. The federal courthouse was swarming with whispers about pending indictments against high-level public officials and powerful members of the state's Democratic party. Reaching near-frenzy proportions, what became commonly referred-to as the "Special Grand Jury" easily overshadowed all developments from the "China Lake" grand jury seated thousands of miles away in California.

Welch assigned Ralph to act as a liaison between the state police and the "Eye," which meant Ralph needed to free up enough of his time to be available at the whim of the FBI, Neil Welch, and the grand jury. The first thing Ralph did was to transfer his surveillance team—which had intensified its watch on Jimmy Lambert—to Colonel Don Powers. Although Ralph would continue to devise the team's strategy, and would stay apprised of the progress of the case, the day-to-day operations would be handled by Powers.

By December 1981, Ralph was pleased with the progress his team was making; he had recruited all of his men and they seemed to be a loyal and competent bunch. Though some of them were already working surveillance, most were in schools or in training.

The Lambert surveillance, while interesting, didn't provide much insight to Drew Thornton's movements. Before his indictment, Drew had regularly dropped by the Old Dobbin residence, but rarely seemed to stay for the parties. It seemed to Ralph as though Drew made routine deliveries of packages to Lambert. The content of those deliveries was but one avenue Ralph intended to explore.

As the state bureaucrats around him began their holiday timetables—coming to work an hour late, leaving an hour early, and sneaking out for last-minute shopping—Ralph's slacked off a bit as well.

He should have known better. History had shown that the Christmas season was traditionally the most active time for his band of smugglers.

CHAPTER THIRTEEN

Andrew Carter Thornton II leaned against the wall in the lobby of the Royal Orleans Hotel. Dressed in a sport coat and oxford shirt open at the neck, his polished Gucci shoes gleaming against the wood floor, he could have been mistaken for a stockbroker or real estate developer. Comfortable amid the opulence of the French antiques, Drew was not the type of man who attracted attention to himself. Handsome in a Marlboro-man way, Drew feigned more self-confidence than he genuinely commanded. He would have been disappointed at how mainstream, predictable, moderately attractive, and insecure, he appeared to those who studied him. His vision of himself was one of grandeur and otherworldly courage. He believed himself to be a man with a mission superior to the mundane designs of common society; a man free of the restraints of civilization; a man immune from the checks and balances of a democracy. He believed he possessed supernatural powers, that he had been sanctioned by a higher force to use those powers in any way he saw fit.

Not even forty years old and larger-than-life rumors had made their way into the intelligence files of a network of enforcement agencies—that he was a lone operator, driven by adrenaline, who made secret parachute jumps into Southeast Asia long after the Vietnam War was over; that his inconspicuous red Dodge van cruised the quiet streets of Lexington, equipped with machine-gun mounts capable of firing rounds at 360 degrees; that men under his direction systematically infiltrated U.S. military bases, stealing explosives, weapons, ammunition, and warfare supplies to be used as a commodity in sundry foreign narcotics and intelligence operations; that he was a participant in a government-directed operation that trafficked drugs from South America to the United States to finance America's covert activities in Nicaragua, El Salvador, and South Africa; that he belonged to a network of renegade intelligence operatives who were running amok across the globe, hiding behind a right-wing ideology, while reaping gargantuan personal profits; that he was a decorated war hero and dedicated soldier who served some shadowy, elite arm of the U.S. Government that was above accountability to Congress and internal oversight; that he possessed credentialed status in some vague, but intensely important, government capacity; that he used his facilities at Triad to train a personal army, consisting of nearly one hundred individuals, who did Drew's bidding in the unsavory warfare of drug smuggling; that he had killed Melanie Flynn, strangling her with his bare hands, deciding she could not be trusted to guard the secrets of his nefarious dealings; or another scenario, that he was a mere accessory to Melanie Flynn's disappearance, risking his involvement because of his intense loyalty to her real killer—a trait of allegiance that had become legendary; or that he was a cold and calculating drug smuggler who thought nothing of ripping off his associates and setting up his competitors and uppity underlings to be killed or busted.

Drew perpetuated much of the mythical status that accompanied him. Careful to maintain subtlety in his boasting, he merely hinted at his larger-than-life exploits and high-level contacts, inspiring the imaginations of others to run rampant.

Ralph Ross, Drew Thornton's nemesis, believed that Drew's psychological makeup was a montage—neither as monumental, nor as petty—as Drew's own fantasies. A legend in his own mind to Ralph, Drew was a dirty police officer. Nothing more and nothing less.

Drew considered Ralph to be a country bumpkin, beneath Drew's social and economic class. To friends, Drew made condescending remarks about Ralph's intelligence and education, claiming Ralph was too inferior to be considered a serious threat. But by Christmas of 1981, Drew was finding it increasingly difficult to dismiss Ralph Ross as a nonentity. Even Drew could no longer pretend that the silver-haired fox could be ignored. He had to admit, at least to himself, that "ole Ralph" was personally accountable for Drew's sudden life on the lam.

■

Drew direct-dialed the 800 number for his Cincinnati answering service, dropping fifty cents in the pay phone slot. After two rings, Drew heard a steady tone on the other end, indicating he should punch in a four-digit code in order to retrieve his messages. Seconds later, a woman's voice came on the line.

"Hello, Mr. Johnson," the woman said, addressing Drew by his most frequently used alias.

"Hello," Drew responded. "Any messages?"

"Several," the woman said. "You haven't checked in for a while." The operator asked Drew to repeat his code. Satisfied, she began listing the calls:

"Matthew called. He said today's quotation is 4955010604. Please call him to confirm.

"Rex called and said it was very important that you return his call collect, as soon as possible at 809/445-3111.

"Mike called. He said the optics will arrive in Lexington at 10:25 P.M., Delta flight number 686.

"Gil returned your call. He said you have the number.

"Matthew called again. He said today's new quotation is 4996952314. Confirmation is number 116.

"Mr. Merrill called. He is expecting you for lobster dinner tomorrow evening.

"Mary Jane Knuckols wants you to call her at 606/846-4521.

"Tim Clark called. He says you have the number.

"Mr. Slone called. It is important.

"Matthew called again. Today's quotation is now 5942063154.

"Chad called. The transponder is finished. But the indicator still has problems. You can reach him at home until 11:30 P.M. tonight.

"Rex called. Call him at Julian's ASAP. It's very important. He says he's doing the best he can.

"Mr. Merrill called. He will be at Allied Marine in Miami until he hears from you.

"Oliver called. Return his call this evening.

"Queen in Chicago called. Call her tonight.

"Bill Canan called. Call him tonight in Lexington at 606/252-8640.

"Lorie called. The girls are checking in and are doing fine.

"Mike called. The valve will not arrive until Wednesday morning.

"Bill Canan called again. He'll try to reach you tomorrow.

"Matthew called. He says he has taken a more conservative point of view. The new quotation is 6070237883. Exercise your option every hour on the hour and you are sure to hit once.

"Henry Vance called. The quote he received is in error. He needs a new quote.

"Ruby called. She's changed her plans. Either come to town to see her, or call her later tonight.

"John Kellar called. Please call.

"Louie called. He has the part that you are interested in obtaining.

"Carl Knight from Knight Aircraft Corp. If he does not hear from you within one week, he is turning his problem with you over to federal authorities. He said you have his address and phone number.

"Rebecca called. She has an important message from a friend of yours.

"That's all, Mr. Johnson. When can I expect to hear from you again?" the answering-service operator asked.

"I'll be in touch," Drew responded.

He hung up the phone and walked out into the warm, humid air. The French Quarter was dotted with tourists who were gawking at the artists. He walked a few blocks to find a different phone booth he could use to call the individuals who were awaiting word from him. In his briefcase he carried rolls of quarters to pay for the long-distance calls so that there would be no charge-card record.

Drew returned his phone calls, only to have his suspicions confirmed that something was amiss. Drew and his associates had established a method for contacting each other, using coded messages. His friend Richard Merrill had failed to comply, instead leaving a vague reference to a lobster dinner.

Becoming increasingly paranoid, Drew returned to the Royal Orleans to check out. He had three hours to kill before he was supposed to meet Merrill in Slidell, thirty miles north of New Orleans, across Lake Ponchartrain. Merrill had rented two rooms at the Slidell Ramada Inn, from which he was supposed to direct the activities of two pickup trucks with covered rear compartments, one van with the seats removed, two rental cars, a fifty-seven-foot converted mine sweeper called The Forty, a twenty-foot fishing boat, an airplane and pilot who was maintaining air-to-ground radio contact with all the vehicles, and a small army of personnel who were facilitating the importation of several thousand pounds of pot in the middle of the night.

Cocky about the competence of his new organization, Drew had the utmost faith in Merrill. Like himself, the forty-year-old Merrill was a blueblood—the progeny of a clan residing in the rolling racehorse grazing land of northern Virginia. The owner of plush resorts in northern California and Florida, Merrill's polished veneer was a far cry from the stereotypical drug smuggler.

No matter how professional and bright his associates were, things could still go wrong for Drew. His instincts must have told him that something had. Indeed, as Drew strolled aimlessly along the banks of the Mississippi River, biding his time, Richard Merrill was being interrogated at the side of a Louisiana highway by undercover Customs agents. During the middle of the night, while Drew meditated in his hotel room, overtaken by a bout of insomnia, Customs agents boarded The Forty under the auspices of a documentation check, and had seized the vessel when they saw marijuana debris in plain view. Agents noticed one of the men on board the boat discarding items from his wallet into the water. Diving to retrieve the items, the feds found printed business cards for *Andrew C. Thornton,* and a yellow sheet of paper upon which had been written an undecipherable code. A search by the federal narcs netted charts with markings indicating directions from South America to Lake Pontchartrain, an aircraft radio, a shotgun, and South American foodstuffs such as Colombian coffee. The strong odor of pine oil disinfectant permeated the craft. Not far from where the boat was seized, agents had also raided a rustic cabin situated on an inlet. At the cabin, which had been rented by one of Drew's subordinates for the purpose of off-loading the pot, they seized twenty-six bales of marijuana weighing fifteen hundred pounds.

Meanwhile, throughout that night the Ramada Inn rooms were

under surveillance by Customs agents, who followed Merrill when he left the hotel early the following morning. They pulled Merrill's car over and searched it, finding an AR 180 weapon, a Bearcat scanner, a VHF radio, and a parachute. Questioned about the items, Merrill admitted a good friend named Drew Thornton had given them to him.

Later that same afternoon, Drew slid into a dark bar and ordered a beer. He drank it down without stopping, placed some money next to the empty glass, and walked down a deserted hallway to the pay telephone. Again, he dialed his 800 number in Cincinnati.

Impatient with the operator's pleasantries, Drew listened carefully to the next batch of messages:

"Rex called. Exchange is overdue. Still waiting. Held up en route. Delay unknown.

"Mr. Joseph has called five times. No message. He says you have the number.

"Tony called. He said it's very important that you return his call tonight because he will be flying tomorrow."

Drew called "Rex," "Mr. Joseph," and "Tony."

Something had gone terribly wrong. Drew, knowing that he shouldn't go near Slidell or the cabin, returned his rental car downtown and took a taxi to a private airfield. He asked the taxi driver to circle the airport a couple of times, searching for anything that resembled surveillance. Once he was convinced he hadn't been followed, and that no one was waiting to apprehend him, Drew approached his plane.

Neglecting to file a flight plan with the control tower, Drew fled New Orleans, reasonably sure he had left no trail. For the first time, Drew was entering a new phase of his life. He was committing himself wholeheartedly to the obscure existence of a fugitive from justice.

As a lawyer, Drew must have known that the China Lake indictment would be a tough one to beat. According to the broad federal conspiracy statutes, every participant in a conspiracy or a continuing criminal enterprise shared equally in liability. Even though the only evidence the feds had against him was that he piloted the DC-4 into Lexington, under the laws of conspiracy, or continuing criminal enterprise, his legal troubles could be as serious as Bradley's—who had been much sloppier. Bradley's tracks were everywhere including on the registrations of the planes and trucks, with the nightscopes stolen from

China Lake, and on phone records. To complicate matters further, twenty-five people were now under indictment for myriad smuggling escapades that dated back two years.

Since that time, Drew and Bradley had split, and the codefendants presented a mixed bag of loyalties. Drew couldn't help wondering how many defendants would be scrambling to make a deal with the government, not to mention how many already *had* made deals in order to avoid indictment. He was amused that Dan Chandler had managed to disappear from the latest indictment—his name stricken, even as an unindicted coconspirator. Drew was relieved but not surprised that Harold Brown had escaped indictment. The DEA would bale Harold out of trouble, considering what an enormous embarrassment the indictment of a DEA regional director would be to the agency. Brown did not emerge wholly unscathed from the scandal, though. The DEA forced him into early retirement, just six months short of qualifying for full retirement benefits.

Drew thought it in his best interest to remain a fugitive for as long as possible and claim, when caught, not to know about the outstanding warrant for his arrest. As long as the government couldn't prove that Drew *knew* he was a wanted man, Drew could not be accused of intentionally fleeing to avoid prosecution.

He didn't know that Ralph Ross was monitoring every call that came in to his Cincinnati answering service. The National Security Agency in Washington was also helping to break Drew's codes. NSA and other intelligence agencies were analyzing the references to *today's quotation* and *confirmation number* in an attempt to understand the language used by Drew and his associates in facilitating their apparent smuggling ventures.

Ralph, while interested in any illegal activities in which Drew might be participating, was becoming increasingly concerned with determining Drew's location.

Ralph wasn't the only one. U.S. Customs in New Orleans had induced the owner of the answering-service company to provide Customs with a complete log of all incoming calls to Drew Thornton's number. Inspired by the recent arrest of Richard Merrill and seven other Thornton associates in November 1981, Customs' incentive to apprehend Drew was heightened by their perception of the Kentucky native as the kingpin of the group.

Even Ralph was slightly surprised at the blatancy with which Drew continued operating, undaunted by the fact that several state and federal agencies were salivating at the challenge of capturing him.

Ralph put on his heavy frame glasses so he could read the stack of papers that had been dropped on his desk by a state police analyst. Either Drew's former associates were now using aliases, Ralph thought, or Drew had a completely new organization. Regardless, it was clear to Ralph that Drew had tightened his circle. Ralph reviewed the calls made to a second answering service Drew had engaged for the month of December. Someone identifying himself alternately as *Mr. Whitt* or *Mr. White* called the number an average of four times a day, asking to have his calls returned to numbers in Los Angeles, Boston, New York, Dallas, and the Virgin Islands. Another individual named *Mr. Graham* also called frequently, leaving various Los Angeles numbers. Gone were the calls from Rebecca, Sally, Mary Jane, Patricia, Ruby, Queen, and various other women who had left regular messages on the Cincinnati service. Rebecca still called daily, but used the initials *R.J.* instead. This new list suggested to Ralph that Drew was more concerned with security, hoping to eliminate potential leaks from his circle of intimates.

Ralph's eye focused upon some of the more interesting messages:

Captain Story called. Return his call as soon as possible. It's a matter of life and death. It is urgent that he speak with you. 809/773-1668.

Dennis the Menace called. He needs to talk to you today.

A woman called and would not leave her name. Please call her back in Delaware.

Lorie called to say Merry Christmas.

Tony called. Go to the place and say "Morgan" and you'll be able to go in. If you have any trouble, ask for Gloria.

On the last day of the year, at 8:30 P.M., a call came in. The only message: *They are ready to move.*

Attached to the list of phone calls was a Kentucky State Police memorandum marked CONFIDENTIAL and entitled "Associates of Andrew Carter Thornton II." That document provided an analysis of all telephone numbers left on Drew's answering service, including the identity and biographical information about the subscriber, and the address where the telephone was actually installed.

"We'll nab him within a few weeks," Ralph said aloud.

CHAPTER

FOURTEEN

It would seem that Ralph had his hands full, as he tried to maintain an alertness to details in the Lambert drug investigation, the continuing China Lake probe of the Company, the Rebecca Moore homicide, the public corruption grand jury, and the Customs search for Drew Thornton. As if those matters were not sufficiently time-consuming, Neil Welch expected Ralph to perform "other endeavors" of a more political nature.

"Sometime in early November 1981," Ralph said, "Welch called me and told me to get my bugging equipment organized so I'd be ready to go at an instant's notice. He didn't tell me what the situation would be—just said that some kind of deal was going to go down and I'd have to be prepared to do a job immediately."

By the time Thanksgiving had rolled around, Ralph marveled at how quickly the past year had come and gone. He had been working directly for Neil Welch for a year and a half, and still felt as though he didn't really know or understand the man. The Jesuit-trained, six-foot-two, two-hundred-pound former FBI SAC (special agent in charge) could have been the prototype for the deadpan expression. His poker face, conservative business suits, tight lips, bland gestures, ubiquitous smirk, and monotone voice constituted the perfect disguise for an undercover cop. While Welch's physical presence was not threatening, neither was it warm and inviting. One walked away from meeting Neil Welch feeling slightly disappointed that the personality did not match up to the reputation. Welch had seemed preoccupied with a book he was writing about J. Edgar Hoover that Welch claimed would "blow the lid off the FBI." He spent hours communicating with his collaborator on the project, a former federal prosecutor. Secretive and mysterious about the details of the upcoming book, Welch frequently trusted Ralph to be a courier of documents between the two authors.

Neil Welch could remain unscorched, no matter how close the fire nipped at his heels. A quote from an FBI agent, which would be published in Welch's book long after Welch's tenure in Kentucky had ended, epitomized this characteristic:

"Welch is smart. He works like a Mafia guy, always keeps himself insulated. He chooses one agent he can trust, and does everything through him."

Unfortunately for Ralph, he was Welch's pick of the litter.

■

Ralph was just nodding off in his chair when the phone rang in his Lexington apartment. It was 10 P.M. on the Friday after Thanksgiving. All his men were on vacation; he could barely move his 230-pound frame, thanks to all he had eaten over the past two days; and he wasn't expecting any calls or visitors.

"Hullo," he said, in a low, sleepy voice.

"Remember when I told you to get your equipment ready for a quick job?"

"Yes, sir," Ralph responded to Welch's voice.

"Well, it's time. Can you catch a plane to Florida tonight?"

Ralph listened as Welch briefed him on the details. Frank Metts, the Secretary of Transportation, had scheduled a meeting with a Frankfort highway contractor named Bill May. As part of Metts's notorious belt-tightening, he had recently canceled millions of dollars' worth of contracts that May had been awarded by the previous administration. May was understandably rankled, and Metts had a feeling that May might attempt to bribe him at the upcoming meeting. As a precautionary measure, Metts had asked Neil Welch to bug the conversation between the two men.

"Sounds fine to me," Ralph said. "Where do I go?"

Welch rattled off a seven-digit number in the 305 area code. "Call Metts when you arrive and he'll give you directions."

"I'll need to take a man with me," Ralph said.

"Whatever you need," Welch replied, and then hung up.

Ralph immediately called the airport to make reservations. The earliest flight he could find was for 10 A.M. the following morning. He booked two seats, then called one of his detectives.

Ralph then called Frank Metts at the Florida number to let him know they would be arriving around noon on Saturday.

"The meeting is scheduled for 1 P.M.," Metts told Ralph.

"There's no way in the world I can get set up by then," Ralph said. "Can the meeting be postponed?"

Metts agreed he would try to stall May until later in the day. "Call me when you arrive and I'll tell you how to get here."

At noon the next day, Ralph and his detective deplaned in Fort Lauderdale, and went directly to the rental car area. While his partner arranged for a car, Ralph went to a pay phone to call Metts.

"Bill May will be here at 7 P.M.," Metts said. "That should give you plenty of time to get ready for him. I'm staying at John Y. Brown's house. Come on over as soon as you can."

Metts gave Ralph explicit directions to follow Highway A1A south along the coastline. "When you come to a sign that says 'Golden Beach' you'll see a big, yellow house on your left. I'll be waiting for you."

They had no trouble finding the mansion. Set back behind a five-foot concrete wall, the circular driveway was empty except for one white Cadillac. The front yard was nothing more than an oblong patch of grass, in the middle of which sat a huge, white fountain. The pale yellow house was trimmed with white wrought iron more typical of New Orleans. The back side of the house faced the Atlantic Ocean, its private beach dotted with expensive outdoor furniture.

"The governor's got a right nice vacation home," Ralph said to his partner, as he pulled his rental car up to the front door. They were greeted at the entrance by a black butler.

Metts, his wife Sandy, and their children were spending the Thanksgiving holiday in the extravagantly decorated residence. "We were just down here on a vacation," Metts told Ralph. "John Y. called and said Bill May was also in Florida, and he had finally been able to set up a meeting between me and May." Metts explained that the governor had "on three or four occasions" tried to get the two men together to settle their differences. "Johnny said to me, 'I want you and May to get this issue resolved once and for all.' "

Metts told Ralph that he had canceled May's contracts and that May, furious, wanted to discuss the matter. "There's nothing to discuss," Metts told Ralph. "They [the contracts] were a big waste of the taxpayers' money." Certain that May was going to offer him a bribe, Metts wanted to record the conversation for his own protection.

Metts then left to take his family out for an air boat ride, promising to return in a few hours. Ralph watched as Metts handed some cash and a set of car keys to the servant, telling him to take off until the following day.

As soon as everyone had left, the state cops set about wiring the living room and den. They placed Nagra recorders in both rooms, taping one to the bottom of a marble coffee table and the second in a flower arrangement on top of a wicker table. They slid the transmitter into Metts's supple leather briefcase that was open at the top. Ralph climbed the stairs to John Y.'s master bedroom, where he attached a receiver to a tape recorder.

The two then waited for Metts to return. When Metts came back to the house, he sent his family out to a movie. As soon as the three men were alone, Ralph described the electronic equipment to Metts.

"If for some reason you can't get May to stay in one of these two rooms," Ralph told Metts, "then be sure to carry your briefcase with you wherever you go."

Shortly before May's scheduled arrival, Ralph and his buddy disappeared to the upstairs bedroom. Punctual, May blustered into the mansion with his mouth moving a mile a minute. Ralph listened carefully to the hour-long conversation, while also monitoring the electronic equipment.

"I want to declare peace," May said to Metts. "This is a privileged conversation. Right? Neither one of us is going to quote the other."

"That's right," Metts lied.

Bill May plunged right in, first detailing at least one prior meeting that had apparently taken place between May and the governor to discuss the highway contracts.

"I told Johnny that Frank Metts was trying to take away my

business. Johnny said don't worry. You two will get along fine. You're just alike."

Bill May presented an arrangement under which Metts and May could settle their differences while both saving face.

"I'm gonna lay it on the table," May said to Metts. *"I want to be paid our arrears, that's $15,000; our 1979 negotiated fee, that's $212,000; or else pay us a lump sum to get us out of the picture . . . twenty-three years at $100,000 a year, or $2.3 million."*

Ralph eavesdropped carefully, as Bill May hinted that he didn't need to bribe Frank Metts because he had already paid his dues. When he contributed $23,000 to the Brown gubernatorial campaign, May claimed he had been guaranteed future state highway contracts.

"Let me get down to hard knocking now of what I'd like to expect of you. First, let's go back to the beginning. Johnny, when he announced for governor at the airport in Louisville, called me and asked me to be for him. Then I talked to Larry [Townsend]. I said 'you're the money man.' I give him $10,000 up front. I give him $3,000 on the final action. I just want to be left alone. I thought I had an arrangement with Larry Townsend where I'd be left alone," May said, referring to Brown's current Secretary of Commerce and former campaign manager. *"That arrangement included Route 3, it included the turnpike inspections. It included everything!"*

May continued, delineating the contributions he had made, including one to Frank Metts's wife, Sandy. *"I put up the 13,000 bucks, I paid off a $7,000 club bill . . . and then, Sandy tagged me for a thousand bucks for Rosalynn Carter and Phyllis [George Brown] tagged me for a thousand bucks."*

Ralph listened as the words rolled off Metts's tongue. Metts contended that any campaign solicitations had been made only because May had the reputation of a big contributor—no strings or promises attached.

"I don't want you to act so fucking naive, Frank."

"John Y. called me on Monday and gave me your phone number. He said 'Frank, if you made a commitment [to Bill May] I know you'll live up to it.' Hell, I didn't make any commitment!"

May hinted to Metts that he had retained lawyers to research the possibility of filing a libel suit against Metts.

"I don't like being threatened," Metts responded, clearly agitated at May's tone.

"I have bought a position to the extent that I ought to be able to maintain the position I had when you all came in," May said.

Ralph's ears perked up when he heard the phrase that would resound through his head for the next several months.

I have bought a position.

"Bill May sure as hell thinks he *already* bribed someone," Ralph said to his investigator as they unhooked the wires.

Upon May's departure, Ralph and Metts dissected the conversation. Both men looked at the tape as if it were a hot potato. Metts picked up the phone to call Neil Welch. He briefly described the taped conversation, and then handed the receiver to Ralph.

"Ship it up here and we'll listen to it," Welch said, discouraging lengthy discussion.

After checking into a hotel, Ralph stayed up until 3 A.M. making a copy of the tape. Early the following Sunday morning, they drove to the airport—the tape in Ralph's satchel. No flights were available, due to the busy holiday traffic. Forced to wait two days for a reservation back to Kentucky, they took the tape over to the freight counter at Delta.

Ralph kept the original tape, and placed his copy in a padded envelope to be shipped to Blue Grass Airport, where Neil Welch awaited its arrival.

"When we returned to Kentucky on Tuesday," Ralph recalled, "Welch told me he and an FBI agent had listened to the tape at the airport in Lexington. They then played it for a prosecutor. 'We don't have a federal case,' Welch told me."

Ralph was nonplussed; the allegations seemed clear enough to him. Once he was back in his orange-wallpapered office, he retrieved the original tape from his briefcase and played it again and again.

Ralph went back to Welch the next day. "The man said he *bought his position.* I think we need to reevaluate this," he said to Welch.

Succumbing to Ralph's determination, Welch directed him to play the tape for the Kentucky State Police legal counsel. "Sure enough, the lawyer ruled that there had been a violation of state law,"

Ralph recalled. "I took the lawyer's opinion back to Welch and recommended that we prosecute Bill May and Commerce Secretary Larry Townsend under the state bribery statutes. I knew it wouldn't look too good for the governor, but I figured let the chips fall where they may. Welch nodded, mumbled something, and said he'd think about it."

Every day, Ralph expected Welch to give him the go-ahead on the case. When the days turned into weeks, Ralph interpreted Welch's silence as a tacit instruction to drop the case. Sensing it would come in handy someday, Ralph took the original tape recording to his apartment and dropped it into a brown paper bag filled with other microcassettes he had saved through the years.

Turning his attention away from politicians, Ralph decided his time would be better spent chasing crooked cops and drug smugglers.

PART

BOOK
ONE

SOURED
MASH

CHAPTER
FIFTEEN

The buxom Kentucky woman called a local attorney from a pay phone in Punta Gorda, Florida.

"Are you sure this is the correct address for Gene Berry?" the woman asked the attorney, rattling off a number located on Melbourne Street in the quiet residential area of Charlotte Harbor.

Satisfied, she returned to the rental car that was idling nearby. To the driver, who thought the woman's name was Brenda Rankin, she said: "We've got the right house."

Richard Hollimon, the driver, once again drove a triangular route from U.S. 41, north to Melbourne Street, over to Harborview Road, and back to U.S. 41. For the second time, they passed the ranch-style house, checking for escape routes. The house sat placidly on the bank of the Peace River, surrounded by a high wooden fence. A tan car was parked in the driveway, its numerous antennas stretching into the air. The tulips that had been so carefully tended by the state prosecutor who owned the house were just beginning to bloom. The dyed-brunette woman squinted in order to read *Berry* on the mailbox.

It was 6:45 P.M. on a Saturday evening, January 16, 1982. Dusk. Many of Berry's neighbors were home, she noted.

In the car, "Brenda" changed into a navy blue jogging suit, pulled on a wig, placed a pair of large sunglasses on the bridge of her nose, and picked up the .38 special that had been given to her by longtime friend Henry Vance. The thirty-nine-year-old straight-laced, top aide to the Kentucky Speaker of the House and respected adviser to former Kentucky Governor Julian Carroll had initially agreed to carry out the assassination, and had even accepted ten thousand dollars as a down payment for the job. Vance had sent two men to Florida to scope out the situation, but two days earlier, they had backed out for some reason. Vance returned Brenda's money, providing her instead with a weapon and instructions.

Shoot the target in the head and in the heart at close range, he had told her, and use *wadcutter,* or hollow point, bullets. He had shown her how to wipe the gun and the ammunition with WD-40 motor oil, so that no fingerprints could be found, and told her to throw the gun into saltwater afterward.

As "Brenda" and Hollimon approached the neighborhood for the third time, the woman instructed her driver to park the car on nearby Shady Lane and to wait for her there. As she walked toward the house, she thought about what Vance had said: "Aim the gun right at his eyes." Nervous, she wondered if she really had the courage to kill someone.

First she prayed. Then she knocked on the front door. Within seconds, Eugene Berry opened it.

"Are you Gene Berry?" she asked.

"Hi, how are you?" Berry politely greeted the woman, recognizing her as Bonnie Kelly—the wife of Mike Kelly, who he had recently prosecuted on drug-smuggling charges.

"You remember me?" she asked, pulling the gun out from behind her. She lifted it up toward his face, but couldn't make herself look him in the eye. Suddenly panicking, she lowered the gun. Berry tried running back into the house and Bonnie opened fire. She shot him twice as he backed away, and one more time in his heart after he fell to the floor.

Trudi, Berry's wife, had been seated on the couch in her living room when the bell rang. As she walked toward the entryway to see the visitor, she heard two gunshots ring out. She dropped to the floor and crawled on her hands and knees to the kitchen and dialed the operator, but then let the phone drop limply, too terrified to speak. Hearing the gurgling, dying sounds her husband made, she ran to him. Over his shoulder Trudi saw his assailant at the same moment she heard one more shot fired. Blood splattered the carpet and walls; their collie and Chihuahua were barking wildly. For a brief instant, the two women were locked in a gaze. Bonnie had intended to kill Trudi as well, but seeing her this way, helpless and vulnerable at the side of her slain husband, Bonnie's conscience bothered her.

Instead, she turned and ran down Melbourne Street looking for her getaway car. As she ran, she found herself yelling, "Call the police," hoping to distract attention from herself.

Waiting for her, Hollimon had heard at least two shots fired from where he was parked. Instinctively, he started to flee, turning his car in the opposite direction. Suddenly, "Brenda" appeared in his headlights. Even then, he considered not picking her up. What was he doing in this crazy situation? he wondered. He was no killer. But reason overtook him. He knew he was a dead man if he didn't follow his orders.

"Is he dead?" Hollimon asked as soon as "Brenda" jumped into the front seat. He whipped the car around and headed for Interstate 75.

"I don't know, but that last shot should have got him. There was blood squirting everywhere. He'll be dead by the time the paramedics get there."

"What happened?" Hollimon asked, not sure he really wanted to know.

"I rang the doorbell and knocked on the door," she answered. "He came to door carrying a puppy. He was smiling, real friendly. I kept my head down. When I pulled the gun out he panicked and tried to run. I shot him and he stumbled." She described how she had crossed the threshold chasing him, and then met the wide, scared eyes of his wife. "She was in a state of shock, like she was wanting to scream. I shot him again and again. I wanted to make sure he was dead."

In her moment of excitement Bonnie Kelly confided in Richard Hollimon. She told him she had considered cutting off one of Berry's ears as a trophy. That's what Henry Vance had suggested to her. She even told him her name was not really Brenda Rankin. She was the wife of the Big Man, she told him. Hollimon had been around the southern Florida drug world for a long time. He knew immediately she was referring to a bushy-haired, 350-pounder named Mike Kelly.

As rehearsed, Hollimon headed north for the county line. Once they crossed over from Charlotte County into Sarasota County, Hollimon drove onto a side road to search for a place to dump the weapon. Bonnie directed him to park next to a canal, where she tossed the gun, her jogging suit, and her wig into the pale blue brine.

■

That night, Drew Thornton, Henry Vance, and others waited at the Lexington residence of Mike and Bonnie Kelly. Bonnie had earlier left a message on the answering machine, saying simply: "It's done."

When she called back later, Stephen Taylor—a friend of the Kellys—answered on the first ring.

"I shot the mother-fucker," Bonnie said, recognizing Taylor's voice. "It's done. I don't know whether he's dead or not." Bonnie did not yet know that the forty-six-year old lawman had died within seconds. "I tried to shoot him in the face but he threw up his arms. I don't know if he recognized me. I don't know if his wife recognized me either."

Taylor nodded at Drew, indicating the mission had been accomplished. Edgy, the full impact of the murder struck Taylor for the first time. He knew the Florida police would suspect him immediately. He was scheduled to go on trial in Florida two days later, to be prosecuted by the dead man—Eugene Berry. Mike Kelly wouldn't be a suspect, since he was already serving his jail time. And who would think of Bonnie? Bonnie had fled to Sarasota, and was scheduled to depart Florida for Lexington on a Delta Airlines flight the next day, using her assumed name of Brenda Rankin.

Satisfied so far with the way events had progressed, Drew and Henry Vance took charge of the next phase: The alibis.

For nearly an hour, Drew had been using a pestle to methodically grind shards of glass. When the mixture was as fine as salt, Drew placed the mortar on the coffee table. Vance took a razor from his briefcase and motioned for Taylor to approach him. Handing him the razor and a Quaalude, Vance told him to channel a gash, first across his face, then down his arms, and then to rub sandpaper on the wound. Ignoring the oozing blood and Taylor's grimaces, Drew poured a layer of glass into the open wounds.

When Drew had finished his laborious carving, Taylor went

outside to the driveway. There, John Kelly—Mike's brother—and Betty Gee—Bonnie's sister—stood next to John Kelly's car. Vance and Thornton had battered the '67 Dodge with a crowbar and smashed the windshield, creating the impression it had recently been involved in an accident.

Under instructions from Drew and Vance, John Kelly and Stephen Taylor, to whom Vance had administered a Quaalude so he'd be groggy, drove to a previously determined Lexington intersection and ran the car into a utility pole.

Then they waited.

Within the hour, traffic detectives arrived to routinely investigate the one-car accident. Taylor feigned unconsciousness. Surreptitiously, he checked his watch. By 2:15 A.M. he was safely ensconced in the emergency room at the University of Kentucky Medical Center. Already, a police report was being filed, referring to his automobile accident. Soon, there would be medical paperwork as well, describing the head, face, and chest injuries he had received in the accident, for which he was dutifully treated by a physician.

Not only had Taylor created an alibi for his whereabouts the night of the murder, but he now had an excuse as well for not appearing in court on Monday.

■

When he was awakened by a midnight phone call—an increasingly common occurrence these days—Ralph was asked to locate all Kentucky members of the Company. "They've shot Gene Berry," Ralph was told by Florida cops with whom he had become familiar during the Mike Kelly drug investigation. "You've got to help us round everyone up."

The night of the murder, police issued a Be-on-the-Lookout, or BOLO, for a car with Kentucky plates. A composite drawing of a woman jogger, based on eyewitness reports, was widely distributed and published in local newspapers and on television stations. Police were pleading for an unknown woman who had been seen jogging in the Berry neighborhood around the same time of the murder to make herself available for questioning. Trudi Berry told police that judging from the inflection in his voice, her husband had recognized his killer, and that it had been a woman. Police had no idea who the woman could be. Her description was that of a five-foot-five woman with an ample bust and wide hips. Investigators quickly learned that a woman matching the composite drawing had been seen in the courthouse the previous week. The woman had been observed removing her wig after leaving the courthouse; she then put the hairpiece inside her coat, fluffed up her hair, and drove away.

Within hours of the shooting, Florida authorities had already zeroed in on Mike Kelly, even though he was incarcerated, and his buddy, Stephen Taylor. Ralph was provided with a physical description, date of birth, and other statistics for Taylor. Taylor, Ralph was told, had met and befriended Mike Kelly in jail—whereupon the two men plotted the murder of the man responsible for putting them both behind bars. Taylor was subsequently released from jail, but was facing prosecution by Gene Berry the Monday following the weekend Berry was killed. To Ralph, it sounded like a replay of the Judge Wood–Jimmy Chagra nightmare.

Initially, evidence was sketchy. Police had found a set of motel keys on a bridge nearby. The motel owner confirmed the patrons had driven a car with Kentucky plates. But divers dragging the Peace River failed to retrieve a weapon.

More than sixty law enforcement officers conducted the largest manhunt in Charlotte County history in search of the mysterious female jogger. Concentrating their search efforts in the area surrounding the middle-class, residential area where the murdered father of five had lived, police boats trolled the nearby Peace River, and trained dogs sniffed the property—all to no avail.

Florida police wanted to avoid the Lexington police, and to work exclusively with the Kentucky State Police, Ralph was told, because of the suspected involvement of several former Lexington police officers in the murder conspiracy.

A group of Florida investigators were going to fly into Lexington the next day, and wanted Ralph to assign some men to assist them. He agreed to give them as many men as they needed. He would locate witnesses, and then accompany the Florida police officers while they conducted the interviews. The case became Ralph's top priority—along with finding Drew Thornton. Ralph suspected Drew had something to do with the death, but had no way of knowing that Drew—still a fugitive from the China Lake indictment—was at the Kellys' house the night of the murder.

The Florida cops had compiled a list of passengers who had traveled by commercial airline from Lexington to Fort Myers, Florida, around the time of the murder. Ralph's men conducted background checks on everyone, interrogating them about why they had gone to Florida. The Florida detectives were swamped, and needed all the help they could get. Kentucky was but one of the angles they were following. They were pursuing every avenue, rumor, and motive that surfaced. A lot of political pressure had been applied upon the police and district attorney's office to solve the case as fast as possible.

The cold-blooded events gave Ralph an eerie feeling. Why would anyone kill a prosecutor? he wondered. Witnesses and informants were occasionally blown away, but it seemed fruitless to kill a prosecuting attorney—an abundance of replacements would always be waiting on the sidelines.

The Company was once again playing by its own rules. Just four days earlier, during surveillance at a favorite Lexington hangout of Drew's, one of Ralph's spies had overheard a conversation between two members of the group. "There's going to be a wave of killings now," one man said to another, apparently referring to reactions to the large number of defendants who were plea-bargaining in the China Lake case.

Even after learning of that comment, though, Ralph assumed the group would begin reprisals against each other. Instead, their first target was a government official. Ralph thought the next victim could be a Lexington television reporter who had broadcast an exposé of the Company's Kentucky members. Recent messages left on Drew's Cincinnati answering service included a thinly veiled reference to a plot against the news reporter: "Desperate situations call for desperate actions," the message said, regarding the reporter who had become a thorn in Drew's side.

Catching Gene Berry's killer became Ralph's obsession, even though the crime had occurred a thousand miles away. Solving the case became a matter of principle to Ralph.

For the first time, Ralph considered Company members a threat to his personal safety. It seemed they had no qualms about killing anyone who got in their way.

Rumors circulated that Berry had accepted a bribe to ensure that Mike Kelly wasn't convicted, and had then failed to produce his end of the bargain. "We bought him [Berry], but he didn't stay bought," one source told Ralph. Revelations that Berry had recently applied for a job with the attorney general in Kentucky sparked conjecture that such a position could have been a payoff. For obvious reasons, the Florida State Attorney's Office did not encourage pursuit of such motives. Ralph didn't believe the bribe story anyway. By all accounts, Berry was a "policeman's prosecutor."

Still, Ralph was convinced it was a highly unusual slaying. "It's not a contract killing," Ralph said to his partner Don Powers one day when the two men were mulling over the various possibilities. "Think about it . . . it takes a special kind of individual to walk up to a guy's front door on a Saturday night and shoot him point-blank in the heart. We're talking about a ruthless, brutal individual who probably had a personal ax to grind with the guy. Not a hired gun."

■

"His life was a brief candle because of a shadowy, faceless creature who crawled out from under a rock last Saturday and committed a cowardly act," the Reverend Henry Galloway told the six hundred people who gathered at the United Methodist Church to pay their final respects to the man who was Charlotte County's chief criminal prosecutor. "Throughout history there have been those who thought they could kill the *idea* by killing the *man*. The principles of truth, honesty, and justice for which Eugene Berry gave his life have not died."

Blasts from a twenty-one-gun salute. A lone bugle. Fifty police cruisers in a mile-long funeral procession. The grief-stricken widow held the American flag in her lap. Eugene Berry's parents and his five children huddled together at the grave site under a green canopy as the casket was carried to the grave. Politicians, judges, lawyers, journalists, and community leaders spoke to each other of the senselessness of the crime. Court dockets in five counties were canceled in official mourning.

"A person has to feel useful in this world," a friend quoted Berry, in his eulogy. "To hit a lick against what's wrong, say a word for what's right—even though you get walloped for saying that word. There's right and there's wrong in this world. You've got to do one or the other."

With that, Eugene Berry—a man who had committed his life to the belief that good will surpass evil in the end—was laid to rest.

Born September 2, 1935, Berry had been a car salesman without a high school diploma until 1970. He had met Trudi and married her the year before—the second time for both. At thirty-five years of age, he decided to fulfill his dream of becoming a lawyer. He moved his five children to Iowa, where he attended four years of undergraduate school while also holding down a full-time job. "This was in a period of unrest on campuses," Berry once said. "I was a man with a family, and in a hurry. I didn't have any time to waste. I picked a college I didn't think was likely to be disturbed by demonstrations. After three years of law school at Vanderbilt in Nashville, Tennessee, he accepted a job offer as a criminal prosecutor in coastal Florida. In a state mired in drugs, it was inevitable that Berry would find himself immersed in drug-smuggling investigations.

"He despised drugs," his widow said at the time of his death. "He saw what they did to people. My only frustration is that sometimes I feel like he was pushing back the wind. Florida needs help. The crime rate is terrible, it's a disgrace, and most of it boils down to drugs."

Quickly gaining a reputation as a tough prosecutor who successfully demanded lengthy jail sentences for major drug conspirators, Berry accepted the rumored threats against his life as part of the job description. Six months before his death, he appealed to his local zoning commission for a variance to build a five-foot wooden fence around his property. "I've had some [security] problems in the past, and I anticipate some in the future," Berry wrote in a letter to county officials. Berry wore a gun holster while at work and was usually armed in public. One week before his death, he had taught Trudi how to use a handgun. But those closest to him said Berry had no idea his life was in imminent danger, nor had he received any direct threats. He probably, however, had heard the street talk referring to vague contracts on his life—most of which was linked to Mike Kelly's sentencing just weeks before Berry's death.

Killing a prosecutor was but one step removed from killing a cop. Thirty-three investigators, working twelve-hour shifts and twenty-four-hour days, appealed to the state for additional funding to continue for an indefinite period. Assisting the local authorities were the FBI, DEA, the Kentucky State Police, other law enforcement agencies in Florida, Texas, Georgia, South Carolina, California, Maryland, and Canada, and more than a dozen civil agencies including the Department of Transportation, telephone companies in three states, car rental companies, motels, and airlines. More than fifty thousand documents were obtained, their data fed into computers and cross-referenced—creating a task-force approach to the most intense criminal investigation in Florida history.

Though the woman jogger had not yet been identified, and other suspects had not yet been located, the thrust of the murder investigation was undeniably focused on one area: Berry's stubborn pursuit of drug smugglers and organized crime—particularly, the Company.

By late January 1982, Kelly's Kentucky associates were the sole focus of the probe, and police were convinced, but couldn't prove, that the mysterious female jogger was in fact the trigger woman.

■

It was a clear and cold winter afternoon in North Carolina. The eleven-year-old Piper Aztec Drew had been flying, which belonged to his friend Richard Merrill, was in dire need of repair of a hydraulic leak. He decided to take it for servicing to the Southern Pines Airport, located near Fort Bragg Army Base, where he knew he would not attract attention to himself. He had flown in and out of the rural airport a hundred times over the past years; Bradley Bryant's mother lived in the area, and the two men used to meet there to discuss their deals.

Drew didn't know that Customs in Louisiana had tracked the twin engine airplane ever since Merrill's arrest months earlier in New Orleans. Though the plane had not been seized in that arrest, radio communication between the smugglers on the ground and Drew Thornton in the airplane had been intercepted. Customs had been stung by

Drew's ability to evade capture that time; to add insult to injury, there had been several near-misses between Drew and Customs in the ensuing weeks.

Customs told local police that an "armed and extremely danger-ous" fugitive who was wanted on federal drug charges in Fresno, Cali-fornia, would be landing in Southern Pines. Described as six feet tall, 180 pounds, with black hair and blue eyes, Drew's nickname was Slick. The Customs agent found himself snickering at the mere mention of that name. Not slick enough, he thought.

Drew was paying the mechanic at the local airport when he sensed warm, unfriendly breath behind him. Remaining calm, he turned slightly. Before he could evaluate his situation and explore his fight-or-flight body mechanisms, several police officers had jumped him.

Maybe it was time to change his nickname, one of them sug-gested.

It was 1 P.M., January 29, 1982. Drew put up no resistance as he was searched. Silently, he must have considered his circumstances. Things had definitely taken a turn for the worse. Their luck had turned as soon as Bonnie blew the prosecutor away; she wasn't a professional. First Bonnie had bungled Berry's murder two weeks earlier, and now this. U.S. marshals were already en route to retrieve Drew and trans-port him to California for arraignment. He knew that his bail would probably be so high that it would take him a few days to round it up. The first thing he did was to call his Lexington lawyer and friend— Randy Reinhardt.

North Carolina police seized all the items in Drew's possession, taking inventory, copying all paperwork, and packing them to be turned over to Customs: A .22-caliber handgun; numb-chucks—a Japanese weapon made of two wooden sticks and joined by a chain, used for grabbing a choke hold on one's enemies; a parachute; and the bullet-proof vest he was wearing at the time of his capture.

In his wallet were two business cards, one for John Carter, a Miami attorney—an alias for himself—and one for his girlfriend, Re-becca Ann Sharp. Written on the first page of his address book were several oriental symbols and the words Monitor; Challenge/Test; Dis-cover/Invent; Realization; Analysis; Requisition; Simulation. His personal philosophy was encapsulated on a printed card that he carried in his shirt pocket.

If a warrior is not unattached to life and death, he will be of no use whatsoever. The saying that "All abilities come from one mind" sounds as though it has to do with sentient matters, but it is in fact a matter of being unattached to life and death. With such nonattachment one can accomplish any feat. Martial arts and the like are related to this insofar as they can lead to the Way.

His address book and personal items were placed into a plastic bag, and Drew was driven forty miles to the Cumberland County Jail.

The next day, Drew was taken to Greensboro, North Carolina, where a federal magistrate set his bond at $1 million and ordered him removed immediately to California. While awaiting his transfer, Drew received two visitors: Henry Vance and Randy Reinhardt.

■

Ralph adjusted his bifocals, furrowed his forehead, and scanned the list of numbers for the hundredth time:

> *606-532—LEX*
> *317-316—SAV*
> *305-789—MIA*
> *215-043—PHIL*
> *1-7*
> *2-0*
> *3-6*
> *4-1*
> *5-4*
> *6-5-1*
> *7-9*
> *8-3*
> *9-8*
> *0-2*
>
> *41-44*
> *3R-35*

2L-79
R-95
4L-35
3R-20
2L-31

The first group obviously referred to a relatively simple series of numbers that transcribed the telephone area codes of Lexington, Savannah, Miami, and Philadelphia. Despite his years of military training as a cryptographer, Ralph had trouble deciphering the next two groupings of codes.

But it was the fourth set of numbers that intrigued him the most: *172.000; 171.450; 172.200; 171.600; 171.825; and 166.500.* Those numbers were the carefully guarded, highly secret radio frequencies used by the DEA to monitor body bugs. Drew also had in his possession codes for DEA transmitters, and a six-digit number referring to "Internal Security."

While it was surprising that Drew Thornton would carry the codes with him, even more intriguing were the nonpublished, home telephone numbers for DEA agents that were listed in his personal address book. One of those agents—Tom Zepeda, from Detroit, Michigan—was the special agent in charge of a task-force investigation code-named CENTAC 26. The target of that special DEA probe was Drew Thornton. Why would the *hunted* be communicating with the *hunter?* Ralph wondered. Only two possibilities would make sense. One, that Drew was working for the DEA as an undercover informant. Or, two, that certain agents in the DEA had been compromised and corrupted, and were assisting Drew in his drug-smuggling activities. Ralph had long ago discounted the theory that Drew was working in either an official or semi-official capacity for the DEA.

Convinced that DEA agent Harold Brown was associated with Drew, Ralph now wondered if Drew's contacts within the DEA were even more insidious and widespread. He turned to a Philadelphia DEA agent working the China Lake case for further information on the subject. The agent insisted that Drew was neither a DEA snitch, nor were any DEA agents partners with Drew in the drug business. Ralph thought the agent seemed more than a little testy when questioned about the issue. Like Ralph, Customs agents also thought Drew's DEA connections significant. They pursued those links through their own channels, and also received emphatic denials from the DEA. Andrew Carter Thornton II was not one of theirs, DEA contended.

Drew's address book contained the personal phone numbers of his contacts throughout the world. Interspersed with the members of Lexington's elite horsey set were the names and numbers of government officials and military generals in Bolivia, Brazil, Costa Rica, Colombia, Equador, Haiti, Mexico, Paraguay, Peru, and Panama. Also listed were the private numbers of Lexington police officers, as well as other law enforcement agents from various parts of the globe—including an officer with the Narcotics Bureau of the Royal Hong Kong Police.

The same phone numbers for the CIA in Washington that Bradley Bryant had had in his possession two years earlier turned up again in Drew's book. One of the CIA numbers—202/449-9944—would inform the caller whether or not the phone he was using was being tapped. As usual, the CIA would neither confirm nor deny the existence of the number, nor any relationship with Drew Thornton.

Then there were the women. Dozens of them, first names only. Bambi, Deborah, Teri, Candi, Julie, Barb, Tanya, Caroline, Donna, Delanna, Sally, Fran, Sue, Lucy, Nancy, Louise, Patricia, Carrie, Nola, Sandy, Kathy, Leslie, Betty, and the ubiquitous, and obviously special, "Rebecca." They lived all over the country. Almost as numerous were the names of lawyers—located in El Paso, Lexington, Miami, New York, Atlanta, Chicago, and Los Angeles.

Not very professional, Ralph concluded. Drew had violated one of the most obvious codes of a covert operative—government-sanctioned or not.

CHAPTER
SIXTEEN

On January 26, an Avis Rent A Car employee in Lee County, Florida, identified a composite drawing as that of a twenty-nine-year-old Lexington, Kentucky, woman named Bonnie Lynn Kelly. Bonnie Kelly had rented automobiles at the airport four times during the past month. During her most recent visit, she had listed her destination as the Howard Johnson's Motor Lodge in Punta Gorda, located within blocks of Berry's home. With this piece of information, Bonnie officially became a suspect in the murder of Eugene Berry. Several leads also pointed to Stephen Taylor: His relationship with Mike and Bonnie Kelly; his scheduled court appearance before Berry on cocaine sale charges; the fact that Mike Kelly had provided Taylor with twelve thousand dollars to bond out of jail; the suspicious one-car accident in a car owned by the Kellys that gave Taylor an alibi; and rumors that Taylor and Bonnie had become romantically involved since Mike's incarceration.

WIFE OF CONVICT SOUGHT IN SLAYING OF PROSECUTOR, the headlines read in the *St. Petersburg Times* on February 1, 1982. Any delusions Bonnie possessed about her immunity from suspicion vanished on that day. Terrorized by the widening net, Bonnie scrambled for an alibi. She turned to her mentor in this sloppy errand—Henry Shelden Vance.

The button-down-collared son of an eminent Lexington family had, so far, escaped being muddied by the negative publicity generated by the disappearance of Melanie Flynn, the murder of Judge Wood, the death of Rebecca Moore, the arrest of Bradley Bryant, and the China Lake indictments. By February 1982, most members of Henry Vance's inner circle—comprised of former high school classmates, boyhood friends of the country club and cotillion set, and police colleagues—had either been indicted, convicted, or were running scared.

His comrades—Mike Kelly, Bradley Bryant, Harold Brown, Drew Thornton, Steve Oliver, and Jack Hillard—were each in a world of trouble. Kelly was serving his sentence in Florida; Oliver and Hillard had pleaded guilty to drug-conspiracy charges in Fresno; Brown had been shamed into early retirement; and Thornton had just been snared. Yet Henry Vance had somehow remained unscathed.

The single skeleton in Henry Vance's closet had been his dismissal from the narcotics unit of the Fayette County Sheriff's Department in 1972. The clean-cut preppy, like his best friend Drew Thornton, had originally been attracted to law enforcement in order to avidly pursue hippies. After numerous internal charges that he was a drug abuser himself, coupled with his overzealous pursuits, his police career came to an end when Vance ordered two dozen .44-caliber pistols from Lexington gun dealer Phillip Gall and forged then-Sheriff Maurice Jackson's name on the voucher. The suspicious gun manufacturer alerted the sheriff. Sheriff Jackson fired Vance, but Vance was never criminally prosecuted in the matter, so only a handful of people knew about the incident. Ralph Ross had never forgotten it.

The day after Berry's murder, Bonnie had reported back to Vance in Lexington. She briefed him on the details of Berry's death— how she had feared she would lose the confidence to carry out the bloody act, how he had slithered back down the hallway, how she had looked into his widow's eyes. She felt pacified by Vance's apparent lack of paranoia and emotion. But as the days turned into weeks, and it became evident to Bonnie that investigators were focusing upon Stephen Taylor, she feared it was only a matter of time until the finger was pointed at her. Vance suggested to her that she kill Taylor, but matters were further complicated in that she had fallen in love with her husband's former cellmate.

By early February, Bonnie had already been interrogated twice about her and Taylor's whereabouts the night of the murder. As she related her fears to Vance, he assured her that he would provide an alibi for her. No one would challenge Vance's word, he told her, for he enjoyed an impeccable statewide reputation as a powerful, behind-the-scenes, political strategist and lobbyist.

Vance suggested to Bonnie that she return to K-Mart in Lexington, where she had purchased the *wadcutter* ammunition that she had used to kill Berry, and steal the records of that transaction.

Following Vance's directions, Bonnie and her sister, Betty Gee, went to K-Mart. Bonnie had signed a registration book using her real name the day she had purchased the ammo. She had watched the clerk place the receipt book in a particular drawer. When she and her sister returned to the discount department store, they were able to locate and retrieve the book and walk out of the establishment escaping notice.

Bonnie, Betty, and Taylor then went to Fort Lauderdale, where they went on a binge of booze, cocaine, and sex—the sisters alternately sleeping with Taylor.

■

The series of events that had propelled Bonnie into this mess had been set into motion the previous December. Stephen Taylor and Mike Kelly had spent several months in jail together, during which they had numerous conversations about Eugene Berry and Linda Bailey. Kelly had been sentenced to forty-five years as a result of his prosecution by Berry; Taylor was facing criminal conviction and a lengthy sentence at the hands of Berry—unless he could dispose of Bailey, the government's main witness.

When Taylor bonded out two days before Christmas, he immediately set about to plot the death of Bailey, enlisting Bonnie's aid. Taylor wanted Bailey killed before January 13—the date she was scheduled to be deposed by Gene Berry in Punta Gorda, Florida, in the criminal case against Taylor. On January 9, Bonnie had traveled to Waycross, Georgia, in an attempt to find Bailey. From there she phoned Vance with a physical description of Bailey—a tall, thin, young black woman—apparently hoping to enlist his assistance in locating her.

She returned to Lexington a few days later, having been initially unsuccessful in finding Bailey. Time was running out. Taylor's trial date was set for Monday, January 18. Home in Lexington, Bonnie dyed her hair and using an alias, flew from Knoxville to Atlanta to Fort Myers. She arrived in Fort Myers at noon, leaving her two and a half hours to get to the Charlotte County courthouse to find Bailey.

She paid for a rental car by charging it to her Visa card—a move that would prove to be a major mistake, as it would later provide a paper trail for investigators. Roaming the halls of the courthouse, she frequently reached into her purse to feel her gun. She found a place to wait which allowed her a direct line of vision to the entrance of the D.A.'s office. A half hour later, Linda Bailey emerged, under the protective custody of a sheriff's deputy. Bonnie scrambled to follow the two, who entered an unmarked police vehicle.

Maintaining an inconspicuous distance behind the police unit, Bonnie watched the deputy drop Bailey off at her home and then depart. She scanned the neighborhood to see how she would escape after shooting her victim. Once certain the police officer was definitely gone, Bonnie turned her attention back to her target. Bonnie watched as the woman walked toward her front door. She felt a pang of envy when several little kids ran up to Bailey, greeting her with hugs and laughter. Bonnie's heart softened as she realized she was incapable of pulling the trigger on the mother of those children.

Never having killed before, she was taken aback by her emotional responses. The business of death was more serious than the business of drugs, she decided. Putting her rental car in reverse, Bonnie retreated from her mission, driving aimlessly until she spotted a pay phone outside a grocery store.

"I couldn't find her," she lied when Taylor answered the phone back in Lexington. She looked at her watch: 3:22 P.M. "I'm coming home," she said.

Two days later, under the assumed name of *Brenda Rankin,* Bonnie had returned to Florida to put Taylor's alternate plan into action —to kill Gene Berry. She chose not to dwell on her inability to pull the trigger the first time. This time it would be different. She had no ax to grind with Linda Bailey; didn't even know the woman. But she hated Gene Berry.

Bonnie was picked up at the Fort Myers Airport at two o'clock the morning of January 16 by Richard Hollimon—a black man she had never met before. Bonnie insisted on telephoning Taylor back in Lexington before proceeding. She had two reasons: To inform him that she had arrived safely, and to confirm that Hollimon was indeed the man who was supposed to be her driver.

She listened as Hollimon spoke to Taylor.

"Watch her back," Taylor told Hollimon. "Take care of her down there and make sure nothin' goes wrong. Can you do that, Richard? You're either in or out."

She listened as Hollimon assured Taylor that he was "in."

Convinced she was in the right hands, Bonnie accompanied Hollimon to a local motel where they registered under the names of Joe and Brenda Rankin. There in the room, Bonnie showed Hollimon the contents of her aluminum attaché case: Two guns and a silver dagger. She bragged to him that she was a professional hit woman who was paid seven thousand dollars per job.

Hollimon was impressed. He was barely able to eke out enough to keep himself alive, much less enough for the court-ordered child support he was supposed to be paying.

Hollimon and Bonnie both slept fitfully that night. Having paid cash in advance for the room, they left in the morning without checking out. They drove to a motel located in Berry's suburban residential neighborhood. Bonnie waited in the car as Hollimon registered, stupidly using his own name. The two then found a K-Mart, where Bonnie purchased a jogging suit and some heavy-duty tape to cover their license plates. Bonnie made her phone call to Mike's attorney to confirm Berry's address, then made a trial run through the shaded streets of Charlotte Harbor, casing the entrances and exits from Berry's home.

The hours passed quickly, and before they both knew it, the darkness they awaited had finally crept upon them.

■

The Merrick Inn sits at the crest of a knoll, as inviting and formidable as the stately mansion it once was. Known for serving some of the best meals in Lexington, the restaurant takes reservations on a priority basis from residents of Merrick Place—a compound of townhouses and condominiums that have been developed on the original farm property. Offering traditional Kentucky fare at moderate prices, its menu includes such classics as beaten biscuits, hush puppies, old-fashioned hoe cakes, corn fritters, wall-eyed pike, country ham, hot browns, and chess pie, served in the elegant splendor of the nineteenth century.

Hung on the darkly painted walls are prints depicting fox hunts, the red-jacketed riders languidly traversing ridges. Oil portraits of famous horses, winners who have won the hearts of the locals with their racing victories or stunning bloodlines, are also displayed.

The bar is less formal, its dark paneling dotted with brightly colored jockey silks like the clubhouse at a racetrack. It is this room where residents of the enclave can meet, bring their guests, and hold court as if at their private club. A back door leads from the bar to an outdoor patio used in the springtime. In the dead of winter, the door usually remains locked.

Among the regulars at the Merrick Inn in the early 1980s were Drew Thornton and Henry Vance. Both men were comfortable in the slightly stuffy environment, for they had been raised in rooms like these.

On the Saturday night of February 27, 1982, the two men had much to discuss. Over dinner and late-night cognacs, their conversation ran the gamut. They were joined at different times by Bonnie Kelly and Sally Sharp—Rebecca's aunt.

Drew had recently returned from Fresno, where, ten days earlier, he had been freed on bail. The judge had agreed to reduce his bond from $1 million cash, allowing Drew to post $75,000 in cash and $920,000 in personal surety. Drew guaranteed the surety with the deed to Triad and conveyed to the court his ownership interest in three racehorses. He was forced to surrender his passport and ordered not to leave Kentucky. He was scheduled to return to Fresno a few days later to enter his plea in the international drugs and weapons conspiracy. Anxious to avoid a jail sentence, Drew couldn't decide how he should plead to the charges. He knew if he stood trial he'd certainly be convicted since the federal conspiracy laws were so all-encompassing. He considered that his best bet would be a *nolo contendere* plea, or "no contest." Though officially considered to be a guilty plea, Drew preferred the sound of it. He would enter it amid hints that, though technically guilty, he had been operating at the behest of an unnamed entity, i.e., the DEA or CIA, or in some other national security capacity. Like his ex-friend Bradley Bryant, one of the legal avenues open to Drew Thornton was to convince the federal judge that he was a "good guy, not a bad guy." He would then have to inundate the court with letters from prominent Lexingtonians and high-level federal intelligence agents who would vouch for his moral character and reputation, and beg for a suspended or probated sentence. Or he could contend that the charges were simply untrue, but that it would be exorbitantly expensive and a drain on his professional and personal life to battle the legal system.

Henry Vance and Bonnie Kelly had their own problems. Neither Henry nor Bonnie knew it yet, but both Stephen Taylor and Richard Hollimon had agreed to cooperate with Florida authorities in the Berry murder investigation. Taylor had been found guilty on cocaine charges and decided to make a deal with the government. In exchange for a lesser sentence, he would tell them everything they wanted to know about the assassination of the Florida prosecutor. Hollimon had found himself in a similar situation, suddenly beholden to the government's demands.

Without knowledge about the deals Taylor and Hollimon had made, Henry and Bonnie had been lulled into a false sense of security. Henry had told Florida detectives that he was with Bonnie Kelly on January 16—the day of the murder. Vance said he had met Bonnie in a Lexington parking lot to discuss an insurance policy that he had sold her. His statement had provided both of them with an alibi.

Bonnie was less confident. She *knew* she was a suspect in the murder; the cops had been all over her. Her freedom hinged upon Henry Vance's loyalty to her, and the decade of dirt they had on each other.

By 11 P.M., Drew, Henry, and Sally Sharp decided to leave the Merrick Inn, selecting the back-door exit from the bar. Drew emerged first, his companions following behind him. As he crossed a boardwalk leading onto the patio, Drew collapsed onto the walkway.

Within seconds, one of Drew's drinking buddies flew out of the doorway. A local veterinarian whom Drew had known most of his adult life hurried to Drew's side in order to administer first aid.

"Drew was in shock," the vet would later tell a newspaper reporter. "I opened up his shirt and there were bruises. Whoever it was must have been using a silencer, and it must have been at close range."

The doctor neglected to mention the fact that the impact of the bullets had been deflected by the bulletproof vest Drew was wearing.

No one in the restaurant had heard a thing.

Moments later, as if by telepathy, since no one would admit having summoned them, a fire department ambulance and *Lexington Herald* photographer arrived upon the scene. Drew was photographed lying on the ground, writhing in agony as paramedics hooked him up to oxygen. Soon he was whisked off to a local emergency room to be treated before undergoing questioning by Lexington Police Sergeant John Bizzack.

Ralph, who was vacationing in Florida at the time, didn't learn of the shooting until the following Monday when Neil Welch called him to tell him that someone had tried to kill Drew and that the Lexington police were working the case.

Ralph called Bizzack to find out what was going on. Bizzack explained that the assailant had stepped out from behind a tree and shot Drew with a .38 using *wadcutter* bullets—a flat-nosed slug such as a *wadcutter* would have a hard time penetrating a bulletproof vest. Bizzack related the sketchy description Drew had provided—Tall, white male, about six feet two, medium build, darkly tanned face, dressed in dark clothing and wearing a ski mask.

"Kind of sounds like me, doesn't it," Ralph said to Bizzack.

"Sure does," Bizzack answered.

"Let me ask you something," Ralph continued. "How in the hell did Drew know the guy had a suntanned face if he was wearing a ski mask?"

Bizzack fell silent. Ralph asked him for a copy of the investigative file, but when it arrived, he found it devoid of any substance, and even lacking witness statements. He wondered why the police hadn't sealed off the scene and interviewed all the people at the restaurant. Why hadn't they asked the standard questions such as *Did you hear any shots? Did you see anything or anyone suspicious? Did you notice anyone standing behind a tree? What did you observe when the shooting occurred?* Basic investigative stuff. Instead, their entire investigative file consisted of Drew's one-page statement to them.

Ralph didn't believe there had been a shooting. It seemed to him that if someone wanted to kill Drew he would have aimed for his head. He thought the whole thing was a well-staged plot. Ralph figured Drew had hung his bulletproof vest on a fencepost earlier that day, and taken a couple of shots at it, then faked some bruises on his chest at the same places as the bullet holes.

Drew had several possible motivations for setting up such a phony act. He might be trying to frame Ralph by describing an assailant who resembled Ralph; or he might be hoping to get sympathy from the judge in California by claiming his life would be in danger if he went to jail; or maybe he was hoping to deflect attention from him and Bonnie and Henry by making it look like whoever killed Gene Berry was also out to get Drew Thornton. It was more than coincidental that the same type of weapon and ammunition was used for both the Berry murder and Drew's shooting. Regardless, Ralph knew that Drew couldn't have pulled it off without inside assistance from someone in the Lexington Police Department who could guarantee the incident would receive but a whitewash of scrutiny.

Henry Vance's name had never been sullied by public association with any members of The Company. But after the "shooting" at the Merrick Inn, Vance's boss—the Speaker of the House—was questioned by the press about Vance's relationship with suspected international drug smugglers.

Speaker Bobby Richardson initially defended Vance's friendship with Drew. "While I may not approve altogether of his friends, it's nothing that I think affects his ability to do his job," Richardson told the *Louisville Courier Journal.*

But when Richardson learned from reporters that Vance had been in regular contact with Drew while Drew was a fugitive, and that Vance had visited Drew in jail in North Carolina and lied on the visitor registration by claiming to be Drew's attorney, then Richardson lost his patience. "I expect him [Vance] to exercise discretion and I would be much happier if he had no further association with Thornton."

Finally, when a Lexington television station reported that Vance had been questioned three times in connection with the Berry murder, Vance was forced to resign his thirty-six-thousand-dollar-a-year position with the Kentucky state legislature.

■

The Special Operations team had been under the direction of Don Powers for several months by the time the Berry murder investigation was
heating up in Kentucky. Neil Welch had put Powers in control in order
to free Ralph up for availability to Welch on other special assignments.
Most of the undercover detectives were working on the Jimmy Lambert
drug investigation and the Rebecca Moore homicide, and though Ralph
was kept informed of the status of the probes, he was not involved with
the day-to-day details.

By March of 1982, Powers had become concerned with "leaks"
from the team. It seemed to him that members of the Lexington Police
Department and Lambert himself knew too much about the team's operations. Powers reported the security problem to State Police Commissioner Marion Campbell. A few days later, Campbell approached Ralph
Ross and practically begged him to retake control of the surveillance
team.

Ralph was skeptical of Campbell's request. The rivalry between
Campbell and Neil Welch had become legendary among the ranks.
Campbell was a "good ole boy" from Morehead, Kentucky, who had
fought long and hard to become state police commissioner—traditionally an extremely powerful position in state government. But Governor
John Y. Brown, Jr., had emasculated him when he recruited Neil Welch
and created a separate Criminal Justice Cabinet under Welch's direction. For the first time in Kentucky history, the state police was not a
fiefdom for the powers that be. Technically, the chain of command
precluded Campbell from exerting any power or influence over Ralph or
any of the men from Welch's special forces—a situation that greatly
irked Campbell.

Though suspecting that Campbell must have ulterior motives,
Ralph decided he could use the group of men he had earlier recruited
and trained to gear up the Bonnie Kelly/Henry Vance investigation. His
only disappointment in the crew was the fact that Terry Barnes—who
he had previously reprimanded—had been returned to *Special Operations* while Ralph had been less involved with the team.

Strategically, Ralph thought it was time to shift attention away
from Lambert onto Bonnie Kelly. If handled right, the Gene Berry
murder case could "open the whole can of worms."

Ralph believed that the Company's Kentucky nexus was finally coming unglued, and that with pressure properly applied upon the right individuals, their world would start to crumble. Everyone was vulnerable: Bonnie Kelly, Mike Kelly, Drew Thornton, Bradley Bryant, Henry Vance, Harold Brown, and a slew of others who were practically stumbling over each other to plead guilty in Fresno. Any one of the Lexington individuals, Ralph felt certain, could help solve Melanie Flynn's disappearance and Ray Ryan's murder; infiltrate Lambert's drug organization; expose corruption within the Lexington Police Department; shed light on the network of mercenaries training at Triad; locate the source of massive quantities of weapons, apparently embezzled from various military bases, and transported to Central and South America; and identify the financial investors in Kentucky who fronted the capital used to purchase the necessary airplanes, landing strips, refrigerated trucks, and yachts, and put up the collateral to give the Colombians in exchange for the loads of marijuana and cocaine.

It was the latter group of individuals who Ralph believed needed to be taken down—the lawyers, bankers, politicians, horse breeders, and prominent Lexington businessmen—who were the *real* kingpins. But they were untouchable, segregated by several strata of underlings who fell under the control of Drew Thornton.

It appeared that the hierarchy of the Company was now headed by Drew and comprised of importers and transporters. Someone else was in charge of national distribution, though it wasn't clear who had replaced Bradley Bryant in that capacity. Still others were responsible for supplying the local elite—the jet-setting racehorse crowd—and for compromising the cops and public officials through bribery and blackmail. That's where the women entered the picture: Girls from Cincinnati, Lexington, New York, and Florida, who lured politicians into dangerous dalliances. Then there were the enforcers—the thugs who killed witnesses, snitches, prosecutors, and anybody else who knew too much and wasn't keeping his mouth shut.

So who did Drew report to? Ralph found himself wondering almost obsessively. He had never considered Drew Thornton to be much of a self-starter. Drew's psychological makeup was one of *allegiance.* Ralph was certain that Drew took his cues from someone else. Like the ninjas he revered, Drew was comfortable only while *serving* a superior system.

How did a guy such as Drew Thornton, reared with the belief that national policy and the American way of life should not be questioned or criticized, justify his activities? How did he transform his personality from the fanatical zealot pursuing long hairs and pot smokers in 1970 to becoming one of the nation's largest wholesale marijuana and cocaine importers? Had Drew's decision to join the police force been a calculated stepping stone for a life of crime? Or were the Lexington Police, as Drew often claimed, merely a cover for his real role as a covert operative for the CIA? Ralph's only hope was to cultivate a source deep within the group.

■

The first time Ralph's eyes landed on Betty Gee he saw a pudgy, timid, sweet-dispositioned girl who was the product of a stereotypical eastern Kentucky upbringing. One of Bonnie's many siblings, Betty was several years younger than her zaftig sister. She had spent her years on the outskirts of Bonnie's more adventurous life, tagging along with her big sister and brother-in-law through their nefarious episodes. Along the way she had seen and heard a lot. She knew Bradley Bryant, Drew Thornton, Henry Vance, and Bill Canan, and all the rest of Mike Kelly's friends. In fact, several of Mike's buddies had made sexual advances to her throughout the years, and some had been successful.

Mike and Bonnie had made her feel a part of their group, though her perpetual status as a kid was so deeply ingrained that it created a permanent sense of inferiority. They trusted her with their secrets in an offhanded way. Through their unguarded remarks, Betty Gee was told what happened to Melanie Flynn; where illegal automatic weapons were buried; which police officers were on the take; and the mechanics of sundry dope deals. Through her own observance, Betty had inadvertently learned the ins and outs of big-time drug smuggling and contract murder.

On the April day in 1982 when Ralph Ross headed across a bumpy country road to interview Betty Gee, even he underestimated the vastness of her knowledge and the potential value of her testimony.

"A friend introduced us," is all Ralph would ever tell anyone, declining to identify the go-between.

Ralph knew that Betty was easy prey. Things were falling apart around her. Hollimon and Taylor had both confessed and fingered Bonnie. Betty had been arrested with Bonnie and Taylor a few weeks earlier in Fort Lauderdale when agents from the FDLE discovered a .44-caliber magnum pistol on the floor of their automobile. Charges had been dropped but Betty felt the heat anyway. By this time Ralph knew that Betty had accompanied Bonnie to K-Mart to steal the records of the ammo purchase. He knew that Bonnie had told Betty of her plans to kill Berry. Facing murder conspiracy charges herself, Betty was a pretty scared kid. She knew it was only a matter of time before she would be arrested and she didn't feel a sense of loyalty or protection from her older sister's organization.

As Ralph played his good-guy routine with Betty, he found she was relatively easily persuaded to cooperate. Finally, realizing she was between a rock and a hard place, and that Ralph Ross had the wherewithal to send her to jail, Betty agreed to talk about what she knew.

After a slow start, she ultimately poured out her heart to Ralph, as handfuls of witnesses—male and female alike—had done before. She succumbed to his unassuming manner, his soft-spoken, fatherly method of interrogation. Terrified of retribution by Bonnie's criminal associates, she found solace in Ralph's promises of protection. Determined not to do anything that would harm her sister and fearful of the wrath of the rest of her family, her tears were soothed away by Ralph. He assured her that now was the time for Betty to think only of herself and the possibility of a lifetime in jail for her role in the grisly murder.

But Ralph worried about Betty's pliability. He had seen plenty of witnesses like Betty Gee before. Vulnerable and uneducated as she was, her cooperation was only guaranteed to whomever had physical custody of her. She could just as easily flip-flop, Ralph thought, and become a double agent—working both sides against each other. The key was to keep control of her, Ralph knew. He immediately arranged to take her to Lexington where her notarized statement could be obtained.

When Ralph Ross and Betty Gee arrived at the office of Commonwealth Attorney Larry Roberts, both were surprised and disappointed by the presence of a Lexington police detective, who had apparently been invited by Roberts to participate in Betty's interrogation.

With good reason, Betty Gee was frightened for her life. She was afraid of her brother-in-law, Mike Kelly, and of Henry Vance and Drew Thornton. Betty was savvy enough to realize that Kelly, Vance, and Thornton would know the details of her testimony within hours, thanks to their spies in the Lexington Police Department. Yet, even as Ralph promised to protect her, he knew she was right. "I'll do everything I can," he told her. "No one will touch you. You just tell the truth and don't worry about anything else." Besides, Ralph thought, you don't have much choice. Betty complied, providing a lengthy, detailed statement that, unbeknown to her, would be the final nail in Bonnie's legal coffin.

A week earlier Bonnie had been arrested in Lexington and charged with first-degree murder. Wearing a bulletproof vest, she had appeared calm and confident at a brief extradition hearing, at which papers signed by Governor John Y. Brown, Jr., ordered her remanded to the custody of the state of Florida. Afraid there would be an attempt on her life, Florida police had asked Kentucky authorities to do everything within their power to guarantee Bonnie's safe arrival in Fort Myers. The Lexington police, under Bizzack's direction, organized two sets of automobile convoys: One to transport Bonnie from the courthouse to Blue Grass Airport, and the other as a decoy to mislead the swarm of news reporters and television crews.

Incarcerated in Florida under intensive protective custody while awaiting trial for the murder of an enormously popular state prosecutor in what appeared to be an airtight case, Bonnie's conviction was nearly a *fait accompli.* Henry Vance's memory had conveniently quavered following Bonnie's arrest, and he was no longer certain he had seen Bonnie on the night of the murder. Ralph had persuaded Betty that there was nothing in the world that Betty could do to hurt Bonnie. There was, however, one thing that Betty could do to *help* her sister, Ralph added. She could save Bonnie from the electric chair.

With the preponderance of evidence against her, Bonnie's only possible bargaining chip would be a sentence reduction. Since murder is a capital offense in the state of Florida, it was highly likely that Bonnie would receive a death sentence if convicted. If, however, she were willing to testify against Henry Vance for providing her with the murder weapon, or to implicate Drew Thornton or any other co-conspirators, Ralph felt certain the judge could be persuaded to spare Bonnie's life.

Ralph's mission with Betty, then, was to induce her to convince Bonnie to talk—not only about the murder of Gene Berry, but about a decade of violence in central Kentucky.

■

Late one evening, Ralph pulled his car up to a stoplight near the Lansdowne Shopping Center. As he reached down to change the radio frequency, he glanced over at a car rolling to a stop beside him. He and Drew recognized each other at the same moment.

Their staring match became more uncomfortable with each passing second. Afraid that Drew might pull a gun, or something equally regrettable, Ralph decided to make the first move. He pressed the button to roll down his window, watching as Drew did the same.

"Hey there," Ralph said.

When Drew accompanied his response with a smile, Ralph continued.

"What are you doing?"

"Oh, just riding around," Drew answered.

Ralph's men had Drew under surveillance, and had been in radio contact with Ralph. Ralph knew that Drew knew that Ralph was in the area because of the surveillance. But both men played out the string, pretending that their meeting had been a chance encounter.

"Why don't you and me go have a beer?" Ralph said, gesturing behind him at a bar called Brewbakers.

Drew nodded in acquiescence and the two rivals headed their cars into the parking lot.

As they entered the bar, Ralph noticed that the woman who was with Drew was accompanying him into Brewbakers.

"Do you mind if she joins us?" Drew asked. Ralph turned toward the woman he recognized as a "Sharp"—but he wasn't sure if it was Rebecca or Sally.

"If we're going to have a conversation, it'll be one on one," Ralph replied emphatically. "There aren't going to be any third parties. We're going to be even up. Otherwise, we might as well forget it."

Drew directed his friend to a seat at the opposite end of the room. Drew and Ralph took seats next to each other at the bar, each intentionally ordering a beer instead of something stronger.

Before they had had time to take a sip, two of Ralph's men entered the establishment and planted themselves at the other side of the bar from Ralph and Drew. Nervous about this unplanned meeting between their boss and their target, the two fidgeted while awaiting some kind of signal from Ralph. Ralph winked at them, and they inferred from his gesture that they should sit tight until further notice. Each ordered a Coke since they weren't allowed to drink on duty. Drew looked in their direction as if to acknowledge that *he* knew they were cops.

"What have you been doing with yourself?" Ralph asked Drew. "Waiting around for your trial?"

"I don't hold anything against you, you know," Drew answered, avoiding getting sucked into revealing anything to Ralph about his activities. "You and I are not that different. You do what you have to do and I do what I have to do. We both have to remain loyal to our personal convictions. Regardless of the consequences."

Ralph was slightly surprised at Drew's amiability and candor. Was his lack of animosity genuine? He listened carefully, often finding himself nodding in agreement as Drew spoke of his ideology and survivalist philosophy. He was a survivalist who thought the world was facing economic collapse, he told Ralph. His actions, Drew emphasized, were *always* in direct accordance with his personal dogma. He never deviated from his beliefs, Drew told Ralph. The ends justified the means.

"Dealing drugs and killing people don't really fit in with any moral convictions I know of," Ralph answered.

"We're just part of two different systems," Drew responded, hinting that his actions were sanctioned by someone or something superior to both men. "We're more alike than you want to admit."

Ralph thought it useless to attempt to extract any valuable information or specific details from Drew. It was obvious to both men that they were playing a mind game in order to defuse what might have been a volatile exchange.

Upon finishing his one beer, Drew stood to leave. "Do me a

favor," Drew said. "No matter what happens, just make sure *she* never gets hurt," Drew said, gesturing toward the Sharp woman.

■

The month of May 1982 would be the absolute worst time in Ralph Ross's entire life. It had started out fine—almost too good to be true. As happens in Kentucky every spring, the landscape that year burst with almost obscene beauty. Accompanying his boss, Neil Welch, to the Derby, Ralph was able to observe the betting habits of the state's big-wigs, who were unaware of being in the scope of Ralph's suspicious eye.

For the first time in a decade, Ralph had a bonafide Company insider in the form of Betty Gee. He had placed her in the protective custody of one of his female detectives, who was shuttling her in and out of motels and safehouses around northern Kentucky. As soon as Betty had given the Florida people everything they wanted on the Berry murder, Ralph started working her on the Kentucky matters. He arranged for a backhoe and went with her to Mike Kelly's farm in Jessamine County. She led Ralph to a spot where she had been told that a machine gun, which had been stolen from the home of a coal company executive, was buried. Ralph's men dug and, sure enough, they found it. She said she had been told by Bonnie and Mike that if Henry Vance or Drew Thornton ever came to her and said they needed the gun that she should lead them to the burial site. She had never seen the gun before, she said, but had been told it was buried a certain amount of steps from the fence line.

One by one, Ralph checked out the particulars of Betty's statement. He had no reason to disbelieve the things Betty had said, for she had enough sense to know the magnitude of trouble she could face if she lied. But Ralph was by nature a cautious man, and was reluctant to become overly excited. In his typically methodical fashion, Ralph focused on the credibility of her allegations and possible loopholes. She claimed under oath that Drew Thornton and several other Lexington police officers had used Mike Kelly's residence as a general meeting place where large amounts of drugs were frequently stored. Betty also said that dozens of two-way radios that had been stolen from the Lexington Police Department years earlier were stored at Kelly's house on

Mount Tabor Road. Ralph had long been interested in the case of the missing walkie-talkies; he had been told by his sources within the Lexington police that Drew Thornton had been the suspect in the theft but the department had refused to investigate the case. Betty also said that Vance, Mike Kelly, and Bill Canan had bombed the home of a chief justice of the Kentucky Supreme Court. Ralph was able to verify that such a bombing had indeed occurred ten years earlier, but had resulted in no injuries and no arrests.

Encouraged by the retrieval of the illegal machine gun, Ralph was anxious to pursue Betty's professed knowledge of Melanie Flynn's disappearance. Melanie had been causing problems for the group, according to Betty's version of events. Melanie was evidently rebeling against doing Drew's dirty work.

Betty said she had been told by her sister Bonnie that Melanie Flynn had been murdered and was buried in a rock quarry at the bank of the Kentucky River. One day, Betty had been in a car with Bonnie driving to Halls-on-the-River—the restaurant and local hangout just downriver from Jimmy Lambert's cabin. As they passed a cave at the side of the road, Bonnie had pointed and said, "That's where Melanie Flynn is."

On a crisp May afternoon, Ralph's men again followed Betty Gee to a remote location, this time with even more excavation equipment. As they pulled to the side of the road, they were less than a quarter of a mile from Jimmy Lambert's cabin where Rebecca Moore had last been seen alive. Ralph found the similarity of the quarry with the description provided by the psychic about Melanie Flynn's death bed eerie. He thought of the psychic's vision—the underwater rock cliff; a deep horseshoe cavern; Melanie's body bag attached to a steel girder.

For hours, the state police team searched the quarry. But five years had passed and the cave had been flooded more than once, making it nearly impossible to find anything. Ralph couldn't hide his disappointment. He knew he had to call an end to the search; but as he did so he sensed that he was saying good-bye forever to the possibility of finding Melanie Flynn. If she ever turned up, Ralph thought, it would be entirely by accident.

Despite the failure to find Melanie Flynn, Ralph's investigations were shaping up nicely. Drew Thornton was subpoenaed to Louisiana where his buddy Richard Merrill had recently been indicted on drug charges. Drew dyed his hair gray, and sported a bushy, fake mustache, platform shoes, and a three-piece suit when he appeared before the federal grand jury in New Orleans so that co-conspirators wouldn't recognize him and think he had become a snitch.

Drew was scheduled to be sentenced the following month in the China Lake case and was certain to receive jail time—despite the fact that Lexington police officers had told federal probation authorities about Drew's sterling reputation as a lawyer and police officer. With Drew Thornton, Mike Kelly, Bradley Bryant, and Bonnie Kelly incarcerated, Ralph felt his job was becoming easier. He split his men between his two main targets, Jimmy Lambert and Henry Vance, with Vance receiving the most attention.

The Lambert surveillance was in full force by May of 1982. Ralph was receiving good information from his sources who had access to Lambert, and Betty's statement had underscored Ralph's belief that Company members associated frequently with Lambert and Lambert's rich horsey-set friends. According to Betty, Drew and the Kellys visited Lambert on a regular basis.

Ralph felt an obligation to notify Neil Welch of the burgeoning Lambert investigation—considering its political sensitivity. The probe had suddenly quickened and a state police raid on Lambert's house seemed imminent.

Ralph found that Welch was not surprised by the information. "Isn't he [Lambert] the guy I see over at Cave Hill all the time with Brown?" Welch asked Ralph.

"That's him," Ralph responded.

"Well then," Welch said to Ralph, "the governor's got a problem, doesn't he?"

"Yep. He sure does," Ralph replied.

Welch told Ralph he considered it his duty to warn John Y. to distance himself from Jimmy Lambert.

Ralph disagreed with Welch's assessment that he should inform the governor about such a delicate probe, assuming that Brown would tip off Lambert and the investigation would be blown. But as it turned out, Welch's warning didn't change anything. Brown adopted the attitude that Lambert had been a friend for many years, and he was not about to discontinue his friendship with Lambert just because Lambert might be suspected of some kind of wrongdoing. When Brown continued associating with Lambert despite the admonition, Ralph, and apparently Welch, decided anything was fair game.

Ralph also made the tactical decision that the lion's share of his investigators' attention should be focused upon Henry Vance. Betty had told him that Vance was a main figure in the Florida murder conspiracy, but for some baffling reason, Florida authorities seemed uninterested in pursuing Henry Vance, despite the existence of an abundance of evidence against him. Even though Florida didn't want him, Ralph did. The fact that Vance was so active as a political figurehead in Kentucky worried Ralph. As a lobbyist, Vance had gone to great lengths to defeat Welch's proposed anti-crime and racketeering legislation, which would have made it much more difficult for organized crime to operate in Kentucky.

C H A P T E R
SEVENTEEN

On the morning of May 18, 1982, Ralph parked his unmarked state police car behind the federal building and entered through the rear door. He took the elevator to the third floor and walked down the long corridor to the United States attorney's office. The receptionist greeted him and gestured toward an open door. "Mr. Trevey's waiting for you," she said.

Ralph entered the office, exchanging pleasantries with assistant U.S. Attorney Robert Trevey. Trevey handed Ralph the court order he had drawn up. Ralph read it, thanked him, and walked down to the U.S. magistrate's office.

Without hesitation, Magistrate James Cook signed the document ordering the installation of a pen register on the telephone line of Henry Vance.

Ralph walked outside into the bright midday sun and headed on foot toward the phone company located a few blocks away. Serving the court order on an official of the company, Ralph instructed him to have a technician run Henry Vance's phone line into Ralph's apartment. Ralph then drove home to get his equipment ready.

The state police had purchased two pen registers under the direction of Neil Welch, and this was not the first time they had been used. Ralph retrieved one of the registers—which looked like a stereo receiver—from the trunk of his car, along with a telephone handset and a bundle of brightly colored wires. He had decided to install the device in his apartment for security reasons. He knew there had been a leak from his team, and if the pen register were installed in the state police office, chances were good that Henry Vance would learn of its existence immediately.

Ralph hooked the register up to his phone jack. From that moment forward, the starting and stopping time for every call made from Henry Vance's telephone line would be recorded, as well as the number called. The device would also denote the time and date of all incoming calls, but not the origination of the call.

Although the content of the phone conversations could be heard through the handset, to listen to the conversations fell outside the legal scope of the court order. Ralph had no authorization to wiretap Henry Vance, but merely to determine the identity of individuals with whom Vance was in contact.

Ralph used the handset to test the equipment. The sound of voices assured him the machinery was operational. He gave a key to his apartment to Terry Barnes and told Barnes to check on the equipment twice a day for the next few days while Ralph went out of town. Despite reservations he had about Barnes's competence, Ralph selected Barnes since he was the highest-ranking officer on Ralph's team and it was a matter of investigative delicacy. The state police were responsible for the equipment in Ralph's apartment, and the phone company was responsible for the rest of the lines. It was therefore imperative that the pen register be checked regularly to ensure nothing went haywire that would alert Vance to interference on his phone line. Ralph explained the equipment to Barnes and told him that if there were any problems he should call the FBI's sound man. Ralph had previously made arrangements with the FBI to be available to help Barnes if necessary.

The next day, Ralph, Don Powers, and Betty Gee boarded a Delta jet bound for Fort Myers, Florida, to meet with Betty's incarcerated sister, Bonnie Kelly. They all hoped that Betty could persuade Bonnie to talk. But Bonnie refused to meet with Ralph and Don, and after two days of tearful episodes between the women, during which Bonnie accused Betty of betraying her, Ralph decided the attempt was futile.

The three were back in Lexington by Friday, May 21.

The minute he walked through the door, Ralph knew that someone had ransacked his apartment. His daughter Christie was living with him at the time, but Ralph had made sure she didn't stay in the apartment alone while he was in Florida. Someone had obviously gone through all of the drawers and closets in both Ralph's and Christie's bedrooms. Their letters and personal effects had been rifled. The first thing Ralph checked was the pen register, which seemed to have been untouched. He then checked his grocery sack full of micro-cassette tapes—recordings that he had made throughout years of undercover investigations. They didn't appear to have been touched. Ralph made a mental inventory and felt certain that nothing was missing.

He assumed that some of Vance's boys were the culprits. Or possibly the Lexington police, trying to find out what he was up to. By this point in time, Ralph felt as if *everyone* was following him: Members of Drew Thornton's group, the Lexington police, and some of Butch Campbell's boys in the state police who wanted to keep tabs on Welch's God Squad. Ralph didn't really give a damn. They could follow him all they wanted, as far as he was concerned. But breaking into his apartment was overstepping the invisible boundaries. Ralph wasn't worried about his own safety, but he didn't like subjecting Christie to danger. He had a shotgun, a magnum, a .38, and a .22, so he felt as if he was in pretty good shape, but the thought of someone boldly entering his apartment angered him.

On Saturday, Ralph left early in the morning to pick up Betty Gee. He had earlier arranged to drive her to Mike Kelly's mother's house because Mrs. Kelly had asked Betty to retrieve all of Bonnie's belongings. With Mike and Bonnie both in jail, Mrs. Kelly apparently didn't want the responsibility of storing their possessions. The contents of the cartons included credit-card receipts, equipment for processing cocaine, and an ATF evidence bag full of gun silencers. Betty turned everything over to Ralph as soon as they left the residence.

The next day Ralph attended a family function in Boyle County. He had placed Scotch tape, sticky side up, on the carpet—staggering the tape throughout the hallways and bedrooms of the apartment so he could tell if anyone entered in his absence. When he returned home late Sunday night, he discerned that someone had stepped on the tape in several locations. Still, nothing had been stolen and the pen register remained intact.

Ralph arose early Monday morning, read the local newspaper, and gulped down a cup of coffee. He dressed in gabardine slacks, an oxford shirt with the sleeves rolled three-quarters length and turned inside, and a pair of polished brown ankle boots.

First he drove by the surveillance team's headquarters—an apartment in the area rented by the state police. The team on duty briefed him on the weekend activities of Henry Vance, Drew Thornton, and Bill Canan. Ralph told them he was en route to a house near Mount Tabor Road that he was considering renting for a new surveillance post. He felt it was time to establish a different headquarters since the investigation was percolating rapidly. The new location was more centrally situated between the Kelly, Vance, Thornton, Canan, and Lambert residences. Ralph purposely neglected to mention the break-in of his apartment, but reiterated his concerns about security. He didn't suspect anyone on his team of intentional leaks, instead blaming any breaches on sloppiness. The worse threat to an undercover investigation of this magnitude, Ralph knew from experience, was a loose mouth over off-duty cocktails. Ralph ordered everyone to tighten up. He asked Barnes to return his house key, but Barnes claimed he had forgotten to bring it to work. Strange answer, Ralph thought.

Fleetingly, Ralph contemplated questioning Barnes about the bizarre entries to his apartment. He eyed Barnes with distrust for a few seconds, as if about to speak, then decided to wait.

"Go get the key," Ralph told him. "I'll be back for it this afternoon."

After looking over the new surveillance post, Ralph headed his car southwest toward Harrodsburg. He was scheduled to rendezvous with Betty at a remote country hideaway in order to return Bonnie's charge-card receipts and drug paraphernalia. Ralph should have realized that he was being followed. But he had trained his men so efficiently that even *he* was unable to detect their presence. He spent several hours with Betty sifting through Bonnie's financial records, then drove twenty-five miles north to Frankfort, where he had a stack of paperwork to sort through, and phone calls to return. He had been away from the office for nearly a week, so he was behind in fulfilling the more bureaucratic duties of his job.

When Ralph returned to Lexington that evening, his daughter Christie was waiting for him. They had been expected an hour earlier at his sister Thelma's house for dinner. Since he was running late, Ralph didn't take the time to stop by the surveillance post to retrieve his key from Sergeant Terry Barnes. Instead, he went to dinner and returned home in time to watch the eleven o'clock news. Just as it ended, Ralph fell into bed with exhaustion.

■

Ralph reached for the phone before it had finished its first ring. He had been sleeping fitfully anyway, half-expecting something to happen.

The digital clock glowed in the darkness of his bedroom, its bright red numerals calling out: 3 A.M.

"I need some help."

Ralph recognized the voice as that of one of his men—Terry Barnes. Why in the hell was Barnes calling at this hour?

"I'm all by myself and I need some help."

"Why don't you call some of the guys on your surveillance team," Ralph responded, assuming there were still a few men on duty.

"They've all gone home for the night," Barnes answered.

"Why haven't you gone home too?"

"I let 'em all go, and I was just fixin' to leave," Barnes said. "I'm out here at the Lansdowne Shopping Center and Drew Thornton and Bill Canan and the whole gang are up here and they have me surrounded. I'm in trouble and I need your help," Barnes pleaded with his boss.

Still struggling to awaken, Ralph couldn't comprehend what Barnes was saying. None of it made any sense to Ralph: Barnes shouldn't have been alone at the shopping center across the street from Henry Vance's townhouse in the middle of the night. What in the hell was going on? Ralph had made little secret of his distrust of Barnes. Barnes's refusal to return Ralph's key the day before combined with the intrusion on his apartment had prompted Ralph to question Barnes's credibility even more. Something didn't ring true with this cockamamy story. But regardless of his distaste for Barnes, Ralph couldn't turn his back on *any* of his men.

"All right," Ralph answered. "I'll be there in a few minutes."

Swinging his long legs out one side of the king-sized bed, Ralph reached to turn on the bedside lamp. He went to the closet and grabbed a pair of Levis, throwing them and a shirt on as fast as he could. He placed his .357 magnum in his briefcase, and slid his .38 into a sheath on his leg.

He bailed out of the front door of his apartment, leaping down the concrete steps toward his parked car. Fumbling for the key to his car, he heard a noise across the parking lot.

"Just as I was fixing to unlock my car door I see two heads pop up from behind a car at the other end of the parking lot. As I looked up, one starts toward me and the other heads in another direction. I didn't recognize either of them and . . . well . . . at this point I'm kind of expecting to get it. I'm still thinking it's Thornton's bunch. So I dropped between the two cars where I could see through the windows. I reached into my briefcase and was trying to get hold of my magnum and at the same time was trying to determine what they were going to do. What I didn't know was they were behind me and all around through the parking lot. They were going to kill me is what they were going to do.

"Then I hear: 'Hey, Ross. This is Larry. You're under arrest. Don't shoot.' And I recognize the voice of Larry Fentress—the state police attorney. Then I didn't know what was going on. They started coming out from all over the place. They were behind me. On the sides. On the front. Five of them, all state police. I had known them all for years and years.

"When I think back on it I know what they were planning. They knew I'd come out of the apartment carrying a gun—especially with the story they gave me about one of my guys being in trouble. They knew I'd be responding to one of my troopers in serious danger, in a life-threatening situation, and that I'd be mentally psyched up for a confrontation. And I know that if I had ever pulled that magnum out of that case they'd have blowed me into a million pieces. That's what they were posed for.

"I didn't know what it was all about. But I just couldn't get over the way they had done it. I kept asking them: 'What's wrong with you guys? Why did you want to do that?' I knew what they were doing. You don't effect an arrest in that manner unless your sole purpose is to try to get the guy to come out armed so you can blow him away and claim self-defense. You know, say the guy fired on a policeman. You just don't do that to someone—especially a fellow police officer—unless you're prepared to kill him.

"They could have walked up to my door and knocked on it. They had a key that I had given to Terry Barnes—they could have come up and unlocked the door. They could have called me on the phone. They could have come there in the daytime. They could have done it while I was at work. They didn't have to call me out in the middle of the night, ready for battle.

"It makes you really wonder why they want you that bad. It's hard to believe that an organization that you've been a part of, devoted your life to, for twenty-six years would do you that way. Very hard to swallow."

■

Ralph accompanied the arresting officers back into his apartment. He wasn't handcuffed, and was allowed to sit on the sofa as the troopers executed what Ralph considered a limited search. He watched his colleagues go to the back bedroom and unhook the pen register. Then they went into a utility closet and took a suitcase Ralph kept that contained various tools: Handsets, screwdrivers, pliers, side cutters, volt meters, telephone wires. They took a Sony dictating machine, a tape recorder, and four tapes that didn't look familiar to Ralph. "They never really searched the apartment. They knew exactly what they were looking for and they didn't want anything else. For example, they left the whole grocery bag full of micro-cassettes," he recalled. From the trunk of Ralph's car the state police seized a brown briefcase containing two telephone receivers and an assortment of electrical devices.

Ralph was careful not to make any statements. He still didn't know what he was being charged with, and decided he'd better keep his mouth shut. Installing him in the back seat of a police vehicle, they drove him downtown to be booked into the county jail. But when the court officials called a judge by telephone, the judge ordered them to take Ralph back home.

Several hours later, at 9 A.M., Ralph drove himself to the courthouse to be arraigned.

"I still didn't know what the charge was. When I appeared

before the judge he was looking at a legal pad. After he read what was on it he said: 'I see here they searched your premises and that there was no wiretapping equipment hooked up. Is that correct?' I answered that was correct. Then the judge said there shouldn't be any problem and he turned me loose on my own recognizance. He said something about waiting to see what the grand jury decided."

Don Powers was waiting for Ralph when he returned home that morning. Together the two of them set about trying to determine what the bottom line was. Who had set him up? Terry Barnes? Commissioner Campbell? Henry Vance? Where was Neil Welch? One thing was obvious: Both the Henry Vance and Jimmy Lambert investigations would come to a screeching halt now that Ralph was out of the picture.

Powers had obtained a copy of an affidavit in support of the search warrant that had been signed at two o'clock that morning. Ralph shook his head in disbelief as he read it:

"Affiant has been an officer with the Kentucky State Police for a period of ten years and this information and observations contained herein were received and made in his capacity as an officer thereof.

"On May 18, 1982, at approximately 10:15 A.M. affiant observed Ralph Ross attach a telephone receiver to a pen register located in the back bedroom of his apartment. After the receiver was hooked up a red light came on and Ross said, 'Someone is talking right now.' Ross then listened to a telephone conversation between two females. After the receiver was hung up Ross stated to affiant, 'Whatever you do, don't tell anyone about this. We could get five years in the pen for it.'

"At approximately 6 P.M. on May 18, 1982, Ross told affiant that 'Vance was burning the phone up. He's calling lawyers and everyone. He said he wasn't going anywhere tomorrow except to Frankfort to pick up some things.'

"At approximately 8 P.M. on May 18, 1982, affiant observed Ross listen to a telephone conversation between persons, one of whom Ross stated was Bobby Richardson [Speaker of the House]. Ross also told affiant that earlier in the evening he had listened to a telephone conversation between Henry Vance and an unidentified party. Ross also said that he planned to hook up a recorder to the listening devices.

"On May 19, 1982, at approximately 11:25 A.M. Ross told affi-

ant that Vance burned the phone up last night. Canan called and the
shit got heavy. They were giving me down the road.

"On May 19, 1982, at approximately 1 P.M. affiant observed the
wiretapping equipment still in place in Ross's bedroom and at approximately 10 P.M. that date affiant photographed the equipment.

"Signed: Sergeant T. C. Barnes."

"The first thing I'd better do is get a lawyer," Ralph said to
Powers, never dreaming such an endeavor would be nearly impossible.

■

Ralph spent that last week of May in a frenetic attempt to comprehend
the severity of his situation. Within days of his arrest, a state grand jury
had returned an indictment against him, charging him with twenty-eight
felony counts: One count of installing eavesdropping equipment, and
twenty-seven counts of eavesdropping. If convicted, Ralph knew he
could face a lifetime in prison.

Almost immediately, it had become evident that Welch had been
the intended target of the investigation. The prosecuter had offered
Ralph a total dismissal of the charges against him if he would implicate
Welch. "You give us Neil Welch and you can walk free," they had told
Ralph. They wanted Ralph to admit to the wiretapping and testify that
he had been operating under Welch's directions and that Welch had
ordered the pen register and wiretap. Those who had framed Ralph also
wanted Welch out of the state of Kentucky before he netted any political
bigwigs, Ralph assumed.

Of alarming concern to him was Neil Welch's reaction—the man
acted as though he had never heard of Ralph Ross. Welch made no
attempt to contact Ralph or offer support, either emotional, professional, or legal. Ralph felt completely in the dark about his situation,
learning more from newspaper accounts than from anyone else. The
simmering interdepartmental feud between Justice Secretary Welch and
State Police Commissioner Campbell became combustible following
Ralph's arrest, as charges and countercharges made front-page headlines every day. "While Welch has admitted being familiar with the
Vance probe," the *Lexington Herald* reported, "he has said that the
State Police were responsible for Ross' activities. State Police Commis-

sioner Marion Campbell has vigorously denied that, saying Ross still reported to Welch." A story in the *Louisville Times* challenged Welch's denials: ". . . Numerous officers say Ross reported directly to Welch and no one else. 'Everybody in the state police knows it,' said one top-level police official. Ross was in Welch's office 'at least three days a week,' and had his own office down the hall."

Reading between the lines, Ralph saw the makings of a scape-goat. The real target was Welch. Irked at being kept in the dark about the Vance investigation, Campbell had relished the idea of arresting Ralph Ross and thereby embarrassing Welch. It had been Campbell who had *insisted* that Ralph retake control of the surveillance team; Campbell who *insisted* that Terry Barnes be reassigned to Special Operations. But why? Ralph wondered.

Ralph's feelings about Welch's public response were mixed. On the one hand, he realized that deniability was often necessary in a criminal investigation. He could understand Welch's need to insulate himself from any alleged illegalities. Such was the nature of the business, and Welch was famous for his ability to distance himself from his underlings when it was expedient to do so. But on the other hand, Ralph felt abandoned by his superior. When he read in the paper that Welch had requested the FBI to enter the wiretap investigation, Ralph thought that maybe Welch was trying to assist him from behind the scenes. Ralph had little faith in the district court system in Lexington where the judges, jurors, and prosecutors had incestuous political and personal affiliations. Ralph thought he could get a fair shake in federal court, and he assumed Welch was trying to help him out by getting the case transferred. But Larry Roberts, the commonwealth attorney, was fighting hard to keep the case. Roberts had never liked Ralph and knew that Ralph didn't trust him. Meanwhile, the FBI found the charges were groundless, and the U.S. attorney didn't want to prosecute the case, so Roberts won out.

The case was a political hot potato. Ralph began to panic when, by late summer 1982, he realized he was not going to be able to obtain first-rate legal counsel. No one wanted to take the case. He approached every major law firm in Lexington and they all turned him down. The reason given was conflict of interest. The lawyers were friends of the Vances. Or the Thorntons. Or the Kellys. Or Jimmy Lambert's. Ralph became more and more depressed as he approached attorneys in other Kentucky cities. Intimidated by the staggering fees of more than a hundred dollars per hour, he feared his defense could cost as much as fifty thousand dollars. The state police maintained a special fund to assist troopers who incurred legal problems as a result of their official duties. But Ralph was hearing rumors that state police officials intended to deny him eligibility for the compensation. Without financial help from the state, Ralph could face personal bankruptcy. But even destitution did not frighten him nearly so much as his inability to retain a lawyer. He knew that he needed a special type of attorney—a fighter, not a fixer.

Finally, a Frankfort attorney named Bill Johnson agreed to take the case. Ralph was initially skeptical of Johnson's close friendship with Commissioner Campbell, and uneasy about the fact that Johnson had defended many of the white-collar criminals whom Ralph had arrested in the past. But Ralph's options were limited. Besides, Johnson's country-lawyer courtroom finesse had earned him a statewide reputation.

Immediately, Johnson encouraged Ralph to accept the state's plea bargain offer to have the twenty-eight felony counts dropped. "Hell no," Ralph said with characteristic outrage. "Let's go fight it out in the courthouse."

In the weeks following Ralph's arrest, a swirl of controversy arose over whether or not Governor John Y. Brown, Jr., had listened to the twenty-seven conversations Ralph had allegedly tape-recorded. Reports circulated that Welch had played the tapes for Brown at Brown's behest. But in his testimony before the grand jury, Welch was vague about the incident, stating only that the governor knew more about the tapes than Welch did.

Governor Brown refused public comment about the tapes, but ordered Welch, Campbell, and Powers to submit to lie detector tests regarding their prior knowledge of the wiretapping. Welch and Campbell both claimed to have passed the tests, though the results were never released to the public, and Powers refused to take the polygraph. Ralph was told that Welch failed one polygraph and the results of the second one were inconclusive. It was during this time that the governor was overheard at a function remarking about Welch: "I can't get him back in his cage."

When United Press International reported that Ross had earlier recommended disciplinary action against his accuser, Terry Barnes, the governor denied that Ross's arrest was a vendetta. " 'This doesn't mean anybody was out to get anybody,' Brown said in a short interview . . . Brown said that he did not want to imply any guilt by Ross, but said that wiretapping 'will not be tolerated in this administration. I don't know anything that is more distasteful.' "

■

In early December 1982, Ralph bellied up to the bar at Brewbakers. Out of the corner of his eye he could see Drew Thornton jumping up from a table and heading out the door. Ralph stole a glance at Drew's drinking partners, and his heart skipped a beat as he recognized Henry Vance and Jimmy Lambert. They were eyeing him and squirming in their seats as if trying to figure out if Ralph had purposely, or accidentally, invaded their territory.

"How you doin'?" Drew said, as he slid onto the barstool next to Ralph.

Ralph figured Drew must have left the bar momentarily to get rid of his "piece"—for Drew had just been released from the Federal Correctional Institute in Lexington where he had spent 120 of his 180-day sentence. If he were caught in a bar carrying a gun, he'd be sent right back to the pen.

"Pretty good . . . considering," Ralph answered. "Let me buy you a drink."

This, their second chance meeting, would be the last time the two men would ever speak. They would see each other one more time, when Drew Thornton would take the witness stand a few days later in Ralph's trial and point his finger across the room at Ralph and say: "That's the man who sent me to prison."

"I can't say that I'm sorry about all your problems," Drew said.

"No," Ralph said, kind of chuckling. "Don't 'spose you would be."

"I *do* hope you don't have to spend any time in the can," Drew said, with uncharacteristic sincerity. "It's not a good place for a cop to be."

"How'd you spend your time in there?" Ralph asked him.

"Mostly trying to keep in shape. I read a lot of books and I worked out all the time. I ran. Lifted weights. Did my *t'ai chi*. It was a long four months."

Ralph nodded his head in understanding if not sympathy.

"Well, good luck to you," Drew said, popping up off his stool so fast that Ralph instinctively stiffened. "Like I said, I hope you don't have to pull any time," Drew said, courteously offering his hand to his arch enemy.

"But I hope you get your ass sued."

■

Snow fell against the windshield as Ralph maneuvered his car into a parking spot near the courthouse. Not until Ralph saw the television stations' vans with their rooftop microwave dishes set up for live shots did he believe that he was really going to stand trial.

For the first time since his arrest, he almost broke down. Ralph had harbored hopes that the judge would dismiss the indictment; that someone would save him from this humiliating circus. But when he saw the swarm of broadcast and print reporters milling about, he realized this was a show that was destined to go on.

The courtroom scene was a microcosm of Ralph's life. Gathered together, as if waiting to watch the gladiators, were his friends, enemies, and family members. An invisible magnet seemed to pull people to one side or another of the courtroom as at a wedding, dividing them in accordance with their loyalties. Ralph's sisters, his daughters, and his mother huddled together, flanked by several of Ralph's surveillance team members who were scheduled to testify as character witnesses for him. Across from them were Henry Vance, Drew Thornton, John Bizzack, Terry Barnes, and prosecuting attorney Larry Roberts. Wearing his uniform of khaki pants and navy blazer, his penny loafers gleaming, Vance paced the halls like a high-strung hunting dog. He scowled at everyone, true to his role as the outraged victim whose constitutional rights and privacy had been invaded by Ralph Ross.

The upcoming trial had the air of the best entertainment in town, promising high drama. A total of sixty-four witnesses—including Governor John Y. Brown, Jr., Neil Welch, two assistant U.S. attorneys, and the state's top law enforcement officials—had been subpoenaed to testify. Because of the political undercurrents, as well as the expected exposure of the inner workings of a fascinating international narcotics ring, the trial provided an arena for curious spectators.

Brown had asked that he be allowed to testify through deposition, rather than in person. But the judge had ruled that the governor would be "well advised" to obey his subpoena. The judge then announced that he intended to hear testimony until late every evening and on weekends if necessary, in order to complete the trial before the Christmas holidays began. Remarkably, the judge only allowed an hour and a half for *voir dire.* A jury was selected and the trial got underway on the first day. Following several motions, the attorneys offered differing portraits of Ralph Ross in their opening statements. The prosecutor described Ralph as an overzealous Lone Ranger cop who trampled on the civil liberties of his targets. Defense attorney Bill Johnson painted a portrait of a conscientious law enforcement officer who had been framed by a disgruntled underling. Johnson admitted that Ralph had monitored Vance's phone calls with a pen register—for which he had a court order —but suggested that Terry Barnes, who possessed a key to Ralph's apartment, was responsible for taping the telephone conversations in question. Johnson described Barnes as a "very disturbed person" who had once told the state police commissioner that he had hallucinations of "ghosts and hands coming out of a wall."

Testifying at night on the second day of the trial were Governor Brown, who claimed never to have heard the tapes, and Welch, who seemed to backtrack on his grand jury testimony, claiming he had no reason to believe that the governor had listened to the tapes.

The question of who had heard the tapes, and when, was of utmost significance to Ralph's defense. He believed that someone had tampered with the tapes before the trial. Of the twenty-seven conversations in question, none substantively reflected Vance's involvement in a murder and drug conspiracy, fueling Ralph's suspicion that the conversations had been purposely selected for their inconsequence. Ralph contended that the tape-recorded conversations were not in sequential order—which he attributed to the fact that the state police had not followed normal investigative procedure. At least two of the conversations were taped while Ralph was in Florida.

But prosecutor Larry Roberts pointed to the lack of substance on the tapes as evidence that Vance was not involved in the murder and drug conspiracy, but was a hapless victim of Ralph's renegade tactics. The prosecution called several witnesses the second day of the trial, who turned out to be better witnesses for Ralph, including several federal prosecutors.

Finishing off the first day of testimony, State Police Commissioner Campbell took the stand and confirmed Barnes's reported sighting of ghosts and hands. With that, Ralph's hopes for acquittal surfaced as Barnes's veracity surged to the forefront of the case.

On the second day of trial, the prosecution elicited testimony demonstrating that the evidence in the case had been properly handled, attempting to dispel notions of tampering. Several state police witnesses who had aided Barnes in setting up Ralph testified that they were afraid and jealous of Welch's God Squad.

In his cross-examination, Johnson intimated that there were locations other than Ralph's apartment where someone could tap Vance's telephone line with a handset. He also asked why the state police never tested the tapes to prove they had been made on Ralph's tape recorder. The state police hadn't even dusted them for fingerprints, Ralph's attorney pointed out.

Barnes took the stand on the fourth day. While admitting that he didn't like Ralph, Barnes denied that he had framed his former boss. During Barnes's testimony, Ralph became concerned that Johnson was not being aggressive enough. When Ralph suggested certain lines of questioning that he thought Johnson should pursue, Johnson reminded Ralph that *Johnson* was the lawyer.

"We've got four police officers who are obviously lying," Ralph said that night to Christie, "and my attorney won't even challenge their credibility."

On that day, the trial was thrown into chaos. Vance pleaded with the judge not to play four conversations in open court: Two of the taped conversations were between Vance's wife and her sister, and related to the emotional problems of Vance's daughter; a third conversation was about a domestic situation involving Vance's sister-in-law; and the fourth tape related to a conversation between Vance and a coworker regarding the job performance of a fellow legislative aide.

In an emotional entreaty, his voice quaking, Vance addressed the court: "They delve into the life of a twelve-year-old girl who didn't ask to have her name thrown around, who didn't ask for Ralph Ross to bug her father's phone." Vance complained that a public airing of the tapes would only serve to further invade the privacy of the participants.

Johnson argued that Ralph's right to a complete defense hinged upon full scrutiny of the evidence. Ralph needed to refer to the entire contents of the tapes in order to prove he didn't record them, Johnson said.

The judge ruled in favor of the defense, creating an air of excitement in the proceedings as spectators anticipated the Vances' dirty laundry being hung on the public line.

But the jurors and audience listened in apparent disappointment and boredom as the twenty-seven conversations were played. Ranging from casual discussions about Mrs. Vance's natural-food diet, to a relative's marital problems and their daughter's instability, the conversations were almost embarrassing in their triviality—common gossip and cattiness that anyone would dread having publicized.

The only suggestion that Vance was involved with the Company surfaced with two long-distance calls from Drew, who had been awaiting sentencing in Fresno at the time. During one conversation, Drew complained about the report prepared by the federal probation officers that referred to the relationship between him and Vance. When Drew asked Vance if things were going well at his end, Vance replied: "There's been more crap in the paper, stuff I'll talk to you about later—the kind of crap you'd expect." A week earlier, news stories had appeared implicating Vance in the Berry murder. The second call from Drew to Vance was brief, only long enough for Drew to ask Vance to return his call from another phone, as if Drew knew Vance's phone was tapped.

But after listening to five hours of recorded drivel, on the fifth day of the trial the testimony took a turn for the defense, as a dramatic fourteen-minute conversation between Betty Gee and Bonnie's attorney was played. The tape had been seized by state police during their raid on Ralph's apartment. Since it had been made with Betty's consent, the taping was not illegal; but because it had been obtained as part of the prosecution's evidence, Ralph's attorney insisted that it too be played.

Whatever stature Henry Vance enjoyed in the community was severely shaken by the Gee tape. For the first time, Vance was linked by testimony to the cold-blooded assassination of a public official.

Vance held his head in his hands as he listened to Betty's voice reverberate through the loudspeakers in the courtroom. At times he patted his wife's hand as she wept soundlessly. The jurors were clearly surprised by the blatancy of Betty Gee's claims, alternating glances from Vance to Ralph.

At the beginning of the conversation, Bonnie's lawyer asked Betty to sign a statement disputing the reports that Vance had given the gun to Bonnie. Betty refused, saying, "I know for a fact that Henry Vance gave Bonnie the gun."

"She told you that?" the attorney was heard asking Betty. *"The* gun or *a* gun?"

"The gun that was used to kill the guy," Betty answered. "Henry Vance is really involved in it all." She asked the lawyer if he knew about Vance "hiring two guys to kill that guy down there"—an apparent reference to an earlier attempt on Berry's life.

Later in the tape, Betty Gee said that both she and Bonnie feared for their lives. "Henry Vance has said he isn't going to jail for anyone. She [Bonnie] said she had signed a contract with several people, and if she didn't do what she was supposed to, that I would be the first to be killed," Betty said.

After another day during which jurors heard testimony from Drew Thornton, Rebecca Sharp, Henry Vance, and everyone else whose conversation had been recorded, the prosecution rested its case on a somewhat sour note.

After the Betty Gee tape, Ralph felt positive he could convince the jury of his innocence. With a sense of security he decided to take the stand in his own defense on the seventh day of trial.

For three and one half hours Ralph calmly answered questions put to him by attorneys for both sides. Exhausted and haggard, his gray suit hung loosely on the massive frame that had lost too much weight too fast. The once jovial face had the appearance of a grieving widower, the dark circles under the eyes belying his stature.

Yes, he had accompanied Neil Welch to the state legislature to propose legalized wiretapping. But no, he had not wiretapped Vance's telephone in retaliation because Vance had lobbied to defeat the bill.

Yes, it was true that the month-long surveillance of Vance had failed to turn up any evidence that Vance had committed a crime. But the purpose of the Vance investigation, Ralph said, was to ascertain Vance's relationship with other suspects in the Berry murder.

Yes, he had installed the court-ordered pen register and used a call-monitoring device to check that the equipment was working properly. But no, he had not listened in on any of Vance's conversations.

Ralph admitted that in addition to the pen register, he had also attached a bird dog—an electronic tracking device—to Vance's Mercedes-Benz sports car. But everything he did in connection with the Vance investigation, Ralph declared, was done within the boundaries of the law.

Asked if he had recorded the telephone conversations that had been played for the jury, Ralph responded: "No, sir. I did not."

To the contrary, Ralph testified, he had witnessed Terry Barnes listening to Vance's conversations on two occasions, and had reprimanded Barnes for so doing.

When the examination turned to the night of his arrest, Ralph paused to gain composure. But as the questioning proceeded, Ralph found he could not maintain control of his emotions. Clearly, he had not yet come to grips with the reality that his own agency had turned against him. As he began describing that fateful night's events, he tried to distance himself from his words. But when he relived crouching in fear in the parking lot of his apartment building, reaching for his magnum to fend off the two men who were moving toward him, his voice cracked. He realized then it had been a grave mistake to take the stand.

His hands quavering, he swallowed as he tried to stifle a sob. When he couldn't suppress the tumult in his mind, Ralph turned to the judge.

"Sir, could we take a recess?" He asked.

Before the judge ruled, Ralph was out of his chair and ducking behind an exhibit stand. His nineteen-year-old daughter Christie ran to embrace him, as the jurors and spectators watched the emotional disintegration of a once solid man.

Ralph listened in disbelief as his attorney told the court he would rest the case without calling more than a dozen of Ralph's character and alibi witnesses.

By the end of his testimony, Ralph felt totally uncomfortable with his legal counsel. He remembered his initial concerns about Johnson's relationship with Campbell and wished he had trusted his instincts. But what had his choices been? He hadn't been able to convince another lawyer in the state to take his case, so what could he expect?

Ralph couldn't shake the nagging feeling that his own lawyer had betrayed him. Suddenly, conviction seemed foregone. He had never felt so vulnerable in his life. He had a sinking feeling that he had placed his future in the hands of his enemy. Whenever Ralph had raised his concerns with Johnson, his lawyer hinted that it was perfectly natural for a man in Ralph's position to experience paranoid apprehension. It seemed to Ralph that Johnson had handled the prosecution witnesses with kid gloves; that he incorrectly decided against calling some of Ralph's best character witnesses and that he failed to raise objections during Ralph's cross-examination. Johnson assured Ralph that he was doing everything within his capacity.

■

The three days of jury deliberation were hell for Ralph Ross. By this point, he was sure the fix was in. He would be convicted, he knew, because everything was against him—even his own lawyer. As do most criminal defendants, Ralph blamed his attorney for the mess he was in. "He's the best prosecuting attorney the state had!" Ralph told relatives.

Ralph thought Johnson had been remiss in neglecting to elicit expert testimony that would have proven the tapes were not made in his apartment. He felt Johnson had not been forceful enough in his cross-examination, and questioned Johnson's decision to rest the case without calling character witnesses.

Ralph paced the halls as he waited for the jurors to return their verdict. They must be hung, he thought, for three days was much too long to decide. He watched as the bailiff popped his head in and out of the room, delivering notes from the prosecutor to the foreman. He watched as the jurors were allowed to come and go as they pleased, not having been sequestered. He had never seen such antics, and wondered at the propriety of outsiders contacting jurors during deliberation. He suggested to Johnson that perhaps they should move for a mistrial. No use, he was told. This was the epitome of bluegrass justice.

On the second day, the jury sent a note to the judge requesting a guarantee that Ralph would serve no jail time if the jurors found him guilty. When the judge responded that it was not within his rights to make such a promise, the jurors returned to their room for another day of battling.

"The jury has reached a verdict," the judge announced finally. It was midnight on the third day—a week before Christmas.

Ralph stared at the jurors as the foreman read their results. Guilty on fourteen counts of illegal eavesdropping. Not guilty of installing the wiretapping equipment, and not guilty on the additional ten counts. Three other counts had been dropped following motions during the trial. The jury urged leniency in each instance, recommending the minimum sentence of one year in prison on each of the fourteen counts.

The verdict made no rhyme nor reason to Ralph. Why would he be guilty of some but not others? To Ralph, it seemed an all or nothing situation.

The judge dismissed the jury, pounded his gavel, and set a sentencing date for after the new year.

Ralph didn't dread the sentencing nearly so much as he expected, so relieved was he that the trial was behind him. After experiencing the most miserable and depressing Christmas of his life, he was happy when 1983 finally rolled around.

In early January, Christie organized a surprise party for her dad's fiftieth birthday. She had invited Ralph's friends from the FBI, the U.S. attorney's office, and the state police. Most responded that they had prior engagements for that particular evening, but their thoughts were with Ralph. Neil Welch didn't even acknowledge the invitation, and there was an unspoken directive in the FBI that it would not be politic for any agent to appear at the event. The federal prosecutors sent their regards, but indicated they felt their presence would not be appropriate at the party of a convicted felon.

Despite the attitude of his colleagues, Ralph was touched by the turnout of friends and family. Wearing a white pullover V-neck sweater and tan slacks, he faced the crowd that had gathered in the recreation room of his apartment complex. As he looked around the room he saw people he had known in high school; loyal members of his surveillance team; his sisters, brothers-in-law, and nieces; his daughters; a few troopers who were proud to be aligned with Ralph; and some informants who had become friends, including Betty Gee. His voice cracked when he tried to speak.

"I just want to thank everyone for coming, and making this a right nice party." Naturally taciturn and slightly shy, Ralph swallowed hard and moved away from the center of attention. For the first time in several months Ralph felt his life returning to him. As he headed for the bar that was set up on a buffet table, he realized that the end of his ordeal was truly in sight. He filled a glass with Maker's Mark bourbon and silently toasted his guests.

On the morning of January 28, 1983, Judge George Barker called his court to order. Nearly every seat was filled in the spectators' section. The day before, Barker had denied motions by the defense for a new trial, a reversal of the verdict, and reduction of the charges from felonies to misdemeanors. "I don't believe Mr. Ross deserves to be put in jail," the judge said, beginning an unusual thirty-minute commentary.

Barker said that in all his years as a judge he had never received so much mail urging leniency for a defendant. He had also been presented with a petition bearing 2,800 signatures that had been circulated in three central Kentucky counties. A grocer from the county seat of Ralph's hometown who had initiated the petition told the judge that "putting a former state policeman in prison would be the same as murdering him."

The judge indicated he had received similar pleas from people who didn't know Ralph Ross personally, including four of the jurors who convicted him. "There is no question but that Mr. Ross enjoyed and still enjoys an outstanding record of faithful service, of dedicated service to his state," Barker said. He then quoted from one letter that referred to the irony of Mike Kelly's recent release from jail upon the reversal of his drug conviction. "Justice is strange," the letter said.

"The courts turn the crooks loose and convict the guys trying to catch the crooks."

Although the judge said he believed that Ralph was "entitled to leniency," he suggested that a request to have his conviction reversed should be directed to Governor John Y. Brown, Jr. "If I were governor," Judge Barker said, "I might be inclined to give clemency in this case."

Judge Barker then sentenced Ralph to a total of six years, but further reduced it to one year of unsupervised probation.

One thing Barker neglected to mention was the six-page presentencing report that had been compiled by probation officers. Delving into Ralph's personal and professional background, the report detailed Ralph's long history of service to both the FBI and CIA. Such intelligence connections lent credence to the theory that Ralph's investigation into Kentucky corruption might have been national in scope. The prosecution had been flustered by the eavesdropping equipment in Ralph's apartment, since it had been stamped: *Property of the U.S. Government.* They wanted to know how Ralph had obtained wiretapping equipment that belonged to the federal government, and whether it belonged to the FBI or CIA. When questioned about where he had gotten it, Ralph would say only that he had picked it up at a federal building in New York City. When asked who owned it, he claimed not to know.

■

Ralph spent the months following his trial in a fog of disbelief, anger, and sorrow. He dwelt constantly on the early days of the Kentucky State Police—back when it was an outfit to make one proud. Now, he felt ashamed to have been associated with such a group. Where could he go from here? The thought of future law enforcement was a moot point, for even if he wanted to, as a convict he could never again be employed as a police officer. His career destroyed and his personal life empty, Ralph somehow managed to preserve his conviction that he was right and that he would eventually be vindicated.

With hindsight vision, he blamed himself for allowing Terry Barnes access to something as sensitive as a pen register. The only guilt Ralph would admit to was the exercise of bad judgment, and he became obsessed with his shortsightedness concerning Barnes. Barnes had been a disciplinary problem more than once. He had falsified reports and lied about the number of hours he had worked. He refused to follow orders, and had once been charged with insubordination. Ralph should have considered the powerful vengeance of a male ego scorned. Ralph knew that Barnes was the type of guy who needed constant supervision; so how did he allow Barnes to insinuate himself into what Ralph thought was a secure system.

Ralph chastised himself for being remiss in checking out Barnes's background. As it turned out, Barnes had worked the streets of Lexington in the early 1970s with Henry Vance, Drew Thornton, and Bill Canan, and had remained friends with them for more than a decade. Barnes had even once been accused by his undercover informants of selling drugs—a fact that Ralph could have ascertained had he taken the time to peruse Barnes's personnel file. Ralph had recognized Barnes as a wild card, but had never suspected him of being a mole. Ralph should have taken more care in choosing his battles and his soldiers.

Ralph dwelled as well on Welch's continuing silence. Perhaps Welch, along with Ralph's many friends in the FBI, would help him in some back-channel fashion. Or had they already done so? Is that why his sentence had been reduced, and he had received special dispensation to carry a gun? After all of his years in service to the federal government—assisting both the CIA and FBI in dozens of investigations—Ralph couldn't believe Welch had left his "right hand man" twisting in the wind. He fostered a secret expectation of salvation in the form of Neil Welch.

At the beginning, on the surface anyway, it had seemed to Ralph that Welch adopted the attitude: "To hell with Ralph Ross. I've got to save my own rear end." But Ralph hoped that had been a facade, and that Welch had failed to respond because he was powerless to salvage his own reputation, much less that of Ralph Ross, in the political atmosphere that surrounded the case.

■

"Mr. Ross?" Ralph turned around from the lunch counter at a Lexington cafeteria.

"Mr. Ross?" the man repeated, holding out his hand and introducing himself. "I don't know whether or not you remember me, but I was one of the jurors in your case."

Ralph narrowed his eyes until he could conjure up a recollection of the man's face. Several months had gone by since his trial.

"I don't know how you feel about it, but I'd like to talk to you a minute if you don't mind," the man said.

Ralph nodded at the stool beside him, but the man remained standing.

"You know," the man had said, "the people on the jury wanted to turn you loose. In fact, we were all going to, except for one person. That's why we kept sending notes to the judge asking if he'd go easy on you. Because this guy insisted that if we didn't convict you that he was going to see to it that we had a hung jury, which would mean the next jury would really sock it to you."

Ralph listened as the man effusively apologized for the jury's actions, intimating he had later come to believe the case had been rigged.

"I just thought you should know this," the guy said, and then turned and walked away.

Ralph had often wondered if there had been jury tampering, for the verdict hadn't made sense. Nothing about the case had made sense, for that matter—the charges or the verdict.

At least this man's version offered a semblance of explanation: The case had been fixed. There had been one holdout determined to hang tough.

CHAPTER

EIGHTEEN

Ralph's diary and personal notebooks, which were seized by state police when they raided his apartment, had thrown a monkey wrench into Ralph's criminal case. Expecting to find references to the Henry Vance surveillance, investigators were stunned to find notations about Jimmy Lambert and Governor John Y. Brown instead.

Ralph obviously had a well-placed informant who was supplying him with information about cocaine use, gambling, and other drug-related activities at Lambert's house on Old Dobbin Road. On one calendar page Ralph had written: *$15,000 changed hands—JYB present.*

After Ralph's arrest, both state police and Lexington police started following him, hoping they'd find out the identity of his source. But Ralph was careful not to blow the cover of Diana Hall—a lithe, thirty-five-year-old Canadian who was employed as Lambert's house-keeper. Ralph urged her to continue working while he sorted out his legal predicament. Meanwhile, he directed her to report to him, assuring her that he would arrange for her continued payment as a state police informant, while keeping her identity a secret known only to Ralph and Don Powers.

"You take care of her for a few weeks until you can get her hooked up with the Eye," Ralph had told Powers. Like Ralph, Powers' substantive days with the state police were nearing an end. His superiors had ordered him to reveal the identity of Ralph's informant in the Lambert probe. When Powers refused, he did so at the risk of demotion and banishment. It seemed to both men that the state police had successfully thwarted both the Lambert and Vance investigations by arresting Ralph. Successful in eliminating Ralph Ross, Powers had remained an irritant to the Campbell factions. The surveillance team had been disbanded after Ralph's arrest, and all its members who were loyal to Ralph had been exiled to remote locations, while Terry Barnes received a plum job with the Criminal Justice Division. Captain Powers was transferred to the Drivers' Licensing Division—an innocuous department located in the basement of the headquarters annex—where he bided his time until he was eligible for retirement.

The two men sifted through a carton of items Diana had absconded from Jimmy Lambert's garbage. Ralph showed Powers several pages of itemized phone statements from General Telephone of Kentucky and South Central Bell. The phone bills, which detailed calls made from Lambert's cabin at Boonesboro and his Lexington home, had been splattered by coffee grinds in the trash can.

Long-distance phone calls had been made to New York, Miami, Chattanooga, Tulsa, and Las Vegas. Next to the numbers, Ralph had made notations identifying the subscribers. Calls had frequently been placed to numbers listed to John Y. Brown, Jr., and his wife Phyllis George in Frankfort, Lexington, Miami, and New York. Several calls were also placed to prominent Lexington and Louisville businessmen, including Paul Hornung.

Diana had also provided Ralph with a list of people and phone numbers who were in Lambert's personal address book. The list read like a Who's Who in sports and local politics, and contained half a dozen unlisted numbers for Magoo and P. G. Magoo—apparent nicknames for the governor and Mrs. Brown—including residential lines to their home in Golden Beach. The home numbers of onetime NFL players—including Randy Burke of the Baltimore Colts and Sonny Collins of the Atlanta Falcons—were listed in the book, as well as other nationally known sports figures such as *Newsweek* writer Pete Axthelm, world poker champ Doyle Brunson, and oddsmaker Jimmy the Greek. Ralph pointed out other familiar names: Dan Chandler; Phil Block—the nephew of former governor Julian Carroll and manager of Trumps; horsewoman Anita Madden; Cornelia Wallace—the wife of former Alabama governor George Wallace; thoroughbred racehorse trainer Leroy Jolley; prominent horse breeder Tom Gentry; Las Vegas designer Suzy Creamcheese; political portrait artist, Ralph Cowan; two Las Vegas casinos—Caesars Palace and the Horseshoe Club; convicted gamblers; and the names of at least three known murder victims.

"Here they are again," Ralph said, referring to two numbers: 202/449-9944 and 202/233-7672 listed under the heading "Tapp Phone." Ralph knew the exchanges were CIA numbers that were used by intelligence operatives in the field. When the numbers were dialed, the person calling heard an electronic signal that indicated whether or not the telephone he was using was secure. The same two numbers had been found in the personal address books of Bradley Bryant and Drew Thornton.

"What do you think of this?" Ralph said, handing Powers a copy of an internal Criminal Justice Department memorandum relating to election fraud. Powers shook his head as he read the memo marked Confidential, which had been sent by Neil Welch to the governor. In the memo, Welch outlined the details of an ongoing investigation into state-wide vote-buying. Ralph wondered aloud if Lambert had been kept apprised by Brown of all investigations conducted by Justice Secretary Welch.

Another memo they found, written by Brown's personal secretary and directed to Lambert, inquired about the status of a pending lawsuit involving Trumps—the Cincinnati nightclub in which Brown had claimed not to have an interest.

Diana had also told Ralph that she had seen a check stub revealing a thousand-dollar payment to Brown for "partnership interest in Trumps," and a checking account deposit slip which showed a thirty-thousand-dollar payment to Lambert from Anita Madden.

Since it is not illegal to retrieve trash, or to read anything that has been left in plain view on desks, tables, or countertops, Diana had legal access to Jimmy Lambert's innermost secrets. Her duties as a housekeeper included cleaning the house and disposing of items in trash containers and destined for the trash.

Diana had also told Ralph a bizarre tale of the entrails of Lambert's personal life: That Lambert routinely snorted cocaine with his morning coffee; that cocaine and Quaaludes were common staples around his house; that there was a drug laboratory in his basement, where Diana had seen football-sized packages of pure, unprocessed cocaine; that she had witnessed Lambert vomit and dry heave for three days straight because of "roller coasting"—getting high on cocaine and then taking Quaaludes to mellow out; that Lambert transported his cocaine in large Thermos bottles; that Lambert regularly hosted flamboyant parties attended by *Playboy* bunnies, mobsters, politicians, and businessmen at which large amounts of drugs were consumed; that she overheard daily conversations about cocaine and that trays of cocaine were regularly placed throughout the house for consumption by Lambert's steady stream of guests; and that Lambert stored a cache of weapons in his house. Lambert had given Diana full access to the house, she told Ralph, and did not attempt to hide anything from her.

Though Diana was interested in financial compensation for her role as an informant, and had long fantasized about working for the FBI, she insisted to Ralph that her motivation in busting Jimmy Lambert was spawned out of concern for him and, especially, the young women in his life. Diana had known Lambert for many years, she claimed, during which time she had grown fond of him. But she feared Lambert would die of a drug overdose unless something drastic occurred, such as his arrest. Of even more concern to her, Diana claimed, was the fate of Jimmy's young female escorts. In them she saw herself at an earlier age—naive, vulnerable, impressionable, intrigued by the glittery fast-lane world of Jimmy Lambert, and totally oblivious to the dangers of that universe.

To Ralph, Diana was the mother lode. For a decade, he had waited for such a source. Betty Gee hadn't quite cut it, for she bent with a shove from any direction. Lambert trusted Diana with every aspect of his life. She cooked his meals, washed his clothes, cleaned his house, planted his flowers, took his messages, protected his house when he went out of town, made his bank deposits, and paid his bills; she babysat and chauffeured his two children when they occasionally visited. The job was perfect for Diana. As a part-time student at Transylvania University, as well as a part-time horse trainer, the hours of 10 A.M. until 2 P.M. allowed her time to pursue her academic and professional interests. Ironically, Ralph thought, now that he finally had an informant who could infiltrate Lambert's infamous horse and sports crowd, Ralph was impotent.

Ralph had confidence in his friends in the FBI, and he knew that he could count on them to treat Diana right. The FBI had been interested in Jimmy Lambert since the mid-1970s; but the fact that Lambert enjoyed a personal and financial relationship with a sitting governor who had made no secret of his intended bid for the U.S. presidency could no longer be overlooked. Ralph was certain the FBI would make the penetration of Lambert's criminal network a top priority. Bolstered by their state-of-the-art investigative techniques, the FBI would surely be able to bring Jimmy Lambert's free-wheeling days to an end.

Unfortunately, Ralph didn't have the same confidence for the conclusion of Henry Vance's illegal activities. Ralph was damned certain that neither the Kentucky State Police nor the Lexington police were continuing the pursuit of Vance. With Bonnie Kelly's conviction in Florida, there seemed to be little incentive to continue a probe into her accomplices. Federal agents in Tampa kicked around the possibility of indicting Vance for violating Berry's constitutional rights, but Ralph had little faith in their efforts. They had enough of their own criminals in Florida without having to worry about a preppy gangster from Kentucky.

■

At some point, reality set in, and Ralph understood that all aspects of his former life had come to a standstill. Even worse than the end of his law enforcement days was the emasculating divestiture of his constitutional rights. Never again would he be able to vote. It came as a surprise to Ralph—the most apolitical person he knew—that being stripped of that right was the most dehumanizing feeling. His family worried as they watched Ralph mope about, devoid of the drive and sense of purpose that had characterized his lifestyle for the past fifty years. He pretended to live a normal life, carrying out necessary daily duties such as paying bills, going to the post office, watching television news, reading the paper. Yet his only connection to his former life was the fear he carried with him every day that Drew Thornton's group would try to kill him. He never left his house without his gun, and slept with one within reach. On the surface, it seemed that Ralph was a free man. But those who knew him recognized the cage within which he was trapped. The phone calls from reporters asking if he intended to appeal his conviction were petering out. Everyone advised him against appealing, the judge had practically set him free anyway. What could be gained? he wondered. Ralph had no guarantee that another judge, another jury, would be any better. When he received a thirty-thousand-dollar bill from Bill Johnson for "services rendered," he tossed it into the trash. He knew Johnson would submit the same invoice to the state police.

Ralph sought out no one and few people called on him. He spoke frequently to Powers, whose refusal to identify Diana Hall had resulted in his exile to the Drivers' Licensing Division. Diana was now being controlled by the FBI, who, at Ralph's behest, had initiated a top-secret investigation of Jimmy Lambert. Though Ralph and Powers had initially consulted with the FBI on a regular basis about the case, they knew it was impolitic to maintain closeness with the federal agents working the case. Federal prosecutors directing the Lambert investigation feared that Ralph's involvement would weaken their legal position. While understanding the lawyers' assessment of the situation, the FBI agents knew that Ralph alone possessed a unique and thorough knowledge of the players—an inside track without which the success of the probe could not be guaranteed.

There came to exist, then, a latent agreement that Ralph Ross was the primary "source" for the FBI's most politically sensitive criminal investigation in Kentucky history.

Ralph, for his part, was less concerned about the perceived impropriety of his involvement. The once-workaholic cop suddenly had an abundance of time on his hands: He had lost his job, his marriage, his youth. His pride and reason for living depended upon his exoneration. His obsessive quest for justice would be mistaken by many as a pursuit for vengeance.

Because of the incestuous local relationships, the FBI operation was kept secret from the Lexington police, the state police, and even from some FBI agents assigned to Lexington. Despite the extreme sensitivity, Ralph was able to monitor the progression of events through his own network of sources.

From his unusual vantage point, Ralph knew as much, or more, about the Lambert investigation as the FBI agents assigned to the case. Ralph knew when the FBI received a court order to install electronic eavesdropping devices inside Lambert's home and a wiretap on Lambert's phones. Ralph knew as it occurred that bugs were being placed in Lambert's living room, bedroom, and basement, and that the FBI had established a monitoring post in a neighboring residence. Ralph knew that when Lambert became suspicious that he was the target of an investigation, he hired Drew Thornton to "sweep" the Old Dobbin house in search of a bug. Ralph also knew that FBI agents monitoring the equipment listened with relief as Drew assured Lambert that the house was "clean." Ralph knew that the FBI was monitoring the conversations of everyone in contact with Jimmy Lambert.

It came as no surprise to Ralph, then, that conversations between Jimmy Lambert and Governor John Y. Brown, Jr., were intercepted in the normal course of events.

■

By April 1983, Ralph had lost his patience with Governor Brown. Since his sentencing three months earlier, Ralph had nurtured the belief that Brown intended to grant him a pardon. But as the Lambert investigation reached its culmination, with less than a week to go before agents planned to raid Lambert's house, Ralph decided that if Brown had planned to give clemency, he would have done so by then. "That S.O.B.'s not going to come through for me," Ralph told Powers one day during the second week of April. "I think it's time to do a number on him," Ralph said, thinking of his bag full of micro-cassettes.

On the night of April 11, thanks to Ralph Ross, Lexington's CBS-affiliated television station scooped the rest of the state's media when it broadcast an explosive tape-recorded conversation. Brown's inner circle cringed in shocked disbelief as they listened to the report on WKYT-TV's six o'clock news broadcast:

"Newscenter 27 has learned that former Transportation Secretary, Frank Metts, secretly tape-recorded a conversation between him and Frankfort engineer Bill May in Governor John Y. Brown's Florida home.

"May, former Chairman of the State Racing Commission . . . made statements during that conversation that he had contributed

$23,000 to the Brown campaign, and had been told that he was guaran-
teed future state highway contracts by so doing.

"May told Newscenter 27 . . . that he was shocked that the
governor would allow Metts to wire Brown's Golden Beach, Florida,
home in order to monitor the conversation. May admitted . . . paying
$23,000 in campaign contributions, but insisted they were donations to
a cause and not to individuals. He said he felt entrapped by the governor and Metts.

"The governor was unavailable for comment."

The airing of the Metts/May tape, as it came to be known,
signaled the beginning of the end for John Y. Brown, Jr. Fulminating,
the governor called an impromptu press conference the following day,
at which he announced that he had fired Neil Welch for Welch's role in
the clandestine taping. "I'm just not going to tolerate secret taping in
my administration," Brown declared angrily. He adamantly claimed
that he knew nothing about the taping incident until the moment he
heard the tape played on the air, and then launched into a tirade against
the "sensationalist journalism" practiced by WKYT's reporter.

Calling himself a soldier in the war against crime, Welch convened a news conference the day after the broadcast to defend himself
and to challenge Brown's contention that he had no prior knowledge of
the taping. Accusing the governor of lying, Welch told the mob of
reporters that Brown had known about the incident for the past sixteen
months. Welch said that such consensual taping was a routine law enforcement practice performed hundreds of times a year by FBI agents
investigating white-collar crime.

"I don't know anything about frying chicken," Welch said, "and
he doesn't know anything about being a cop!"

Responding to Welch's allegations, Brown reversed himself and
suddenly recalled having been told several months earlier about the
taping. But Brown said he assumed Metts had recorded the conversation using a pocket recorder. It was, therefore, the sophistication of the
equipment and techniques that angered the governor and made the
operation smack of the greatly feared Abscam-type "bugging."

Within hours of the television broadcast, Ralph Ross's name
was bandied about by reporters who were playing catch-up to the televi-

sion story. The Louisville and Lexington newspapers quoted "unnamed sources" who said Ralph was the one who had wired the governor's house. The mere mention of Ralph Ross—the notorious, convicted wiretapper—sent Brown into a rage. The thought of an expert sound man such as Ralph invading the governor's residence and planting electronic transmitters sickened Brown who thought tapping an invasion of privacy.

At this point in time, Brown's intentions to enter the Democratic presidential primaries were no secret. His name was regularly mentioned by the national media, including the *New York Times*, as a hopeful; and he was unabashedly using his role as chairman of the Democratic telethon as a pole vault for a nationwide campaign. The Golden Beach house was the base of operations where Brown's political brainstorming and fund-raising efforts occurred. Hundreds of privileged strategy discussions about Brown's presidential aspirations and the activities of the Democratic National Committee had been held at the beachfront property. Had any of the conversations occurring at that location been secretly recorded it could prove devastating beyond belief for Brown's political future.

Speculation bubbled that Neil Welch—the man known as Jaws —had pulled off the ultimate sting operation. Perhaps Welch and Ross were working from within, infiltrating the Brown administration in an Abscam-type operation. Perhaps Welch had never *really* retired from the FBI. Perhaps he was part of an FBI intelligence-gathering operation into a U.S. presidential contender whose known associates included organized crime figures and drug dealers. *Does* the FBI routinely investigate contenders for such high-level government positions? observers wondered. Is that why Welch had wormed his way into Brown's cabinet? To keep abreast of the activities of Brown and his allies?

Amid the conjecture that often bordered on the absurd, a phrase was repeated frequently around the state: *The stupidest thing John Y. ever did was to hire Neil Welch. The second stupidest thing John Y. ever did was to fire Neil Welch.*

Using the Metts/May tape as evidence, a federal grand jury seated in Lexington launched a probe into the fund-raising habits of Brown's 1979 gubernatorial campaign. Brown's administration was thrown into total disarray when three of his cabinet members were subpoenaed. Fending off reporters and critics, Brown circled his wagons and tried to salvage his fast-dwindling presidential expectations.

Little did Brown know that one week later any semblance of national credibility would disappear, as federal drug agents descended *en masse* on the home of his best friend, Jimmy Lambert.

C H A P T E R

NINETEEN

More than a dozen FBI agents surrounded the ivory, ranch-style residence on Old Dobbin Road that had long been Mecca to Lexington's jet-setting party-goers. Simultaneously, agents were raiding Jimmy Lambert's cabin in Boonesboro, and the home of Arnold Kirkpatrick—an officer of Spendthrift, one of the most famous Thoroughbred racehorse farms in the Bluegrass. Lambert himself was nowhere to be found, having fled to Europe after reportedly being tipped off about the undercover investigation.

Operating on a hint from someone in the FBI, Ralph had parked his car early that morning near Mount Tabor Road, where he had a bird's-eye view of Lambert's. Nothing happened for several hours. Then, in the early afternoon, Ralph recognized the swarm of unmarked, antennaed FBI cars heading in tandem toward Old Dobbin Road. He reached for the quarter he had placed on the dashboard, and stepped out of his car. The WKYT reporter answered Ralph's call on the first ring, having expected such a call for weeks.

"You better get on over here," Ralph told the reporter. "Lambert's going down right now."

By the time the television van arrived on the scene, there was no sign of Ralph. The camera crew shot an hour's worth of footage of undercover G-men carrying cartons and trash bags of evidence out of the house. The search and seizure continued all afternoon, but the feds refused to comment about the contents of the cartons.

That evening, Ralph poured himself a bourbon-and-Seven in the den of his sister Thelma's colonial mansion. He was anxious to watch the six o'clock news, knowing that the station would air the first of a multipart series about the year-long probe into narcotics, weapons, and gambling. He knew that the story, which linked the governor to Jimmy Lambert, had been "in the can" for the past several weeks—thanks partially to his role as a news source.

Ralph was but one of thousands of viewers who watched with awe as details of the Lexington millionaire's secret life were unveiled. Among the items and documents that rolled across the television screen were internal Criminal Justice Department memoranda signed by Neil Welch; Lambert's telephone toll records that reflected calls to Brown and First Lady Phyllis George; flight records that revealed Lambert had accompanied Brown on a state-owned helicopter to the racetrack; Lambert's personal address book, which referred to Brown and his wife as *Magoo* and *P. G. Magoo;* confidential FBI reports stating that Lambert had been the target of a prostitution, corruption, murder, extortion, and narcotics investigation since 1979; and information about Lambert's initial refusal to take a polygraph in connection with the disappearance and death of Rebecca Moore.

Also shown was a check stub indicating a payment from Lambert to Brown referencing "partnership interest in Trumps—the Cincinnati nightclub in which John Y. Brown had denied involvement. That stub would prompt the IRS to question why the asset had never been declared as income by Brown. Brown countered that he had loaned Lambert thirty thousand dollars to buy the club. But Trumps landlords contradicted Brown's claims, and said they considered Brown to be the owner and responsible party for any debts incurred by the business.

Ralph watched the explosive broadcast with a mixture of satisfaction and yearning. In a small way he felt vindicated by the imminent arrest of Lambert and the devastating embarrassment of John Y. Brown, Jr. But still, he had a hunger for more. He wondered if he had the stamina and patience to await what he believed would be the inevitable demise of Drew Thornton and Henry Vance.

■

The raids on Lambert's houses threw John Y. Brown, Jr., into a quandary. Though Lambert remained in Europe, it was but a matter of time before he would be indicted on criminal charges.

At a hastily called press conference, similar to the one a week earlier at which he had announced Welch's firing, Brown again lashed out against the television station—WKYT. "I think what has happened in Lexington makes [the movie] *Absence of Malice* look like *Puffball.*" Brown defended his twenty-five-year friendship with Lambert, and claimed never to have seen "Jimmy do anything illegal." Brown stated further that he had never even *seen* cocaine. Questioned by reporters about rumors that Lambert was the governor's bookie, Brown responded: "Jimmy likes to bet on everything. He bets on everything that walks, talks, or wiggles. Everything but wrestling matches. So you can use your own imagination if Jimmy and I ever bet each other."

Fortunately for Brown, little significance was attached to the Lambert raid by either the *Lexington Herald* or the *Louisville Courier Journal*—the state's two most influential daily newspapers. Except for reporting on the initial raid, neither followed up with any in-depth stories. The problem then, for both Brown and Lambert, appeared to be the reports on WKYT. A subsidiary corporation of Kentucky Central Bank and Kentucky Central Insurance Company, WKYT fell under the cloak of state-regulated industries—and, therefore, particularly susceptible to political pressure.

Lexington's nobility was also united in its disapproval of such "investigative-type journalism." Though it is said that no official social register exists, it is no secret that the state is controlled by those of high descent—the invisible names etched on the nonexistent register. Lexington's aristocrats, rising to Lambert's defense, snubbed federal prosecutors and their wives. The posh country clubs and service organizations known for their snobbishness blackballed anyone associated with the government's side of the probe. None of the enclaves is more exclusive than the Idle Hour Country Club, whose restrictive policies are discussed in hushed tones, so as to avoid publicity about the racist and anti-Semitic policies that are still pervasive a quarter of a century after the passage of civil rights legislation. With Idle Hour as the unchallenged benchmark, other organizations followed suit. So the families of federal agents faced censure from a host of social events.

In a state where politicians are often considered bought-and-paid-for puppets, holding public office has never guaranteed social stature. But Brown's daddy had been *somebody,* so the governor made the grade.

Though Jimmy Lambert was an outsider, he had taken cover under the wing of a member—namely, John Y. Brown, Jr. Perquisites from such sponsorship thereby extended to him. Ralph Ross knew that a social novitiate in Lexington would remain indebted to his protective squire for life. "He *owes* me," is a phrase heard more than once around Lexington as bluebloods coveted the newcomers whom they take credit for "introducing around." Such introductions are priceless, as the guardian tacitly vouches for the outsider's credentials. Breaches of such relationships were rare, and for that reason Ralph knew that Lambert would never turn against Brown. Ralph had told his friends in the FBI that they would be wasting their time if they waited for Lambert to implicate the governor in order to save his own skin.

Horsewoman and socialite Anita Madden was one of the first to crusade against the raw deal Lambert was getting from the government. Draped in a royal blue jogging suit, her brassy mane drenched by the pouring rain and her pale face stained by running mascara, she formed a one-woman picket line at the entrance to WKYT's television studios. Protesting the news stories broadcast about her "good friends, Lambert, Kirkpatrick, and Brown," Mrs. Madden carried signs that read: "Trial By TV" and "Presence of Malice."

The *Herald* published letters to the editor that reflected a deep-felt sympathy for, and protectiveness of, Lambert and Brown.

"Lambert Due an Apology," said one letter. "Other than defamation of character, emotional strain on family members, intrusion of privacy (legally or not), possible ruination of political ambitions of a close friend, Gov. John Y. Brown, Jr., and generally just enraging Jim Lambert and friends, the FBI has accomplished little in its investigation and has created an unfortunate situation.

"Because the news media—television, radio, newspapers and magazines—contributed to the unfounded innuendos against Lambert, I feel they owe him an apology when this is all over. Knowing this probably will not happen and would not be enough to undo the harm that has been done to his family, close friends, and Jimmy himself, I want to say to him: 'Remember, life will always love you.' "

Even the "news" stories were often slanted in support of Lambert. One profile of the prominent businessman began, "He's a laid-back guy who likes to sip beer and listen to Willie Nelson records. He

loves children and buys Christmas presents every year for orphans at
the Bluegrass Boys' Ranch . . . Jimmy Lambert: drug figure or victim
of innuendo spawned by a scurrilous federal fishing expedition?"

Society columnists turned Lambert into a folk hero. When the
FBI, in accordance with the law, notified forty individuals that their
conversations had been bugged, the following appeared in the paper:
"The disclosure that there allegedly is a list of '40 prominent Kentuckians' who may be subpoenaed in connection with a federal investigation
of a well-known Lexington nightclub owner has caused mixed emotions
in the class-conscious Bluegrass. On the one hand, nobody wants the
inconvenience of going before the grand jury. On the other hand, nobody wants to be left off any list marked prominent. Obviously it would
help if these prominent figures had a way of identifying each other. May
we suggest a new bumper sticker for Lexington? 'Honk If You've Been
To Jimmy Lambert's House.' "

Laudatory references to Lambert's contributions to charitable
organizations appeared in the newspaper. "Not many people know
this," one article said, "but for the past eight years the Library Lounge
. . . has donated all the bartenders, napkins, cups and setups and
coordinated buying the liquor for . . . the fund-raising event for Car-
dinal Hill Hospital . . . The person who gets all the credit for the
Library's generosity is the owner, Jimmy Lambert."

By Derby time—the first Saturday in May—the momentum in
support of Lambert and against WKYT was at its peak. The Lambert
drug investigation disappeared from the pages of the newspapers, and
WKYT ordered its reporter to stop covering the story. Lambert was still
"vacationing" in Italy, and the U.S. attorney's office was conspicuously
silent about the progress of the case, sparking supposition that the
judicial system was succumbing to political and social pressure.

Brown's reputation appeared to remain intact, despite the guilt-
by-association insinuations. He and his wife continued their lives as
though Jimmy Lambert's problems were unrelated to them. They moved
from Cave Hill—their posh racehorse farm—into the recently restored
governor's mansion located in Frankfort. When the driveway at the
mansion was being paved, Phyllis is said to have made inquiries about
the dimensions of the driveway at the White House for the sake of
comparison. To a casual observer, life seemed to be as it should be for

the regal first family. State workers busily planted five thousand bloom-
ing tulips the first lady had ordered to line the entrance to her new
home, and two hundred state troopers were on hand to chauffeur the
Browns' guests to and from Derby festivities—including the annual
gala held at Hamburg Place hosted by their good friend Anita Madden.

So distraught was Anita over Lambert's predicament that her
fans had feared that she would not host her annual shindig. But tradition must have gotten the better of her, for she appeared in top form on
Derby Day 1983. Wearing a daffodil-colored, transparent Suzy
Creamcheese creation, Anita distributed two hundred Derby tickets to
her guests. Some of her more famous admirers, such as Dennis Cole
and Connie Stevens, milled through the crowd trying to determine
which of the fifteen limousines, five luxury vans, and three buses would
transport them from Hamburg Place to Churchill Downs.

The Browns exuded the aura of royalty throughout the Derby
season, and announced that their toddler son—Lincoln Tyler George-
Brown—would soon have a sibling. During their tenure in the state
house, Phyllis had been more visible than her husband. She had
orchestrated the purchase of Kentucky crafts by Bloomingdales in New
York; published a book called the *I Love America Diet;* convinced Neiman-Marcus in Beverly Hills to sell quilts made in the mountains of the
Bluegrass State; hosted Derby parties attended by Andy Warhol, Kenny
Rogers, Armand Hammer, and Barbara Walters; enticed Hollywood studios to film movies in Kentucky; and had won the hearts of constituents
when she claimed to have sung "My Old Kentucky Home" at the exact
moment that her son was born.

Seemingly undaunted by the continuing rumors that the Lambert probe would "blow the lid off Lexington," Brown kept his presidential aspirations on track. He was frequently mentioned in national
newspapers as an attractive candidate, and the couple launched an international "sell-Kentucky" program that served as a Brown-for-Presi-
dent springboard. Full-page, four-color advertisements in national magazines, paid for by the state Commerce Cabinet, promoted KENTUCKY &
COMPANY—THE STATE THAT'S RUN LIKE A BUSINESS. But Brown was count-
ing on the much-ballyhooed Democratic telethon that he had coordinated to guarantee him even more exposure. As chairman of a successful telethon, Brown hoped to be propelled into the limelight as a serious

national contender. He had been working for more than a year on the scheduled seventeen-hour, $6 million extravaganza, and had raised the $1.5 million in seed money from Kentucky Democrats. Brown, with help from his wife, had arranged for the appearance of television and movie stars, and scheduled a coast-to-coast series of rock concerts for the event. The show, ironically dubbed "Vigil for America," was to be nationally broadcast live from the Hollywood Bowl and Madison Square Garden.

■

On June 13, 1983, Ralph drove to the Hyatt in downtown Lexington to buy a *New York Times.* From the hilltop vantage point of the glitzy hotel, Ralph thought Lexington's main drag looked the way he imagined boomtown Houston had before it went bust. All the charming old buildings, Victorian and pre-Civil War, were being bulldozed and replaced by twenty-story concrete and glass towers. Billboards offering space for lease and "build-to-suit" dotted every corner. Ralph was naturally suspicious about all the "new money" pouring into town.

He turned his car into the driveway of the hotel and left it idling while he ran into the gift shop to pick up a paper. Ralph knew that *Times* reporter Wendell Rawls, Jr., a Pulitzer Prize winner, was working on a story about Brown's links to people involved with illegal drugs and gambling. Rawls had interviewed Ralph and it was obvious that Rawls grasped the magnitude of the story. There, on the front page, was the story Ralph thought would devastate Brown, for it was in New York that Brown intended to raise money for his national campaign. LEADING KENTUCKIANS LINKED TO DRUG AND BETTING INQUIRY, read the headline. For the first time, the debacles of the Brown administration were delineated for a national audience: The Lambert raids and the connections between the governor and Lambert; the fact that Lambert was a courier for Brown, carrying hundreds of thousands of dollars from Las Vegas back to Kentucky; the arrest and conviction of Ralph Ross; the firing of Neil Welch; and the demotion and transfer of Don Powers. "Some investigators," the story said, "have said Kentucky has a history of thwarted investigations of prominent people and have expressed fears that 'political pressures' would stunt this one."

Brown downplayed his relationship with Lambert to the *Times*, claiming he had only seen his friend "three, four, five times a year." The governor was apparently unaware that state phone records contradicted him, revealing that Brown had called Lambert on a weekly, often daily, basis throughout his tenure, and that state police assigned to guard the governor's private residence had noted Lambert's regular visits.

But the most volcanic and damaging aspect of the lengthy article was the reference to a federal grand jury in Miami that was investigating Brown for withdrawing $1.3 million in cash from a Florida bank. The incident had been reported nine months earlier in the *Miami Herald*, but had received little attention in Brown's home state. The *Lexington Herald* had carried the story, but had not followed up with any substantive stories about the status of the probe.

On an unspecified number of occasions, in 1981 and 1982, Brown had sent couriers to the All American Bank of Miami to retrieve several hundred thousand dollars in cash from the tiny institution. At least twice, Brown went to the bank after closing hours to retrieve brown paper sacks containing tightly bound one-hundred-dollar bills. The grand jury was investigating the deposits—ranging from $300,000 to $785,000—which had been wire-transferred from Kentucky financial institutions, and then picked up in cash by Brown.

The withdrawals were the subject of Operation Greenback—a cash-tracking effort of the IRS, DEA, and Customs—which was probing the laundering of money used in illegal drug smuggling. The All American Bank had failed to report Brown's deposits and withdrawals, as required by federal law, which had set off alarm bells to the federal task force. Meanwhile, employees of a second Florida bank that was used by Brown—Great American Bank of Dade County—were indicted for laundering $96 million in proceeds from narcotics trafficking.

When the cash withdrawals were first reported, Brown had called the investigation a political "dirty trick" spawned by the Republicans because of Brown's potential presidential candidacy. After complaining of harassment to then-Vice President George Bush, Brown told reporters he was assured by Bush that the investigation had come to a halt. Brown deflected difficult questions by claiming the public's right to know did not extend to his private life. Facing mild inquiry by Ken-

tucky reporters, Brown contended, once again, that his personal financial affairs were nobody's business and put it off on Phyllis, joking that
his wife maintained an expensive lifestyle. "You know you can't take a
trip overseas, not with Phyllis anyway, without getting into large
amounts. I think a cheap trip with Phyllis would be fifty thousand
dollars." Apparently satisfied with Brown's jocular response, the Kentucky press corps politely dropped the matter.

Brown was only slightly more forthcoming when interviewed by
Rawls, who pressed for an answer. Confronted with inferences that the
cash withdrawals were the profits of a drug-smuggling operation, Brown
apparently decided to choose the lesser of two evils, hoping voters had
forgotten his earlier campaign statements that he was not a big gambler.
To Rawls, Brown for the first time admitted publicly his reasons for the
withdrawals: "One real bad night" gambling in Las Vegas in 1981.

Maybe gambling had long been a staple of Kentucky life, but
the revelation that a sitting governor had dropped $1.3 million in one
night at a Vegas casino aroused even the most apathetic constituent.
Perhaps the irony of Brown's actions would have been lost on more
Kentuckians if their state had not been one of the poorest in the nation.

" 'I operate in cash, which is my right,' " the governor told the
New York Times, regarding the withdrawals and transfers of large sums.
" 'I worked hard for my money, I made it legally and I paid the taxes
on it. If I want to take it out of a bank in wheelbarrows, that's my
business. It's my money and I can do with it what I want.' "

He described his betting habits as "recreational": " 'Sometimes
I forgot I was governor and had some fun, but I never made a bet I
couldn't afford. I've taken care of my responsibilities, provided hand-
somely for my first wife, set up trust funds for my children, given $3
million to charities. If somebody wants to fault me for poor judgment
that's fine, but there is nothing illegal in my activities.' "

The *New York Times* story signaled the beginning of the end for
Brown. The proverbial icing on the cake was the telethon disaster.
Officially declared a bust, grossing only $2.75 million, Brown had in-
curred the wrath of Democratic party chairmen from numerous states.
Brown seemed to fall apart—both emotionally and physically. He refused to appear at a press conference, issuing a statement instead in
which he belittled the federal probe and alluded to unspecified discrep-

ancies in the *Times* story. Infuriated by an earlier *Times* story that had been critical of his administration, Brown had fired off a letter to the publisher of the *Times* offering to pay a million dollars to the newspaper's favorite charity if it could find a state "better run" than Kentucky. "Apparently the *New York Times* doesn't know how to accept a gentlemanly Kentucky challenge," Brown told reporters after the *Times* failed either to respond to his letter or to publish it.

But the *Times* story was only the beginning as the state was suddenly inundated by a barrage of national reporters who found that Brown's high-stakes gambling and cash withdrawals made good copy.

The *Los Angeles Times* reported that the Miami grand jury was considering evidence that Brown had encouraged the bank not to report the withdrawals. That story also quoted sources with the Nevada casino regulators who said Jimmy Lambert was an associate of J. Dan Chandler, who was under investigation in Nevada.

The *Las Vegas Sun* reported that Brown had lost more than a million dollars in a baccarat game at Caesars Palace. The European card game famous for its fast pace was Brown's game of choice, according to the *Sun*. That same story revealed that Brown had lost half a million dollars at the Horseshoe Club and had taken more than five years to repay the outstanding debt.

Time magazine published an overview of the controversy, focusing on Brown as the common link between the elite and the netherworld. "Lexington, Ky, has always had a pretty high opinion of itself. The Idle Hour Country Club, the inner sanctum for Thoroughbred horse breeders and other bluebloods, is about as smugly exclusive as such places get. Lexington's upper-class chat just now should be preoccupied with the annual Keeneland yearling sale . . . Instead, each day the conversations are thicker with unsavory gossip."

Newsweek too drew attention to *"The Woes of John Y. Brown."* Recounting an earlier incident when Phyllis was conducting a televised interview of Muhammad Ali, the weekly news magazine portrayed Brown as a politician who tactlessly acted on impulse. "[Phyllis] Brown asked the former heavyweight boxing champion about his best fight. While Ali pondered the question, Kentucky Gov. John Y. Brown, Jr. wandered over to give his wife an assist: 'Why don't you ask him about his fights with his wife?' Ali, who has had his share of marital strife, was stunned. 'Man,' he said to the chief executive of the commonwealth of Kentucky, 'you really are stupider than you look.' "

By late June, Brown-bashing by the media was chic. Finally, the local papers got into the act. BROWN'S FOIBLES TEND TO OBSCURE HIS ACHIEVEMENTS, pontificated a *Courier Journal* columnist. "Matters have come to an astonishing pass when the state's highest elected official spends the better part of an hour answering questions on virtually nothing else except his gambling habits, other aspects of his personal lifestyle and his association with people under investigation."

Presumably uncomfortable at having been scooped by the national media, the *Lexington Herald* published a sanctimonious prediction that Brown's career in national politics had come to a standstill. "One of the startling things that can befall a politician," wrote editor John Carroll, "is to discover, after years of seeking national attention, that the nation is actually listening. Some have been pained to learn— as Gov. John Y. Brown Jr. is now learning—that the floodlights can shine without mercy, illuminating one's weaknesses in terrible detail . . . Four years ago, Brown was mildly embarrassed when it was discovered that he, a candidate running as a businessman, did not know the meaning of the term *affirmative action.* Such a gaffe in a national campaign could be damaging, if not fatal."

MIGHTY STRANGE BEHAVIOR FOR A STATE'S HIGHEST OFFICIAL, declared the venerable *Courier Journal.*

Jokes became rampant about Brown's cabinet slogan, "Kentucky Company—The State That's Run Like a Business." T-shirts and bumper stickers popped up that said: KENTUCKY & COMPANY—A STATE YOU CAN GAMBLE ON; or, with apparent reference to the Company, KENTUCKY & COMPANY—A STATE THAT'S RUN LIKE A DRUG OPERATION.

Unamused, Brown apparently decided it was finally time to face the music. His eyes bulging with tension and rage, the governor answered questions put to him by a mass of state and national reporters. Brown promoted his image as a gambler, apparently to dispel suspicions and rumors regarding his friendship with drug smugglers. But it seemed nearly as impolitic to recklessly wage staggering amounts of money. Vowing to give up gambling for the rest of his term, Brown refused to answer specific questions about his gambling losses or the cash withdrawals.

Four days after the press conference, Governor Brown underwent emergency open-heart surgery after complaining of chest pains. When he suffered respiratory failure after the operation and lapsed into a coma, even his medical condition became rife with sordid rumors.

Ralph Ross couldn't help feeling sorry for the guy. Ralph could relate, better than anyone, to a man whose life was suddenly in shambles.

■

Closed-circuit television monitors were camouflaged in the gigantic oak trees near the gateposts. The white mansion was hidden from the busy road, more than a quarter of a mile down a curved asphalt driveway. Ralph inched his new Subaru sedan up to the gate, reached a long arm out of the window to push a button that would be undiscernible to an unknowing visitor. The front gate, heavy as a barn door, swung open to allow Ralph's entrance. At that moment, a bell rang in the main house, alerting its occupants to an intruder. Within seconds, two seemingly vicious Doberman pinschers—aptly named Napoleon and Gideon— bounded across the manicured lawns toward the entrance. Ralph had already pushed the second button that was mounted on a post twenty feet inside the property. Behind him, the electric gate closed slowly. His car window glided up just as the guard dogs reached his car. Their menacing scowls turned to playful barking the moment they recognized Ralph.

"Get off me, you sorry animals," Ralph joked as the dogs attacked him with affection, running circles round his legs.

"Anybody home?" he yelled through the back screen door of his sister Thelma's house.

It seemed awfully quiet to Ralph, considering the number of cars parked out back. Thelma responded from across the yard.

"We're all out here by the pool," she said. "You'd better get over here. You've got a lot of explaining to do."

Ralph lumbered over, the sun beating down on his head.

The massive rectangular swimming pool was crystalline blue.

He had helped Thelma with the annual cleaning and preparation for summer, which entailed days of vacuuming and chemical testing. Lounging on the expensive outdoor furniture was an unlikely crew, looking hot and uncomfortable in their professional clothes. He nodded at the two reporters who had come by to check out the story. They seemed out of context there, drinking gin and tonics prepared for them by Thelma, file folders stacked on the umbrellaed round table, anxiously awaiting Ralph's arrival.

"At least you're alive," Thelma said to Ralph.

Ralph's teenaged niece floated on a raft in the pool. "Hi, Buster," she yelled to her uncle, using Ralph's nickname from his youth. "Glad you're back."

Ralph was slightly embarrassed and ashamed. He knew that everyone present had been up most of the night panicked, believing that he had been killed. At that very moment, his daughter Christie was in the protective custody of police in South Carolina. Ralph's ex-wife Vivian and her new husband were en route to the Myrtle Beach resort area to retrieve Christie—a terrified coed.

It had started the night before, around 1 A.M., with a phone call to Christie's hotel room. She and some friends had driven to the vacation spot famous for its onslaught of college kids. They had gone out to dinner that evening, then to a local bar for a couple of beers, arriving back at their room just after midnight.

The moment they entered the room, the phone rang.

First inside the door, Christie ran to answer it.

"Hello," she said.

"Is this Christie Ross?"

"Yes it is," she replied, not recognizing the male voice.

"We've just shot your dad, and you're next."

Christie hysterically summoned the local police, and efforts began immediately to locate Ralph back in Kentucky. Awakened in the middle of the night, Don Powers went to Ralph's apartment when the telephone had failed to rouse him. When Powers found a vacant apartment, calls rang out to everyone Ralph knew. Have you heard from Ralph tonight? Have you seen Ralph tonight? Do you have any idea where Ralph could be tonight? A BOLO, be-on-the-lookout, was issued, and state police searched roads in the Lexington and Lawrenceburg area for Ralph's car. Ralph's friends in the FBI were alerted to the incident.

It wasn't until 6 A.M. that Ralph dragged himself home from a date, to be confronted by a "bunch of cryin' kin."

■

Ralph may have sat idly by as Henry Vance and Drew Thornton played their mind games with him, but he was not about to allow his children to be victimized.

He took the Myrtle Beach incident as a warning, and though it hurt his pride to do so, his good sense told him it was time for him and Christie to get the hell out of Kentucky. Otherwise, someone was liable to end up dead.

"Too hot in Dodge," he joked with his friends before leaving. "Reckon I'll be back when things cool off." Packing his car with the bare necessities, Ralph and Christie headed West in search of a remote location in which to temporarily land. Settling in a small town in the Rocky Mountains that had only one road leading in and out, Ralph rented a condominium with two bedrooms and a fireplace, bought them each a pair of skis, some longjohns, and parkas, enrolled in private ski instruction, and burrowed in for a long, cold winter a thousand miles from home.

Ralph found the same kind of solace in the West as had generations before him. He spent his evenings at one of a handful of cowboy bars where he blended in with dozens of others who had sought out a less complicated life. No one recognized him or asked him personal questions, and he never mentioned that he was a cop. Only a handful of friends and family members knew his whereabouts, diminishing his chances of being tracked down by Drew's boys. Though he carried his gun at all times, for which he had a permit from ATF, Ralph looked over his shoulder less often. He couldn't forget the look in Drew Thornton's eyes when Drew testified for the prosecution at Ralph's trial. From the witness stand, Drew had pointed his finger at Ralph and said: "That man's the one who put me in jail." At the moment Ralph had realized that someday Drew would try to have him killed. Ralph also knew that Drew and Henry Vance had discussed murdering Ralph, and that Vance had said he wanted to "personally" take care of the job.

Every day, he rode the chairlift to the top of the mountain and awkwardly maneuvered his cumbersome, middle-aged body down the steep slopes, cursing his ineptness every inch of the way. Every night, he drank whiskey or wine and contemplated his remaining days. Although he found peace in the majestic beauty of the mountains, he knew it was but a temporary respite. Ralph didn't want to spend the rest of his life skiing and boozing it up, spending his retirement income on older divorcées, but he felt powerless to change anything.

His friends kept him apprised of events in Kentucky, making it easier for Ralph to gauge the necessity for his continuing absence. He was not surprised to learn that Drew's girlfriend, Rebecca Sharp, along with four of Henry Vance's relatives, had filed a $1.2 million civil suit against him claiming their constitutional rights had been violated by Ralph when he wiretapped Vance's phone. Ralph scoffed at the appearance of Randy Reinhardt as the attorney for the plaintiffs. He never ceased to be baffled by the fact that an attorney with obvious ties to the likes of Drew Thornton and Henry Vance could enjoy reputable standing in his profession.

Once again Ralph was faced with the unpleasant task of retaining an attorney. This time, the thought of spending thousands of dollars to defend himself was disgusting. If the lawsuit had been brought anywhere else in the country, Ralph would have shrugged it off, certain any judge would throw it out. But he knew from experience that the damnedest things could happen in Lexington. He began worrying about his legacy. What would he, a convicted felon, leave to his daughters when he died? A successful civil suit would wipe him out. Not only had he lost his job, but his lifetime of financial savings was in jeopardy.

Small victories temporarily elevated his spirits. Right after the turn of the New Year, Jimmy Lambert was indicted by a federal grand jury in Lexington. Charged with fifty-nine counts of possession or distribution of cocaine, marijuana, or methaqualone, one count of conspiracy to distribute cocaine, and one count of violating federal firearms laws, the governor's friend faced a lifetime in jail. Named as co-conspirators with Lambert were Phillip Block—nephew of former governor Julian Carroll—and Spendthrift executive Arnold Kirkpatrick.

In a surprise accompanying indictment, Anita Madden was charged with conspiracy, obstruction of justice, and theft of government property in connection with the leak of more than a hundred pages of grand jury testimony to Lambert. She had allegedly been the recipient of stolen carbon copies of grand jury proceedings, from which she then typed a transcript for Lambert.

Ralph read with amusement the newspaper accounts sent to him by his sister Thelma. ". . . a confident and sardonic Lambert, wearing cowboy boots, jeans and a hat that advertised Red Man chewing tobacco, joked with reporters about the investigation and needled federal prosecutors as they passed by," Ralph read in the *Herald.*

In a profile of the hostess laureate of Kentucky, reporters speculated about Anita's age. "In 1981 she took an accidental overdose of medication and was found unconscious at her home. She was listed in critical condition for two days before regaining consciousness . . . Mrs. Madden had long kept her age a secret, but the paramedics who took her to the hospital listed her as 48 years old. That was later disputed by her husband, who said she was 39."

Ralph assumed that would be the end of it. Lambert would never stand trial. His collaborators would never allow their shenanigans to be bandied about in open court. The FBI was hoping Lambert would point the finger at some of his more prominent co-conspirators. But Ralph knew better, Jimmy Lambert would never flip. He'd be a dead man if he did.

Ralph also suspected that charges against Anita would be dropped, as in fact they were.

Brown—who had completed his gubernatorial term and announced plans to run for the U.S. Senate—issued statements denying that he had ever been a target of the Lambert drug probe. Hedging his bets though, he retained former Watergate prosecutor James Neal to accompany him to an interrogation by the FBI.

Pleased as he was with the culmination of the Lambert investigation, Ralph felt little personal satisfaction or mitigation. Remarkably, he still believed that the bad guys *usually* got caught. Some just took longer than others.

(Subsequently on June 7, 1984, Lambert, under a plea bargaining agreement, pled guilty to a single drug conspiracy charge, the fifty eight other counts against him were dropped. In pleading guilty, Lambert admitted using cocaine and giving it out to houseguests and others.)

PART

BOOK TWO

T W O

BLUEGRASS JUSTICE

CHAPTER
TWENTY

By the time the Jefferson County homicide unit arrived at Harold Brown's Louisville apartment on March 20, 1984, the grisly scene had already been compromised.

The forty-three-year-old former regional head of the DEA was lying in a pool of dried blood—dead of a single gunshot wound to the head. The entire episode had gotten off to a bizarre start. Brown's estranged wife told police she and Brown were quarreling on the telephone when a shot rang out. For some unexplained reason, she first called C. Fred Partin—a former federal prosecutor and close friend of both Brown and Drew Thornton—rather than the police. Partin, instead of summoning the police, proceeded directly to Brown's condominium where he claimed to find the doors and windows locked from the inside.

Partin later told reporters the death was not suspicious—it was indisputably a suicide. Brown left three suicide notes, Partin said, and had been despondent about his marital strife. But Captain James Black, commander of the county's special investigations and narcotics unit, didn't believe it. He thought Brown had been murdered. Black questioned Partin's objectivity in the matter, citing Partin's friendship with Harold Brown, Drew Thornton, Bill Canan, and Henry Vance, which dated back to the early 1970s when Partin was an assistant U.S. attorney and the others were narcs.

Captain Black had also been in law enforcement in those days, and, like Ralph Ross, had come to suspect Harold Brown of dealing drugs. It had seemed to Black that Brown had only busted smuggling groups that competed with the Company. In the days leading up to his death, Brown publicly and frequently blamed Sergeant Ross and Cap-

tain Black for his forced resignation from the DEA, both having testified to Brown's cover-ups.

Ralph learned of Brown's death shortly after it occurred. Making inquiries from his remote mountain hideaway, Ralph learned that at
the time of his death Brown was on the verge of arrest for the manufacture and distribution of exotic poisons. Through a company he called
Aardvark Industries, aptly named for the weird, burrowing animal,
Brown was selling ricin—a poisonous protein extracted from the castor
bean. Advertising in mercenary magazines such as *Soldier of Fortune*
and *Shotgun News,* he sold the poison to assassins. Police in Oklahoma
and Florida had implicated Brown in at least one death.

When Black's narcotics unit gained access to a cabin owned by
Brown located in Dead Horse Hollow—a canyon outside of Louisville—
they found Partin had again beaten them to the scene. Under the cloak
of attorney-client privilege, Partin confiscated guns and files that Black
considered germane to the investigations.

A battle began on the pages of the local newspapers, in which
Black and Partin shot barbs, each accusing the other of overstepping
boundaries. Partin contended the police had no right to Brown's personal belongings as long as the death was a suicide; Black countered
that as a subject of criminal investigations, the circumstances surrounding Brown's death warranted closer scrutiny. Still intact when Black
had arrived at the cabin was an intricate drug laboratory. Having begun
his career as a chemist with the Food and Drug Administration before
joining the DEA, Brown had apparently reverted to his earlier calling.
Found in the search were ether, nicotine, sodium, ammonium nitrate,
tear gas, and explosives.

In addition to ricin, the police found a supply of curare-type
drugs. The presence of curare raised Ralph's eyebrows, for the substance had also been listed in a pamphlet entitled *Ten Lethal or Incapacitating Drugs Stored by the CIA* that had been found three years earlier
in Bradley Bryant's possession. The strange drug is most commonly
used by African hunters on poison-tipped arrows.

Brown's laboratory produced a poison called P-2-P—a substance sold on the streets as cocaine, and which can be obtained legally
only by individuals possessing a DEA registration number. Providing a
"rush" similar to that of cocaine, the poison is deadly to unsuspecting

users. Items found at the cabin led police to suspect Brown was also distributing mescaline—a hallucinogenic derivative of a Mexican cactus for which there was a flourishing market among urban high school kids.

Brown had also founded Dead Horse Hollow Publications, police learned. Booklets in the cabin instructed drug smugglers how to operate without detection by the DEA, and advised them to "deal big" because the DEA is only after the "little guys." *Clandestine Laboratory Seizures in the U.S.* told readers how to synthesize drug labs using common solvents, while also evading investigation by the DEA. *The Underground Chemist* published confidential information from internal DEA documents, provided a "DEA Watchlist," and gave detailed instructions for the manufacture of P-2-P and methamphetamines. Pricey, the publications were marked at twenty-five dollars each.

Brown's personal diary reflected regular and frequent meetings with Drew Thornton in the weeks prior to Brown's death. Most of their rendezvous occurred at the Sportsman in Louisville—a gun club where police officers and weapons enthusiasts went for "social shooting." Entries also reflected several trips "to West Point." Personal notes seized by police suggested a desire, if not intention, to carry out the murders of Ralph Ross, Don Powers, Jim Black, and an FBI agent named Mike Griffin.

Shortly before Brown's death an infamous marijuana smuggler, deep-sea diver, treasure hunter, and soldier-for-hire who had participated—along with some ex-Green Berets and Ku Klux Klansmen—in the unsuccessful takeover of the Caribbean island of Dominica, had approached one of Black's undercover narcs. Evidently unaware of the narc's true identity, the smuggler claimed that Brown was attempting to steal a marijuana field under his cultivation. Hoping to net Brown in the act, Black had assigned his undercover team to surveil Favergill's Hardin County marijuana farm, and had found the allegation to be true. For years, Harold Brown had been to Jim Black what Drew Thornton had been to Ralph Ross—a crooked cop too slippery to catch. With Brown's implication in the Favergill marijuana scandal, Black thought he would finally be able to ensnare his nemesis.

But Brown had used death to slide out of yet another encounter with Black.

Despite Partin's claims that Brown died at his own hands, the coroner decided there was enough mystery surrounding the death to warrant an inquest. Six jurors considered a number of bewildering occurrences that coincided with the death—an unidentified individual had driven off in Brown's car several hours after the body was found, and then returned the vehicle to its parking spot the following morning; a "substantial sum of money" had been removed from Brown's apartment sometime after the shooting death; and someone had stolen tape recordings from Brown's apartment that contained conversations incriminating Brown in illegal drug transactions. But the death was ultimately ruled a suicide, and the unanswered questions remained just that.

By far, the most fascinating pieces of information uncovered in the investigation of Harold Brown's death were hints that Brown's illegal activities had in fact been sanctioned by the DEA. Internal DEA documents and statements found at Brown's cabin alluded to a secret CIA team housed within the DEA, and hinted that Brown had been a part of that elite cadre. The elaborate scenario depicted in the documents allowed the CIA, through the use of DEA overt and covert agents, to infiltrate narcotics organizations with a secret purpose of gathering military intelligence vital to U.S. national security interests.

Ralph Ross was reluctant to give credence to the farfetched scheme.

■

On the heels of Harold Brown's death, Ralph received a manila envelope full of what purported to be DEA documents. Sent to him by an anonymous source, the documents were accompanied by a handwritten note that read: "Could Harold Brown and Andrew Thornton have been part of this scenario?"

Marked *Classified,* the hundred pages detailed the existence of a quid-pro-quo arrangement between the CIA and DEA that allowed large-scale narcotics activities in return for intelligence information on Latin American countries. Such a system was an outgrowth of the CIA's participation a decade earlier in a clandestine narcotics network hidden within the DEA. Since the early 1970s, the documents suggested, the CIA had used the DEA for cover, and had employed known drug smugglers and mercenaries, called "assets," who were allowed to continue their illegal activities in return for information on groups and individuals of interest to the United States.

Because of the CIA's relationship with the defendants, prosecution of several major drug dealers and soldiers of fortune had been jeopardized or thwarted.

The original unit housed within the DEA was apparently code-named Operation Buncin, an acronym for the Bureau of Narcotics Clandestine Intelligence Network. That pilot project, which provided cover for CIA covert operations at home and abroad, was the forerunner of Operation Deacon—Drug Enforcement Administration Covert Operations Network. Because many Latin and South American governments and economies were integrally tied to cocaine and marijuana production and export, the secret operation's stated purpose was to infiltrate the international drug organizations under the auspices of fighting drugs, while really monitoring political activities of those governments.

The details of the operation were painstakingly outlined in the documents. Through a mind-boggling design, Buncin would utilize covert operatives, overt operatives, and assets. The "overt operative would be the DEA agent who presented his face in the community." The covert operative was the "deep cover person" who reported to the overt operative. The "asset" was the individual who obtained the intelligence information from foreign governments, and provided it to the "covert operative."

Ralph plugged the players into the formula: Was Harold Brown the "overt operative" who "presented his face in the community" as head of the Kentucky DEA office? Was Drew Thornton the "covert operative" who reported to Harold Brown? Were Bradley Bryant and Drew's sundry smuggling conspirators the "assets" who reported to Drew? Was Colombia, where the Company purchased cocaine and sold weapons, the foreign government being infiltrated?

According to the plot, only the "covert agent" was allowed to know the identity of both the "overt operative" and the various "assets," thereby insulating the DEA agent who "presented his face in the community" from the actual smugglers. The project was monitored by the Office of Security of the CIA, and all information originating from the unit was considered top secret. The intelligence information was hand-delivered to Homestead Air Force Base in Florida, flown on classified Defense Department courier planes to Andrews Air Force Base in Maryland, and retrieved personally by DEA agent Lucien Conein—the super-spook renowned for his expertise with an intelligence device known as the "Moscow cell structure."

Ralph had never heard of Conein—the former Office of Strategic Services (OSS) and CIA agent credited by some with orchestrating the 1963 overthrow of South Vietnamese President Ngo Dinh Diem—so the significance of Conein's involvement escaped Ralph.

One of the documents, entitled *CIA Narcotic Intelligence Collection*, referred to twenty-seven U.S. drug prosecutions that had to be halted because of the CIA's involvement.

A confidential Justice Department memorandum attached to the documents stated a policy of falsely blaming other American agencies, or even foreign governments, if the operations were exposed.

Ralph contemplated the questions raised. Would such an arrangement explain why Drew Thornton had possession of DEA codes, coding devices, and body transmitters? Would it explain why Bradley Bryant contended he was a participant in a "classified CIA operation"? Why Harold Brown busted most drug-smuggling organizations, while protecting Drew's group? Why the DEA never pursued charges against Bradley Bryant or Drew Thornton in 1979 even though Harold Brown seized the DC-4 belonging to Bradley Bryant that had been used to smuggle ten tons of dope into Kentucky? Why Bradley Bryant told Lance Alworth and others that the CIA allowed him to smuggle drugs? Why Drew had nonpublished, home telephone numbers for DEA agents in his possession? Why the name the Company was selected? Was it a euphemism for the CIA? Why Drew and Bradley had CIA phone numbers in their wallets and CIA publications in their homes? Why Drew and Bradley were well versed in spy tradecraft, using telephone scramblers, state-of-the-art electronic surveillance and countersurveillance techniques, silencers, daggers, exotic poisons, explosives, disguises, assassination kits, electronic dart guns, survivalist rations, and false identification. Would it explain how the group was able to embezzle weapons and radar equipment from top-secret military installations such as China Lake? Would it explain how a Kentucky boy such as Drew Thornton had cultivated high-level intelligence and military contacts in Bolivia, Brazil, Costa Rica, Colombia, Equador, Haiti, Mexico, Paraguay, Peru, and Panama? Would it explain why Bradley vehemently claimed "we're good guys, not bad guys"? Would it explain why such seasoned spies as Colonel James Atwood, Ed Wilson, and Frank Terpil would befriend such a motley crew? Would it explain why Triad operated unabated? Was it a training ground for Third World police forces who were secretly supported by the CIA? Would it explain why the Company had escaped detection and apprehension for so long?

Were Drew and Harold and Bradley not only drug smugglers, but also members of an elite cabal of contract assassins who performed their services for the highest bidder—government and private industry alike? Documents retrieved from Harold Brown's apartment at the time of his death pointed to such a possibility, as did the apparent obsession with exotic weapons and poisons.

To believe that the Buncin-Deacon scenario applied to the Kentucky crew would ascribe lofty motives to a bunch of criminals—something Ralph thought attributed undue beneficence.

Admittedly, Ralph was more naive than was justified by his training and experience, but he found it hard to believe that his own government would rely upon men the caliber of Drew Thornton and Harold Brown. Then again, Ralph thought, maybe he just didn't *want* to believe it.

Ralph had done his own share of work for the Agency and knew that an effective intelligence-gathering apparatus must sometimes resort to unorthodox methods. But, as a matter of policy, did the government *really* engage in drug smuggling and assassinations?

Ralph liked to believe it did not.

Perhaps it was true, Ralph decided, that Brown used members of the Company as "assets." Perhaps it was also true that Drew Thornton engaged in acts that benefited the CIA, such as flying a planeload of weapons to the Nicaraguan contras. And perhaps the CIA turned its cheek when Drew flew the same airplane back to the U.S. loaded with drugs. Why waste cargo space on a return trip?

Ultimately, Ralph decided that Drew Thornton and his wayward accomplices had to be independent contractors whose actions rarely, if ever, fell under the protective cloak of the U.S. Government.

"Drew Thornton is dead," the male voice said to Ralph Ross, awakening him at the crack of dawn on September 11, 1985.

Ralph thanked his source for the information and dialed the number of a friend in the FBI. After relating details of his phone conversation to the federal agent, Ralph dressed in a pair of Levis and a flannel shirt. He started the engine of his used Lincoln Continental and waited briefly for the car to warm up in the brisk autumn morning. As he drove the five miles to an old-fashioned Southern diner located on Main Street in the county seat of Lawrenceburg, Ralph listened to the radio for reports of Drew's death. Nothing.

Outside the café, he bought a *Lexington Herald* and a *Louisville Courier Journal.* Again, no mention of the bizarre free-fall. He wondered momentarily if perhaps his source had been wrong. Then he realized that the incident must have occurred after the newspapers had been put to bed.

Seating himself at the counter, Ralph ordered a cup of coffee and biscuits 'n' gravy—the common Kentucky breakfast of patty-sized buttermilk biscuits swimming in a creamy pork-laced gravy. Awaiting the meal that would sit like a lead balloon in the pit of his stomach for the rest of the day, Ralph decided to call Don Powers.

"Come on down to the Anderson Grill," he said to his longtime buddy. "I've got some interesting news for you."

By the following day, Ralph's "news" was splashed across the front pages of every newspaper in Lexington, Louisville, Knoxville, Nashville, and Atlanta. Stories and sidebars probed Drew Thornton's wild life and crashing death. The national newsfeed from CBS, NBC, and ABC broadcast accounts of the tragicomic fate of the millionaire, racehorse breeder, lawyer, pilot, jumper, and cop-turned-drug-smuggler.

"I sure don't want to wake up to *that* every morning," eighty-five-year-old Fred Myers told the *Knoxville Journal,* referring to finding a broken Drew Thornton lying stacked on his paraphernalia near Myers' strawberry patch.

The heavily armed cocaine commando was wearing Army-issue night-vision goggles, a money belt with forty-five hundred dollars, and a bulletproof vest when he hit the gravel driveway. In his wallet was a membership card for the Lexington Fraternal Order of Police, identification in the names of Andrew Thornton and Andrew Bourbon, fifty telephone numbers—most of which were listed in code—and a personal address book containing fewer than a dozen names. Tied around the neck of the 82nd Airborne veteran were ten bandanas of different colors.

Lying on his back, Drew's arms were stretched over his head. A trickle of blood from his nose had dried on each cheek. Four of his teeth had been knocked out, and he clutched the ripcord to his partially deployed reserve chute in his right hand. Under his knees, which were elevated by the bulk, lay a three-and-a-half-foot-long duffel bag containing seventy-five pounds of pure, unprocessed cocaine. The thirty-four football-sized parcels of cocaine were wrapped in brown paper, and were labeled USA 10—the logo that had become the trademark of the Medellín Cartel. Another duffel bag tied to his waist contained his weapons and survival materials.

When police responded to the old man's reported sighting, they were struck by the seeming incongruity of Drew's apparel: Gucci shoes with combat fatigues. But to those, like Ralph Ross, who had known and studied Drew for many years, for Drew to be fully outfitted for battle, and yet wearing lightweight Italian shoes, only underscored the enigma of Andrew Carter Thornton II.

"On the plains of hesitation lie the blackened bodies of countless millions who, at the dawn of victory, sat down to rest, and resting, died," read one of the epigrams Drew carried in the pocket of his jacket. "Believe nothing," read another, ". . . believe what yourself judge to be true."

Ralph immediately began to piece together the information on the circumstances surrounding Drew's death.

In the year and a half since Harold Brown's suicide, Ralph had returned to Kentucky from his Rocky Mountain hideout. Though he hadn't actively pursued Company members, he continued to light fires under his friends in the FBI. He particularly encouraged them to try to make a case against Henry Vance for Vance's role in the Gene Berry killing.

Sources continued to call Ralph to relate information about the group. It seemed that the Company had become fragmented between 1982 and 1985, and that Thornton worked for the Carlos Lehder faction of what had come to be called the "Medellín Cartel."

Acquaintances of Drew's told Ralph that Drew was even more paranoid than before, and that he had alienated many of his former associates. A tight circle now existed, Ralph was told. Following the conviction of Jimmy Lambert, Bradley Bryant, and Bonnie Kelly, it seemed that Drew distrusted everyone. His core group consisted of Henry Vance and Bill Canan, and he now bragged of being an independent operator.

Simultaneously, Ralph was told by the FBI that the Colombians controlled cocaine smuggling now, and that the Company had been swallowed up by that foreign enterprise.

A fellow mercenary of Drew's had told Ralph that Drew had been hanging around Ilopango—the Salvadoran air base where weapons from the U.S. were transshipped to the *contras*—and that he had quickly gained the reputation of a "down-and-out, pissed-off soldier of fortune looking for action." Drew had also been seen in Tegucigalpa—the capital of Honduras and center of American military action in Central America—hobnobbing with *contra* leaders.

It was unclear whether Drew intended to land in Tennessee, or was on his way to Kentucky. There was also confusion about whether Rebecca Sharp had identified him, or if his parents traveled to Tennessee to view the body. Some even questioned if it was really Drew Thornton.

Ralph read the autopsy report over and over again, searching for that which was not obvious: "The body is that of a very well developed, muscular, well-nourished adult white male," began the report.

Combining the pathological findings with the FBI laboratory reports and the examination of Drew's parachute, the Tennessee medical examiner created the following scenario: "The victim jumped from the aircraft and opened his main chute, but for an unknown reason got a streamer. By this time he was at terminal velocity and did a crosshand release of the reserve chute which destabilized him in a head-down position. The abrupt deceleration by the emergency chute—from 120 miles-per-hour to 40 miles-per-hour in four seconds—decelerated the victim but not the bag attached to his waistbelt. He was then struck by this bag, inflicting the abrasions of the neck and chin and fractured teeth, which produced at least semi-consciousness. Because of this semi-conscious state, he did not release the brakes on the reserve chute which caused oscillation, during one phase of which, the leading edge of the chute stalled allowing him to essentially freefall an unknown number of feet."

Why did the medical examiner's findings fail to mention the possibility of what Ralph's sources in the FBI had told him that Drew had been hit by something either before or during his jump. Had he been beaten on board and then thrown out? Had he been hit by the tail of his own plane as he came out the door, which would explain the swath of lacerations across his face and fractured teeth? Or had he been hit by a wingtip, either intentionally or inadvertently, by a Customs chase plane? If so, was a cover-up underway?

Parachute experts called to the scene were in a quandary, unable to determine if the main chute had malfunctioned, or if Drew had failed to open it. Authorities ultimately decided that Drew had been struck by a part of the aircraft as he jumped out its door, and that he never attempted to open his main parachute. Knocked unconscious, they concluded that Drew was clinically dying while falling, and that his deployment of his reserve chute was a purely reflexive act. Though the reserve opened, it couldn't handle the weight of Drew and the cocaine. The rapid deceleration caused Drew's body to collapse from the inside out, rupturing his aorta, which led to massive hemorrhaging. Drew had landed on his heels before falling onto his back, the cocaine beneath him. His spine and most of his ribs then fractured. He was alive for two minutes after he hit the ground.

Parachutists—both recreational and combat—who had jumped

with Drew in the past, were shocked. Known for the meticulous care he took in packing his two-thousand-dollar chute—considered the "Cadillac of gear"—Drew's mishap seemed incredible to fellow jumpers. His chute had been specially rigged to open fast, and he was notoriously fanatical about packing his own chute. Basing their theories on the indentations in the driveway, and the condition of Drew's corpse, experts decided that Drew had hit the ground just a few seconds after his Pioneer Reliant reserve canopy opened. Drew had a reputation for "pulling low," or waiting until he was well under the standard minimum altitude of two thousand feet to pull his ripcord. In the weeks prior to his death, he had been seen practicing such jumps at skydiving centers in Georgia and Kentucky.

Since Drew's airplane had last been seen in Miami, experts wondered if perhaps his altimeter had been set at sea level—a potentially fatal mistake considering Knoxville's mountainous terrain and 832-foot elevation. Some speculated that Drew might have waited until the last possible moment to open his parachute in order to avoid being detected by Customs chase planes. But Ralph Ross considered that explanation absurd, since he believed Drew was familiar with Customs' sophisticated infrared capabilities. Ralph was positive that Drew realized a Customs chase plane could illuminate the sky with what they called "night sun." Only an amateur would think he could parachute from a plane and not be sighted by such equipment.

Drew had belonged to a group that called themselves "BASE jumpers"—an acronym for Building, Antennae, Span, and Earth. Drew had recently completed his certification in the group by jumping from a skyscraper (building), a broadcast tower (antennae), a bridge (span), and a Norwegian cliff (earth).

He was an expert who had jumped more than a thousand times into situations considerably more complex and dangerous. A few days before his death, Drew had jumped onto the Kentucky riverbank, narrowly missing a maze of electrical wires and a grove of trees.

Ralph didn't believe that Drew had intended to jump into the midnight sky, loaded down with cocaine, and relying solely upon his reserve chute. He didn't care how brave Drew claimed to be, such an act just didn't make sense. Something, Ralph was convinced, had forced Drew into his contingency plan.

Rebecca Sharp had been waiting for Drew in Knoxville, so that had apparently been his destination. Who was his off-load crew? Where were they now? Who and where were Drew's countersurveillance crew? Ralph knew that Drew didn't bring loads into the U.S. without a ground crew who maintained surface-to-air communication and who monitored Customs radio frequencies in order to detect a chase.

Had Drew miscalculated his altitude? Or was he so pumped up on adrenaline and cocaine that he jumped with too heavy a load? Stories indicated that Drew had an increasing dependency upon cocaine. One source told Ralph that Drew's habit of more than a gram a day was making him even more paranoid than usual, and that in the weeks prior to his death he was agitated and high strung. He had become fanatical in his preparations for Armageddon and the impending race wars, further tightening security around his farm, Triad. His strenuous preparation and disciplined physical endeavors were eerily prescient in their intensity. His close friends said that Drew had become a "different man" in the days before his death, that he trusted no one, confided in no one, and had lost his organization.

If that was true, then for whose organization was Drew transporting cocaine? Had Drew intended to drop the cocaine attached to parachutes in specified locations for later retrieval? Could he have been part of a rip-off scheme in which he was attempting to steal from a larger load the $15 million worth of cocaine he had on his body? If so, where was the rest of the load?

Drew had made a significant error in judgment a few months earlier when he dropped a load of cocaine onto the Hawk's Nest side of the Bahamas instead of on the other side of the island where the ground crew was waiting. The Colombians who had commissioned that flight were not happy when Bahamian authorities seized the valuable contraband.

On the night of his death Drew's fantasies may have metasticized into a full-fledged case of paranoid delusion. Probably with reason, Ralph thought. Ralph could not be convinced that Drew Thornton would voluntarily jump into a black sky in a populated area carrying seventy-five pounds of cocaine.

Someone was chasing him, Ralph felt certain. But who? Customs or the Colombians?

■

At 1 A.M. on September 11, two men were fishing in the remote western North Carolina recreational area of Nantahala Lake. They heard an airplane pass over. Then, the cool, clear night air was suddenly ripped open by an explosion. Both men turned in the direction of the sound, and saw a ball of fire on a nearby mountainside. Fifteen minutes later they reported the incident to the Clay County Sheriff's Office.

Investigators from Tennessee, North Carolina, the DEA, FBI, and the National Transportation and Safety Board (NTSB) hiked nearly five hours through fog and rugged terrain to the crash site. Located sixty miles from Knoxville, the plane crash was immediately linked to Drew's last sky dive. The twin-engine had been placed on automatic pilot and smashed into the mountain when it ran out of fuel. Because of the lack of flammable gasoline, the plane had only burned slightly by the time police arrived on the scene. Worth $250,000, the Cessna 404 was described as a "smuggler's dream." Among other things, it was equipped with long-range fuel tanks. Not surprisingly, the plane's identifying number—N128SP—matched the key found on Drew's body. A half-mile from the site, police found a mysterious red sleeping bag rolled up against a tree, and a blue bandana, resembling those worn by Drew, tied to a tree limb.

FAA inspectors immediately set about to trace the murky ownership of the aircraft. Originally owned by buyers in Gabon, Nigeria, and Zimbabwe, it had been sold in 1984 to Opex Aviation of Santa Paula, California. Since that time, the plane had changed hands through brokers in Tucson, Arizona, Shreveport, Louisiana, and Fort Lauderdale, Florida, within a two-month time period. Two days before Drew's jump, the plane was purchased in Florida by a company called Key Air. That company was traced back to Bertram Gordon—the elderly Miami Jockey Club resident who would pay Rebecca Sharp a visit nine days after Drew's death. Immediately before Key Air bought the aircraft, a company called South Air contracted with a Florida airport to have the extra fuel tanks installed. Other modifications included removing the back from the pilot's and copilot's seats in order to accommodate wearing parachute gear while flying the plane.

All evidence at the crash site linked the plane to Drew's venture earlier that night. No bodies, no luggage, and no blood were found. The seat belts were fastened on the six passenger seats, but were open on the pilot's and copilot's, prompting investigators to theorize that a second person had indeed been on board the aircraft. None of the registration documents, airworthiness certificates, or various licenses required to be aboard an aircraft were present.

One item was found on board, however, that would haunt Ralph Ross for years to come: In a briefcase was a hit list, complete with dossiers and photographs, of three men whom Drew wanted dead. At the top of that list was the name "Ralph Ross." Two other Kentucky cops were on the list—Captain James Black and Bud Farmer from the Jefferson County Police Department.

Why had Drew taken the hit list on this drug run? Had he hired a contract killer in Colombia to do the job?

When police searched Drew's Lexington residence located in the Merrick Place compound near where Drew had been shot three years earlier, they found an arsenal of death. By the time Lexington police and the FBI arrived at Drew's apartment, though, someone had obviously removed any incriminating evidence from the townhouse. What was left behind for the detectives' perusal were the same types of exotic poisons and explosives that had been found in DEA agent Harold Brown's cabin following Brown's suicide. They seized tear gas, smoke grenades, flares, ether, nicotine, hydrochloric acid, and sodium and ammonium nitrate.

On Saturday afternoon, September 14, two U.S. Forest Service employees were on routine patrol in northern Georgia when they spotted a white parachute hanging from a tree. They drove past the tree, located seventy-five feet from the road, and then decided to return to inspect the odd sight. When they examined the chute—marked Okinawa 9—they found three black nylon duffel bags attached. Inside were a hundred and fifty pounds of cocaine—wrapped in the same exact way and with the identical locking devices as the cocaine found on Drew. The green military-type canvas duffel bags within the nylon bags were marked USA 30, while the individual cocaine parcels inside were marked USA 10. That same afternoon, in the Chattahoochee National Forest in Georgia, more duffel bags and cocaine were found. Not coincidentally, witnesses had heard a low-flying aircraft in the areas of the cocaine drops the night Drew made his last flight, leading investigators to conclude Drew had thrown numerous parachute-laden drug bundles along a flight path from South America to Tennessee.

Dispatching helicopters and airplanes, federal agents began searching for what they thought would be at least another six hundred pounds of cocaine—since DEA's informant, Bertram Gordon, claimed Drew had picked up eight hundred pounds the day before in Colombia. The only distinguishing similarities in the drop sites appeared to be their proximity to bodies of water, so federal agents set about to re-create a flight path that used remote lakes and streams as landmarks.

■

A Georgia farmer's wife walked out to her turnip patch to pick some vegetables. There, in her garden, was a plastic shopping bag.

Mary Kitchens had heard lots of stories about drugs being smuggled into central Georgia. So her first thought upon finding the bag was that it would be filled with dope. "I looked at the stuff only briefly because I didn't want to get involved. I didn't even want it in the house," she later told reporters.

She returned to her house to notify her husband. J. B. Kitchens —a sixty-two-year-old Butts County farmer—was less reluctant to get involved. When he peered into what he called "the bag of goodies," its contents puzzled him. Inside the bag, which was labeled National Health and Nutrition, were packages of sunflower seeds, nuts, raisins, and chewing gum, candy bars, books listing landing sites across the United States, a pilot's aviation guide to the Bahamas, and maps of Jamaica.

That morning, Mrs. Kitchens called the Butts County sheriff. "I'm afraid we got something that doesn't belong to us," she told the dispatcher. But the law enforcement agency seemed uninterested, and didn't bother to investigate further.

The next week, Mr. Kitchens spotted a black nylon garment bag with a Brass Boot label floating in his fish pond. When he retrieved it and examined its contents, he found a polo shirt, men's underwear, a pair of swimming trunks, an extra-large jacket, keys to a pair of hand-cuffs, a lock-blade knife, two bottles of sterile water for contact lenses, and a bottle of nasal spray.

They again called the sheriff's office, which expressed only a tad more interest in the incident. A deputy visited the farm and confiscated the items. He let Mr. Kitchens keep the knife as a souvenir because Kitchens "thought he should get something out of all this."

When Mr. Kitchens called the sheriff for the third time, on September 16—five days after Drew Thornton's death, investigator Mike Riley responded immediately—his interest having been piqued by the earlier findings and press reports about Drew's drug-laden parachute jump. Kitchens' fifteen-year-old grandson, Dale, had found a pilot's manual on the property.

In the Cessna 404 manual was the plane registration number: N2678D. Though that number differed from N128SP—the number on Drew's pilotless plane that had crashed into a North Carolina mountain—a record search revealed the plane had originally been registered under N2678D.

With the latest discovery, a profusion of federal and state agents arrived to search the forty-eight-acre farm located forty-five miles south of Atlanta. But efforts were later abandoned when no additional evidence turned up.

"There is nothing startling about the Thornton case," said Atlanta DEA special agent Thomas Cash to reporters. "But the method he used seems to have tickled the public's fancy. There was cocaine . . . literally falling from the sky. This isn't *Chicken Little.*"

∎

Kentucky's newspapers rushed to publish profiles of the decorated Army paratrooper and progeny of a well-heeled Bluegrass family.

" 'Sure, I'll tell you about him. Just don't print my name,' " was the typical response of the men and women who were asked about him, wrote the neighborhood *Chevy Chase Chronicle.*

His friends and enemies chose adjectives to alternately describe Drew as "tough," "courageous," "intelligent," "charming," "loyal," "a light drinker," "a heavy drinker," "a cocaine addict," "a dangerous man," and "a gentle man."

Immortalizing their native son, the *Courier Journal* quoted the president of a local parachute club, who said: " 'Drew and I had basically the same code. He was quiet, he didn't brag. And he believed in an eye for an eye, and that revenge is sweet.' "

The *Lexington Herald-Leader* wrote: "Some saw a karate master who became deeply impressed with Asian philosophy and a true friend who would bear any burden for those close to him. Others saw the daredevil skydiver who was always the last to pull his chute, the survivalist who played war games with live ammunition and the weapons fanatic who always wore a bulletproof vest. 'I never wanted to say anything against Thornton because I was afraid he would firebomb my house,' said a man who asked not to be identified."

His expensive clothing and white Jaguar sparked one acquaintance to comment: "He reminded me of a rich polo player, a jet-setter, a Paul Newman type."

Drew's generosity proved to be slightly unsettling for some of his friends. A two-page, handwritten will shone an unmerciful light on Drew's beneficiaries. Bequeathing the lion's share of his estate to long-time friend Henry Vance, other assets were divided among friends and family. One thing was certain: Each of Drew's heirs would become subjects of the federal government's inquisitive eye. Such scrutiny would prove embarrassing for U.S. Customs agent Jay Silvestro, among others.

The will, dated June 18, 1984, provided for the distribution of assets without placing a value on the total estate:

> *I, Andrew Carter Thornton II, do this 18th day of June 1984 set pen to paper to write my last will and testament.*
>
> *Being of sound mind and body at the time of this writing I leave the following monies and properties to the following people. I leave J. Randall Reinhardt, Attorney-At-Law, as my Executor, and specify that he receive $5,000 as his fee.*
>
> *To my father, mother, brother and sister—my horses, to share + share alike.*
>
> *To my neices (sic) + nephews—the proceeds of my whole life insurance policies with Northwestern Mutual Life Ins. Company.*
>
> *To Sally Ely Sharp McCloud [Rebecca's aunt], a personal*

communication in the form of a letter, which will be left with Phil
Clements, Randy Reinhardt, or my parents.

To Rebecca Ann Sharp, a personal letter to be left with Phil
Clements, Randy Reinhardt or my parents.

To Henry Vance, my Jessamine Cty. property, my Jer-
rico + Eli Lilly stock + my oil well interests (Contact Richard
Harris, Fresno, Cal.)

To Louis Andrew Silvestro, son of Jay Joseph Silvestro, my
godson, my interest in Pino Altos Limited Partnership.

To Tony Dehner, my interest in 411 Kenilworth Ct.

To Billy Rhodes, my parachute gear.

To Henry Vance, Jamie Thackaberry, Tim Thorn-
ton + Rebecca   Sharp + Phil   Clements,   my   weapons,
share + share alike.

To Rebecca Sharp those stocks remaining at my death other
than those given to Henry Vance.

The remainder of my personal property to include but not
limited to cars, clothes, books, etc. is to be disposed of by Sally Ely
Sharp McCloud + Rebecca Ann Sharp as they see fit.

There is to be no funeral. After useable body parts (eyes,
kidneys, etc.) are removed I want to be cremated. Release my ashes
in air over my parents farm + then have a party.

Each page of this two-page document is signed by me.

Randy Reinhardt—a partner in the prominent Lexington law
firm of Bullitt Kinkead Irvin and Reinhardt—was conspicuously absent
in the immediate days following Drew's death. Though Drew had
named Reinhardt executor of his estate, Reinhardt begged off, citing a
hectic schedule. Drew's family then asked the Probate Court to appoint
Louisville attorney C. Fred Partin to take Reinhardt's place.

Drew's death was also dicey for his retinue of loyal allies.
Though he had specifically requested that there be no funeral, his parents, who were deeply religious, overrode his wishes. In a poignant
ceremony on a chilly Kentucky morning, two hundred mourners paid
their respects. Despite certainty that drug agents would infiltrate the
funeral, shooting photographs and recording names and license numbers, the bereaved braved their way to the Bourbon County grave site—

filing past the giant wreath signed *I will always love you, Rebecca.* Among those grieving, the media noted, was Jimmy Lambert. Not among them, reporters observed, was former Governor John Y. Brown, Jr.

"He went out like an Eagle Scout," said his former wife, Betty Zaring. "He loved the concept of the warriors who fall from the sky."

The family requested that in lieu of flowers donations be sent to the United States Parachute Association in Alexandria, Virginia. A month later, the association had received only one contribution: A dime taped to a blank piece of paper.

Threave Main Stud—Drew's childhood home and serene adult retreat—assumed a dark, mournful appearance as autumn turned to winter. True to their character, the Thorntons contributed to the mystique surrounding their strange son. They refused to be pitied, withdrawing further and further into their code of silence. That year their standing studs were named "Silent Dignity" and "Best of It."

■

Drug agents continued their multistate search for the remainder of Drew's cocaine shipment for several weeks. But they weren't the only ones engaged in the treasure hunt. Forest Service officials reported record numbers of "hikers" combing the Chattahoochee Forest. Pilots in private airplanes used binoculars to scout the rugged countryside. A two-hundred-pound bear discovered one of the duffel bags, and died of an overdose after burying his face in the powder. In Cherokee County, Georgia—north of Atlanta—a parachute with its straps cut was found in a residential backyard that was adjacent to a vacant field. Neighbors remembered a maroon car that was parked nearby on the night of Drew's last jump.

That car was traced to David "Cowboy" Williams, who had been a member of Drew's off-load crew and who was to be responsible for driving the nine hundred pounds of cocaine from Knoxville to the "stash house" in Daytona, Florida, where it would be turned over to the Colombians' distributors. But, like so many others whose paths intersected with Drew Thornton, the owner of the maroon Mercedes-Benz with vanity plates that read SKYDIV would not live long enough to provide clues.

At noon, on September 29, 1985, "Cowboy" was doing what he did every weekend: He boarded himself, a pilot, and fifteen recreational sky divers onto his commercial Cessna 208 Caravan. Operating out of the West Wind Sport Parachute Club—a remote landing strip located three miles from the Kitchens' farm in Jenkinsburg, Georgia—"Cowboy" regularly ferried loads of jumpers on his $750,000 single-engine turboprop. He charged the sky divers a standard rate of $1.00 per thousand feet of altitude. The plane, which had been purchased by Williams four months earlier, was coveted by Williams' competitors, so admired was it for its speedy climbing capability. Williams regularly took the plane to so-called "jump-boogies" in various parts of the country, where it was the envy of everyone.

On this particular Sunday, two and a half weeks after Drew's deadly jump, Williams—a Vietnam helicopter pilot and longtime associate of Drew's—intended to parachute in formation with the other jumpers when the plane reached twelve thousand feet. The plane barreled down the runway at seemingly normal speed, but was airborne only a few seconds before witnesses on the ground heard sputtering. When they looked up, they saw the expensive aircraft spiraling downward in an uncontrollable nosedive.

All seventeen people on board were killed instantly when the plane crashed into the ground.

Investigators swarmed to the scene. From the meadow where the plane crashed, officials held a press conference at which they announced findings almost too weird to be believed: The plane's fuel had been contaminated. Someone, it seemed, had added sugar to the gas tank.

The FBI's Atlanta office assigned twenty agents to investigate the suspected sabotage.

Gary Scott, a Savannah pilot and former associate of Drew Thornton's who had been convicted in connection with the DC-4 seized in Lexington five years earlier, speculated from his jail cell about the events. Admittedly bitter at taking a fall for one of Drew's deals, there was no love lost between the two men. "A lot of people were glad when Drew died," Scott said. "He was kinky and greedy, and known as a rip-off." In Scott's scenario, the Colombian cocaine suppliers had sabotaged "Cowboy's" Caravan to avenge the botched cocaine scheme. "It was a classic scam," Scott said in an interview with the author shortly after Drew's death. "Drew would pick up the coke in Colombia, deliver it to the distributors in the U.S., then return to Colombia short of money. He'd lie to the Colombian suppliers who had fronted him the coke, telling them that certain distributors had refused to pay. The Colombians would retaliate by killing the people Drew had fingered."

Scott was not the only Company insider speculating about a massive cocaine theft attempted by Drew Thornton, "Cowboy" Williams, and their co-conspirators. The *Macon Telegraph & News* reported that the Caravan was sabotaged because of a "sizeable amount [of cocaine] skimmed from the shipment going to Tennessee." The thought that Colombian drug dealers would kill sixteen innocent people in order to eliminate one man—"Cowboy" Williams—was to many people incredible.

Law enforcement analysts familiar with the Colombians' more standard *modus operandi* discounted the revenge theory.

Still other "anonymous sources" hypothesized to newspapers that "Cowboy" Williams was suspected by Drew's organization of being the snitch who was responsible for Customs following Drew's plane. So vengeful and cold-blooded was Drew's faithful Kentucky cadre, that killing sixteen innocent victims would serve as a powerful message to any future Judases.

Conjecture in this vein did not seem farfetched to Ralph Ross. He knew that Drew's group was capable of anything. He believed with all his heart that if "Cowboy" bore any responsibility whatsoever for Drew's death, then he would pay with his life.

On the other hand, Ralph was puzzled by the DEA's attempts to downplay "Cowboy"'s relationship with Drew. He knew that the two men had been associated for more than a decade, and that surveillance reports in the possession of the Kentucky State Police Intelligence Division would prove such a connection. But neither the DEA nor the FBI seemed to want to pursue those links.

C H A P T E R

TWENTY-TWO

AUGUST 1989.
Eindhoven, Holland

The tulips were at their peak, the fragrance of hyacinths permeating the countryside. But Bertram R. Gordon—the dignified Miami millionaire and pilot—could not appreciate Holland's beauty from his solitary confinement cell. Suddenly, a man accustomed to blanketing the globe, living on yachts and island estates, charging high-priced items at Neiman-Marcus and maintaining a life of luxury at his Jockey Club apartment, flashing a Canadian passport and socializing with leaders of Caribbean and South American countries was ensconced in secrecy.

To an undiscerning eye, the sixty-two-year-old man would appear to be a refined grandfatherly type individual; an international financier who was said to have made a fortune as an airplane salesman; a gray-haired, balding, affable fellow with a light heart and animated tale. "The nicest guy in the world," said a longtime acquaintance.

But to listen to a rash of American and international law enforcement agents tell it, Bertram Gordon was the most wanted man in the world.

Bert Gordon bought airplanes. Lots of them.

The DEA believed that Gordon provided aircraft for the entire Medellín Cartel—the Colombian cocaine import and distribution network responsible for 80 percent of the cocaine entering the United States and Canada. Gordon, according to the DEA, worked directly for Carlos Lehder—the convicted Colombian billionaire whose cocaine empire was part of his political vision to destabilize America.

The reason the DEA knew so much about Bert Gordon was because Gordon worked for them. Or did, until one of his planes crashed, unmanned, into a North Carolina mountain.

Gordon had been on the lam for several years before his appre-hension in February 1989 in the Netherlands. Though frequent sight-ings of him had been reported in Spain and the Bahamas, he was apparently always one step ahead of the authorities. Following a 1988 federal indictment in Florida charging him with importing cocaine from Paradise Island into Fort Lauderdale, Gordon had decided to skip out. That indictment, according to friends, was but one more thorn in Gor-don's side.

Perhaps the least worrisome of his myriad problems was a sec-ond indictment charging him with the death of Andrew Carter Thornton II. But this charge was also the most perplexing, for Bertram Gordon didn't believe that the body that fell from the sky over Knoxville, Tennessee, four years earlier was really Drew Thornton.

■

Ralph Ross wanted to get to Bert Gordon before the talkative old con man was killed by one of his vast circle of international enemies.

What had begun with the death of Drew Thornton had risen to a level of international intrigue that surpassed even Ralph's active imagi-nation and musings.

Ralph sat in the living room of his Anderson County, Kentucky, home. Out the window, he could see the vivid green grass spreading before him down to the fence line that ran along the creek, separating Ralph's land from his neighbor's. A few newborn leaves were barely attached to the tree limbs, struggling to survive until all threat of snow and ice storms had passed.

Ralph had built what he hoped would be his last home. He had designed and constructed his two-story house to provide enough space for separate living quarters for his daughter, son-in-law, and first grand-son.

Downstairs, Ralph had built a bachelor's apartment to match his needs—a bedroom, a bathroom, a living room, a kitchen, and a garage large enough to house a tractor. Equipped with heavy, masculine furni-ture, an antique oak dining table, an electric coffee maker, a television, VCR, stereo, telephone-answering machine, and a few decorative items, the dwelling provided Ralph with a stable sense of "home" that he had been lacking for nearly a decade.

Propped up against one wall, as if awaiting Ralph's judgment as to whether or not it deserved a place of prominence, was a limited-edition print depicting the hat and accoutrements of the Kentucky State Police trooper. Ralph's mixed feelings about the artwork that had been presented to him following his wiretapping conviction by his daughters, Connie Zoe and Christie Jo, were as unreconciled as his thoughts about law enforcement.

On this spring day in 1989, Ralph drank a glass of Chablis as he listed the questions he intended to ask Bert Gordon. Although Gordon's visitation rights were severely restricted, Ralph had decided to use whatever connections were necessary to invade Gordon's privacy. For it was Gordon, Ralph had come to believe, who held the key to the mystery of Drew Thornton.

Fighting extradition back to the United States, where he faced a slew of federal drug trafficking charges, Gordon was said to be offering deals right and left with the DEA, FBI, Florida Department of Law Enforcement, Interpol, and Dutch officials.

Further complicating matters was the ubiquitous presence of a CIA operative from Miami who floated in and out of the various investigations, a man described by DEA agents as a "close family friend of Gordon's," and with whom Gordon had apparently been in regular contact for many years.

Ralph's mind was once again in overdrive. When he first learned of Gordon's arrest the previous spring, Ralph was only vaguely familiar with the name. He had read in the newspaper a couple of years earlier that Gordon was the man who had posed as a Colombian representative, along with an undercover DEA agent, to elicit information from Rebecca Sharp about the circumstances surrounding Drew's death. That confession had resulted in Sharp's indictment in Tennessee, but a federal magistrate had dismissed the charges, ruling that Sharp's "confession" had been coerced by the two men.

The DEA in Knoxville had somehow co-opted the Drew Thornton investigation, and Ralph thought they had pursued it from the beginning with a minimum of enthusiasm. It would have made more sense for the federal authorities in Florida to direct the investigation, since Drew's drug run had originated in Fort Lauderdale. Ralph found it particularly odd that DEA made so few inquiries with state or federal agencies in Kentucky about Drew. One would have thought, considering Drew's long-standing history of smuggling activities in Kentucky, that such exploration would have been *pro forma.*

Ralph set out to reconstruct the events leading up to Drew's death. He contacted sources in FDLE who were spearheading the investigation against Gordon. The thrust of their investigation, Ralph was told, was based upon the following set of facts: Gordon, a DEA informant of many years standing, was in charge of transport for the Medellín Cartel. In that capacity, he provided the airplanes and pilots for most of the cocaine importation into the United States. One of Gordon's most agile and experienced pilots was Drew Thornton.

Gordon was in the unique and enviable position of having cocaine fronted by the Colombians, having money fronted to him by the cartel's American distributors, receiving thousands of dollars in compensation from the DEA for his informant services, and eliminating his competitors in the drug business by snitching them out to DEA.

The similarities in methods and personalities between Gordon and Drew were striking.

Drew had been living with Gordon at the Jockey Club in the weeks prior to the September 1985 drug run, and, according to friends, was edgy and nervous about the planned operation. As late as the day before he flew to Colombia, Drew was trying to round up a companion for the trip. He told friends that he didn't need a copilot, but merely someone who could "watch his back," or conduct countersurveillance.

Gordon, meanwhile, had been yanked from his DEA "control" agent, who internal inspectors had come to believe was allowing Gordon to run rampant. Reassigned to DEA agent Kieran Kobell, Gordon found himself suddenly under enormous pressure to produce a significant case for DEA—not to merely throw them a bone by informing on a competitor.

Gordon reluctantly agreed to inform on a deal in the works involving Drew Thornton. But Kobell would find that Gordon continued to dig in his heels, insisting on telling Kobell only bits and pieces of the plans. According to Gordon, the following scheme was underway: Bert Gordon had purchased a Cessna 404 for Drew, and had introduced

Drew to the Colombian suppliers; Drew was to fly to Colombia and pick up four hundred kilos of cocaine, for which he would be paid four thousand dollars per kilo, plus the airplane; the cocaine would be brought into Knoxville, Tennessee, where it would be off-loaded by Drew's crew, and trucked back to a stash house in Daytona, Florida, where it would be whacked up by the Colombian cartel's American distributors.

Drew, meanwhile, would travel from Knoxville back to Lexington with Rebecca Sharp.

Tennessee had been selected by Drew, according to Gordon, because it was the hub for Federal Express, and he thought he could avoid radar detection by blending in with the courier planes.

Although Gordon consistently failed to hold up his end of the agreement with Kobell, Kobell learned independently that a few days before the drug run Gordon had purchased the aircraft and had it ferried to Fort Lauderdale International Airport, where Drew arranged to have the plane modified to accommodate extra fuel tanks and the removal of the seats.

Gordon had promised to notify Kobell when Drew took off, so that Kobell could arrange to have the plane tracked. Distrusting Gordon, however, Kobell took the initiative and alerted the U.S. Customs Air Support division in Miami that an aircraft, tail number N128SP, was preparing for a run to Colombia.

It was shocking for Kobell, therefore, to be watching the national news two days later and to learn of Drew Thornton's death, since Gordon had never told Kobell that the plane had taken off. Gordon claimed to be as surprised as Kobell, and, in his defense, Gordon explained that he had intended to inform Kobell about the load after it was trucked into Daytona. Such a decision was not Gordon's to make, Kobell told him, as it became obvious to Kobell that Gordon had intended to let Drew get away, while busting the underlings in the conspiracy.

Kobell's angst was but one of Gordon's mounting problems, as the Colombians held him responsible for the millions of dollars' worth of cocaine that was missing. The Colombians dispatched Gordon to Kentucky to talk to Rebecca Sharp to find out where the coke had gone.

"I'm going with you," Kobell told Gordon, in no uncertain terms.

Kobell ignored Gordon's protestations, insinuating himself in Gordon's every move.

Identifying himself as James Vincent—a representative of the Colombians, Kobell watched as Rebecca pulled on her white gloves. For a split second Kobell thought maybe she was about to pull out a gun and blow them both away. But instead, to Kobell's relief, she recounted what seemed to him to be a remarkably pat story: Drew and his mysteriously anonymous companion were being "chased by two Citations and a Black Hawk helicopter," and were forced to throw the cocaine out, set the plane on auto pilot, and jump.

Further, the attractive, well-groomed blonde said that she would kill anyone in Drew's organization who failed to hold up his end of the bargain.

Surely, Rebecca was mortified to learn, many months later that the two undercover DEA operatives would use her statements against her, that she had unwittingly confessed every detail of the smuggling conspiracy to two undercover DEA operatives who, prior to Rebecca's statements, possessed zero knowledge about Drew's tragically thwarted mission.

Kobell was as baffled as anyone when Customs denied having launched any chase planes the night of September 10, 1984.

It wasn't until April 1989 that Ralph Ross learned the details of Rebecca Sharp's statement, and recognized their possible implications.

Ralph thought that the report of Rebecca's story seemed too specific about the aircraft. She didn't say that the two men *learned,* perhaps by monitoring Customs channels, that they were being chased. She said they *saw* the three airplanes out the window. But Ralph's research indicated that in September 1985, only a handful of Customs pilots were certified to fly a Citation jet, and that the agency was still using the Cobra helicopter—not the Black Hawk.

Further, Customs consistently maintained that they were not chasing Drew Thornton. If any log reports or radio transmissions existed regarding such a chase, Customs denied their existence to DEA. Even had Customs "gone up," as they refer to a launch, it is highly improbable that Drew Thornton would have seen them out the window, as they usually fly at least two thousand feet higher than the suspect aircraft.

What reason would Customs have for denying such a chase? Ralph wondered. Had one of the pilots decided he'd teach the smuggler a lesson by whacking him with a wingtip? Would that explain why Drew's body had been mutilated from top to bottom when it was found in the old man's driveway, and why he was half-dead during his fall?

Ralph pulled out the autopsy report and pathologist's findings, and examined them once again—Drew's back was broken in two or three places, 70 percent of the circumference of his aorta was lacerated, his pelvic area was separated from his abdomen by a gaping hole, his chin and neck were full of bruises and abrasions, his teeth were fractured, several of his ribs were broken, and his spinal cord was torn.

It sounded more like a man who had been run over by a Mack truck, than an experienced sky diver who had jumped out of an airplane with two chutes in perfect working order.

Those who examined the corpse, Ralph learned, had speculated privately that perhaps Drew had not died in the scenario put forth, and generally believed, by the medical examiner: That the bag of cocaine knocked Drew semi-conscious, leaving him incapable of maneuvering.

So what had happened? Had Drew been knocked across the chest by a chase plane? Had he been hit across the face by his own plane's stabilizer? Why was he wearing expensive Italian shoes if he intended to jump? Was he killed on board and thrown out?

One mystery, however, could be eliminated: That the body was indeed that of Drew Thornton, and was neither a "double" nor a convenient "stiff." The Knoxville Police Department had matched the corpse's fingerprints to the FBI's prints of Drew.

Ralph racked his brain for a plausible explanation of the circumstances. Although the DEA denied publicly that they had ever identified Drew's accomplice, Ralph knew that they had, and that the man was a Lexington bodybuilder and martial arts expert named Bill Leonard. Why hadn't Leonard ever been charged in the conspiracy?

The DEA in Knoxville had concluded that Drew had intended to throw the cocaine out of the airplane in designated areas, to be retrieved by the ground crews and trucked back to Florida. But Ralph had problems with that theory, considering it too risky to drop millions of dollars of cocaine into national forest attached to parachutes. It seemed like a needle in a haystack.

Maybe it had indeed been a rip-off scheme, in which Drew planned to throw the dope out in previously specified areas, using remote bodies of water as landmarks, to be picked up by his organization on the ground, then sky-diving to safety while pretending to have died in the plane crash.

What about "Cowboy" Williams and the crash of the Caravan? It was strange that the feds had reneged on their original determination that the plane had been sabotaged. Was one agency protecting another government agency? Was "Cowboy" killed by Drew's people for failing to fulfill his obligations? Or by the Colombians for participating in the rip-off?

Ralph suspected that Drew had not flown an empty plane to Colombia, he was much too shrewd to waste such an opportunity. Drew had probably taken a load of weapons south. For it was Ralph's conviction, having pursued Drew Thornton for nearly two decades, that he was a gunrunner first and a doper second. It was clear to Ralph that Drew fancied himself an elite soldier in Lieutenant Colonel Oliver North's formerly secret war. If Ralph was right, then where had the guns gone? Was that why his smuggling escapade had not been pursued with vigor, and why Customs denied any knowledge?

∎

In the years that had transpired since his criminal conviction in 1982, Ralph Ross had finally grown comfortable with his new role as an "unofficial adviser" to the various law enforcement agencies whose investigations led them to Lexington.

It had been at Ralph's urging that the FBI supervision of the organized crime and narcotics squad in Lexington instigated a dogged pursuit of Henry Vance. In December 1986, FBI agent James Higgins had persuaded Bonnie Kelly to testify against Henry Vance. On January 12, 1987, Henry Vance was indicted by a federal grand jury in the murder conspiracy of Florida prosecutor Eugene Berry. The indictment came just four days before the statute of limitations would expire.

Ralph had felt a strong sense of personal satisfaction and completion when, on October 29, 1987, Vance was convicted and later sentenced to fifteen years in a federal penitentiary.

Vance's conviction and Drew's death were but a blip on the screen as far as the continuing criminal conspiracy was concerned. Ralph knew that Drew's associates continued to operate at full force, perhaps with even more sophistication. Lexington remained a hotbed of drug smuggling and murders. Drew's organization might have dissipated when it lost its most notorious member, but his enforcers were still roaming the territory, and planeloads of cocaine were landing regularly on Kentucky's remote airfields. The group was still favorite sons in the community, as evidenced by Henry Vance's inclusion in the 1989 edition of *The Society Registry: Blue Grass Blue Book.*

But now, with Bertram Gordon's detention in the Netherlands, Ralph saw the denouement of the dramatic odyssey that started in 1970 when Ralph Ross and Drew Thornton were thrust into conflict. He sensed that Gordon's arrest was the climax before the resolution. Finally, the promise of a just conclusion to years of bloody battles seemed imminent. Ralph saw the possibility of hitting the group at its core. He made plane reservations to Amsterdam, dug out his passport, and cleared his schedule. As soon as he received word that he would be granted an audience with Gordon, Ralph was ready to take off.

Ralph actually felt excited about the group's vulnerability. They had dismissed him as a threat years ago. But he was just gearing up for the final scene. Armed with the knowledge of Rebecca's statement and the identity and whereabouts of mystery man Bill Leonard, he knew he could convince the FBI and the U.S. Attorney of the need for a specially convened federal grand jury to be seated in Lexington. DEA in Knoxville had just announced it had closed its investigation, so they couldn't claim an invasion of turf.

Though Ralph had suspected it all along, now he had proof— the smuggling conspiracy that resulted in Drew Thornton's death had been spawned and fulfilled in Lexington. The three main players— Drew, Rebecca, and Bill Leonard—lived in Lexington. What had convinced Ralph more than anything else that Rebecca Sharp was a more significant player than the little-girlfriend-keeping-the-homefires-burning image she struggled to project was her statement: ". . . *they know I will have them killed.*"

Pretty strong stuff, he thought.

Though his legal pad was full of questions for Gordon, there was only one to which he felt he absolutely must know the answer: Why had Drew Thornton taken the "hit list" on board his last flight? Had there been a contract "let" on the life of Ralph Ross? Had Drew taken the dossier with him to Colombia and hired cartel assassins to get the job done? Or had he taken it to Miami to be turned over to a Mafia hit man? Had the contract been voided with Drew's death? Or was it still pending, unfinished business for one of Drew's foot soldiers?

Despite his hope for a grand jury before which Rebecca, Leonard, Kobell, and Gordon would be called to testify, Ralph Ross's realism reminded him that anything could happen in the hands of bluegrass justice.

On a personal level, Ralph was totally comfortable with his life. He had a thriving private investigations business—having teamed up with his longtime partner, Don Powers. Ross and Powers Associates charged a high hourly rate, and served clients from around the United States.

His bitterness had subsided, and he was now able to look at the decade's tragedies with a sense of irony and humor. He spent his free time trying everything he had ever fantasized about. He dated regularly and, finally, was a happy and free man.

It had been a tumultuous and trying seven years since his felony conviction; and even a rocky four years since the death of his nemesis, Drew Thornton. But now, he was back in the game.

Ralph knew he had survived intact when he realized that once again, the chase was fun. Though he couldn't deny his subjectivity, he recognized his pursuit of Bertram Gordon for what it was. A game that he was winning. Not a war that he had lost.

ACKNOWLEDGMENTS

This book could never have been written were it not for the overwhelming support and involvement of Harry and Pat Miller. Without Harry's keen legal eye, subsequent endorsement of the veracity of the material, and personal guarantee to WKYT executives that the stories were thoroughly substantiated and documented, my original reporting would have stopped dead in its tracks years ago. As if that were not enough, Harry and his wife, Pat, offered me safe harbor in an increasingly tempestuous sea. They opened their home to me and incorporated me into their lives at a time when being a friend of Sally Denton's was highly unpopular.

Likewise, special thanks are due John Schaaf and Mary Jane Gallaher, who loved Kentucky enough to want to improve it, and who believed in the First Amendment enough to withstand the resulting heat.

Most of the supporting documentation for this book is found in government documents. Still, my sources are the cornerstone of my endeavors. Many of my sources in the FBI, Customs, DEA, IRS, Kentucky State Police, and the Lexington Police Department do not wish to be publicly acknowledged. They know who they are, and they know how appreciative I am.

My thanks to the following current and former law enforcement officers: DEA—Bob Brightwell, John Burns, Dennis Dayle, Ralph Frias, Kieran Kobell, Lowell Miller, Al Overbow, Lou Perry, Cindy Schultz, Don Ware; FBI—Jim Blasingame, John Crisp, John Denton, Bill Henshaw, Jim Huggins, Neil Welch; U.S. Customs—Houston Allman, Art Donelan, Bill Paul, Marvin Walker; ATF—Dennis Dutch, Frank Eddy, Bob Pritchett, Sam Simpson; Captain James Black, Jefferson County

Police; Pete Caram, New York Port Authority; Bud Farmer, Jefferson County Police; Billy Gallinaro and Nick Navarro, Broward County Sheriff's Department; Colonel Don Powers, Kentucky State Police; Ron Rohlfs, Georgia Bureau of Investigation; John Sampson, Dade County Metro Police; Arthur Bohanan, Knoxville Police Department; Danny Dominguez and John Buhrmaster, Miami Police Department; Corky Dwight, Louisiana State Police; Bill Wolf, Florida Department of Law Enforcement; and to Steve and Harry.

My thanks also to the following reporters, writers, editors, and researchers who contributed their time and support to me throughout the years: Joanne Bario; Dan Baum, Tom Burton, Tom Chester, Ken Cummins, Jan Fisher, Jeff Frank, Jim Grady, Patricia Griffith, John Hill, Jim and Carolyn Hougan, Robert Blair Kaiser, George Knapp, Ken Kurtz, Jonathan Marshall, Greg McDonald, Jay Peterzell, Wendell Rawls, Bill Rempel, Kevin Sacks, Jim Savage, Albert Scardino, Tom Scheffey, Quin Shea, Curt Suplee, Nicholas Von Hoffman, and to the memory of Ned Day and Bob Brown.

I am grateful to the following friends and acquaintances who offered assistance in this project: Tom Baynard, Dennis Blewitt, Karen Brannon, Maxine Champion, Paul Cody, John Davis, Gregory Bruce English, Larry Forgy, Ed Garland, Dottie Goffstein, Bonnie Goldstein, Pat Hallinan, Chris Jurgenson, Steve Koch, Dr. and Mrs. Thomas Hobbs, Guy Mendez, Dr. and Mrs. John Moore, John Paustian, George Ratterman, Howard and Ruth Samuel, Robert Samuel, Larry Weinberg, Dr. Doug Wilson, and Betty Zaring.

The following current and former state and federal prosecutors provided valuable insight: Louis De Falaise, U.S. Attorney, Lexington, Kentucky; John Gill, U.S. Attorney, Knoxville, Tennessee; Mark Johnson, Florida Statewide Prosecutor; Robert Trevey, Assistant U.S. Attorney, Lexington, Kentucky; Steve Wehner, Assistant U.S. Attorney, Philadelphia, Pennsylvania.

I appreciate the time taken by sundry librarians, archivists, and FOIA officers who assisted in my research.

Thanks to Mabel Mitchell, who taught me how to write, and to Bob Trapp, who taught me how to report.

Thanks to my agents, Arnold and Elise Goodman, for their

commitment to this project; and to my editor, Patrick Filley, for grasping its significance.

The mystery that unfolds in The Bluegrass Conspiracy was explored by a hard-working, sensible, idealistic cop named Ralph Ross. He received little assistance in his endeavors, and was faced with a multitude of personal and professional obstacles more unfair and difficult than most of us ever face in a lifetime. Words cannot express the depth of my gratitude to him.

INDEX